"For many years, I have hoped t edition of this valued compendiu.. .. .. of family living. In a day when many Christians are confused about the callings of Christian living in the home, Baxter gives clear job descriptions for husbands, wives, and even children. It is my prayer that Baxter's robust biblical vision for the family will inspire and encourage many, just as it did in the seventeenth century."

Tedd Tripp, pastor, conference speaker,
author of *Shepherding a Child's Heart*

"Richard Baxter's *Christian Directory* was one of the most compendious books of spiritual advice to be published in the seventeenth century. Its massive size, however, has hindered its usefulness in engaging a wide, evangelical audience. In *The Godly Home*, Randall J. Pederson has sought to remedy this by producing a volume that, with fresh urgency, presents Baxter's wisdom on family life and worship. Pederson's sensitive editorial care is to be commended. This is a work to be read and reread. I hope it reaches a wide audience and serves to awaken Christians to the need of an enduring godly legacy."

Crawford Gribben, Long Room Hub Senior Lecturer in
Early Modern Print Culture, Trinity College, Dublin;
author of *God's Irishmen: Theological Debates in
Cromwellian Ireland*

"Baxter's *The Godly Home* is a treasure of godly information and advice desperately needed in today's world. Few areas are more in need of reformation than the home and family, and this updating of Baxter's prose is very welcome indeed. For too long, this excellent piece has been buried in the massive *Directory*, and its resurrection under the skillful hand of Randall Pederson is both timely and welcome. Let us hope that a new reformation begins in the home and that this publication will aid to that end."

Derek Thomas, John E. Richards Professor of Theology,
Reformed Theological Seminary (Jackson);
Minister of Teaching, First Presbyterian Church,
Jackson, Mississippi

"The Puritans elevated the concept that our homes and families should be like little churches and godly enclaves more than anyone else in church history. They preached scores of sermons and wrote numerous books on how to live as Christian husbands, wives, and children. One of the most important among these books was written by Richard Baxter and has long been buried in miniscule print in his *A Christian Directory*. In *The Godly Home*, Randall Pederson has masterfully edited Baxter's *tour de force* on the duties of husbands, wives, children, and teenagers in building God-glorifying homes. Though a few items in this book may seem outdated, the vast majority of it provides solid, convicting, and instructive biblical advice. If every Christian family, by the Spirit's grace, conscientiously practiced the godly piety Baxter commends in this book, homes, churches, and nations would be truly transformed for good and we would see better days ahead."

Joel R. Beeke, President, Puritan Reformed Theological Seminary, Grand Rapids, Michigan

THE
Godly Home

RICHARD BAXTER

Edited by Randall J. Pederson

Introduction by J. I. Packer

WHEATON, ILLINOIS

Cover design: Amy Bristow

Cover photo: iStock

First printing, 2010

Printed in the United States of America

Unless otherwise indicated, Scripture quotations are taken from the ESV® Bible (*The Holy Bible: English Standard Version*®), copyright © 2001 by Crossway Bibles, a publishing ministry of Good News Publishers. Used by permission. All rights reserved.

Scripture quotations marked KJV are from the King James Version of the Bible.

Trade paperback ISBN: 978-1-4335-1344-2

PDF ISBN: 978-1-4335-1345-9

Mobipocket ISBN: 978-1-4335-1346-6

ePub ISBN: 978-1-4335-2041-9

Library of Congress Cataloging-in-Publication Data
Baxter, Richard, 1615–1691
   [Christian economics]
   The Godly home / Richard Baxter ; edited by Randall J. Pederson.
     p. cm.
   Includes bibliographical references.
   ISBN: 978-1-4335-1344-2 (tpb)
   1. Family—Religious life. 2. Christian life—Puritan authors.
I. Pederson, Randall J., 1975–   . II. Title
BV4526.3.B39   2010
248.4—dc22   2009015136

VP		20	19	18	17	16	15	14	13	12	11	10
15	14	13	12	11	10	9	8	7	6	5	4	3	2	1

Dedicated by the editor to
JAMES DOLEZAL,
a friend and kindred spirit in the things of
God and men

Contents

Introduction

J. I. Packer

If someone was planning to produce an encyclopedia, that is,
an exhaustive work of reference, on some subject, or indeed,
like the *Encyclopedia Britannica*, on all subjects together, how
would you expect him to go about it? Surely, by recruiting a team of
assistants, by ensuring access to a good library, by stocking up with
some lavishly equipped computers, and by acquiring for comparative
purposes copies of all those earlier works of reference that the new
project was intended to outclass. How could one hope to do a good
job otherwise?

Back in the eighteenth century, when a group of booksellers-
publishers (in those days these two trades were one) engaged Samuel
Johnson to produce a definitive English dictionary, they gave him
money to hire and pay a team of researchers, to rent premises in
which they could all work together, and to purchase what they
needed for their task. The investment, we know, paid off. Johnson's
dictionary was a landmark from the start and became the foundation
on which all later English dictionaries were built.

When the Puritan Richard Baxter (1615–1691) produced his
encyclopedia of the Christian life, however, the story was rather
different.

In 1664 Baxter was a pastor out of a job. His ministry at
Kidderminster in the English Midlands, where he had served (with
a five-year absence as a Civil War chaplain) since 1641, and which
had been marvelously fruitful in evangelism, nurture, and church
community-building, had been terminated by the anti-Puritan Act of
Uniformity in 1662. Since then he had resided in Acton, a few miles

outside London, living, it seems, on book royalties and rents from the small property he owned. He was married to a woman twenty years younger than himself who had some money of her own. His mind went back to urgings from the late Archbishop Usher that he should "write a directory for the several ranks of professed Christians" and to his own plan, formed some years before, of writing "a Family Directory," which he began to compose. The project took him something like a year. He had no secretary, copyist, or pastoral peers to help him, and he was "far from my library and all my books, save an inconsiderable parcel which wandered with me, where I went." But what came out of the hopper of his fantastically fertile and fast-moving mind was a treatise of a million and a quarter words that, when finally published in 1673, bore the following title:

A Christian Directory
Or
A Sum of Practical Theology, and Cases of Conscience
Directing Christians
How to Use their Knowledge and Faith;
How to Improve all Helps and Means, and to Perform all Duties;
How to Overcome Temptations, and to Escape or Mortify Every Sin;
In Four Parts.
I. Christian Ethics (or Private Duties)
II. Christian Economics (or Family Duties)
III. Christian Ecclesiastics (or Church Duties)
IV. Christian Politics (or Duties to our Rulers and Neighbors)

Do not treat this title as grandiose or inflated. In the days before dust jackets and blurbs, title pages were regularly fulsome, since it was only there that information as to what you would find in the book if you bought it could be given. Baxter's title is a factual inventory of what he believed his book contained. It is worth noting that when it was reprinted in 1990, the dust jacket carried Timothy Keller's estimate of it as "the greatest manual on Biblical counseling ever produced."

Three points in particular need to be noted.

1. *Baxter's scope.* The *Directory* announces itself as a *sum* of practical theology—that is, a *summa*, in the medieval sense, a single,

comprehensive presentation dealing with everything, "all helps and means," "all duties," "every sin"—in short, all that is involved with living before God as a faithful disciple of Jesus Christ, our Savior and Lord. Baxter's exhaustiveness can be exhausting, but it would be foolish to criticize the monumentally thorough work for being too long. Its scope warrants its length. It is, in fact, a triumph of close-packed clarity; and it is, after all, a work of reference.

2. *Baxter's method.* The *Directory* announces itself as a sum of *cases of conscience. Case* means here a specific uncertainty and trigger of inward debate as to where one stands with God and what one should do to know him and keep his favor, to please him and to show him honor and bring him glory. Baxter asks us to observe "that the resolving of practical cases of conscience, and the reducing of theoretical knowledge into serious Christian practice, and promoting a skillful facility in the faithful exercise of universal obedience, and holiness of heart and life, is the great work of this treatise." Many of the externals of Baxter's world have changed over the past three and a half centuries, but God and man and the principles of godliness remain just what they were, and the relevance of Baxter's "cases" and case-oriented directions to our own relationships with God and our various neighbors will, I think, startle thoughtful readers. Within his seventeenth-century frame, Baxter is handling the things that abide.

3. *Baxter's readership.* The title tells us that the *Directory* is for Christians as such—and more particularly, so Baxter says in his introductory remarks, for "the younger and more unfurnished and unexperienced sort of ministers" and "the more judicious masters of families, who may choose and read such parcels to their families, as at any time the case requireth." But anyone who is prepared not to yield to twenty-first-century panic at seemingly seventeenth-century Anglo-Saxon, to let Baxter's passionate persuadings do their work, and to allow each point to hit the conscience as it was meant to, will find here a glowing sense of God, unending food for thought, and constant incentives to self-assessment, self-humbling, and true repentance and reconsecration, to one's own lasting benefit. Read, and you will see.

The present book is a slightly edited version of the opening chapters of the *Christian Directory*, Part II, "Christian Economics," on marriage partnership, family worship, parents, and children. "Economics" here means not commerce as today but management. Godliness at home, in the life of the married couple and their family, is Baxter's theme, and he develops it with steady concentration and haunting power.

But one might ask, why reprint this material now? Why should anyone expect today's readers to take an interest in it? To this perfectly fair question a twofold answer must be given.

The first answer is that in the Western world at least, and increasingly elsewhere, the family is in deep trouble. Relentless pressures arising from the centralizations of urban life are eroding domestic relationships, so that their intrinsic primacy in human life is no longer being appreciated or lived out. Instead these pressures cut off husbands and wives from each other, cut off children from their parents and grandparents, and cut off the nuclear family from uncles, aunts, and next-door neighbors. And from being everyday life's focal center, a sustained source of warmth and joy ("there's no place like home") the home turns into a dormitory and snacking point from which family members scatter for most of most days. Awareness that this state of things is not happy is widespread, and on the principle of scratching where it itches, many blueprints for rebuilding the family get into print, particularly among Christian people, whose sense of family life being out of joint is most acute. In this situation, it would be mere chronological snobbery, to borrow C. S. Lewis's phrase, to assume that only contemporary treatments of Christian family life are worth reading. When the boat is leaking and taking in water fast, the time-honored word of wisdom has been, all hands to the pumps; and when healthy family life is under threat, the call should be, let all wise persons in this field speak and be heard. On this basis alone, we shall do well to listen to Richard Baxter.

The second answer, which follows on from this, is, quite simply that on this topic, no less than on many others, Richard Baxter was superb. Though a bachelor during his Kidderminster pastorate and still childless after two years of marriage (the marriage was permanently childless, which Baxter regretted), he knew very well what he was talking about and was able to speak as a real authority on it. A well-read man with quick intelligence and a virtually photographic memory, an autodidact whose mental energy seemed endless, and a Puritan Christian whose God-centeredness, devotion, zeal, mastery of Scripture, and passion for holiness were truly awesome, he inherited from his predecessors in the Puritan pastorate a great deal of wisdom on home and family life, which his own pastoral acumen and insight enabled him first to absorb and then to surpass. Down-to-earth, humble humanity, thoughtful and prayerful care for those he served, and an abundance of common sense and shrewdness on people's motivations, personal and relational dynamics, and the short- and long-term consequences of actions had further equipped him for his hands-on years of parish ministry. Further he was effortlessly clearheaded, lucid in thought, and eloquent in speech, a master communicator on any subject. His talents were fully on display as he wrote about the tasks, ideals, and problems of Christian family life.

In typical Puritan style, Baxter viewed all human life, and here specifically all domestic life, through three grids: the grid of doctrine, that of duty, and that of promise. All three were sourced directly from Scripture. The *doctrine* grid set forth the purposes and goals of God, first in creation and then in redemption, for each person and for each department of his or her existence and activity. The *duty* grid spelled out the moral commands of God, his will of precept as Reformed theologians called it, as pointers to and as shaped by God's objective in each case. The *promise* grid deployed God's offers of help for faithful obedience, aimed at achieving his specific target in each case. In the chapters reprinted in this book, Baxter assumes that readers have a working knowledge of the relevant doctrine—namely, that the family is for God-honoring partnership and mutual service, for character-molding in and through love, and for the continuance of our race through the producing and nurturing of children; that sex is strictly for procreation, with affectionate playfulness and pleasure; and that every family should be a mini-church, with its male head as the pastor. (This is the standard Puritan view.) Baxter assumes also that we know how to plead and rely on the promises of God in relation to our hopes, fears, endeavors, and bafflements, a subject that he had already treated at length in *The Life of Faith* (1670). What he concentrates on is the duty grid, stating and clarifying standards by which we humans are called to live. His thought moves rapidly, and he crisscrosses each area of duty many times, filling in all the angles, hammering each obligation home in the conscience. Readers will soon see why the editors of the first reprint of *Christian Directory*, in 1707, sixteen years after Baxter's death, spoke of it as "perhaps the best body of practical divinity that is extant in our own and any other tongue."

It is good, and a matter for thanksgiving, to have Baxter back in print on the domestic topics with which the following chapters deal, and it is to be hoped that in the ongoing contemporary conversation about them his contribution will be heard and heeded.

J. I. Packer

Editor's Preface

Richard Baxter (1615–1691) influenced the English Protestantism of the seventeenth century in ways that may never be known. Largely self-taught, Baxter wrote to be read and reread. His chief aim, even amid seventeenth-century controversies, was to be useful and peaceable. Arguably the most popular author of his era, Baxter's works continue to be read today, as they have been in every century since the seventeenth, though often their size and language (reprinted with nineteenth-century archaisms) diminish their usefulness to a modern, broader, more popular audience.

This new edition of Baxter's "Christian Economics," or teachings on family life, is taken from the second part of his massive, 1,143-page book *A Christian Directory*. Part of Baxter's practical corpus, *A Christian Directory* was designed for young ministers, masters of families, and private Christians; it was written to be as thorough as possible and to address as wide an array of questions and cases as feasible. We are hopeful that this volume, renamed *The Godly Home*, will widen Baxter's influence throughout the church today and will be used for teaching, training, and inspiring Christians to renew their zeal for godly homes.

The task of editor is filled with many difficulties. Not only does one have to work through a language barrier, but one must get into the mind, as it were, of a seventeenth-century author and try to decipher, in certain cases, the sense and meaning of obscure prose (what a professor of mine once called "breaking the historical sound barrier"). The political and religious upheavals of the seventeenth century are always in the background and inform not only the words chosen but the emphasis placed in repetition and reiteration. Baxter was a product of early modern England and, as such, teaches us what life was like, and what was to be expected of a Christian living not only on the borders of the Atlantic Ocean but on the edge of eternity. Thus this work will be useful for Christian pilgrims of all denominations and creeds, for the establishing and maintaining of godly conduct in our ordained spheres. I have found much profit in Michael Hunter's *Editing Early Modern Texts: An Introduction to Principles and Practice* (New York: Palgrave Macmillan, 2007), and would recommend it as a guide to the editing of early modern texts.

I have striven to remain as close to original texts as possible, given the limitations of evolved English. I had three editions to compare, all printed in various quarters in London: Robert White's 1673 edition, for Nevill Simons, printed at the Prince's Arms in St. Paul's Churchyard; Thomas Parkhurst's 1707 edition, printed in Cheapside; and William Orme's critical edition of 1830 (Volume 4 of a twenty-three-volume edition), printed at Fleet Street. All three editions were nearly the same, except for variances in punctuation, spelling, and emphases. Both White's and Parkhurst's editions had numerous italics and emphasized words, whereas Orme's imposed an early consensus of nineteenth-century English usage and removed most italics, limiting them to section headings. I have for the most part left the italics out. My reason for doing so is that in seventeenth-century usage, the abundance of italics obscures any intended emphasis; there is also the lingering question of whether the italics were the product of authors or printers. Spelling and punctuation have been modernized, and inconsistencies in presentation have been regularized. I have striven to make as few corrections and emendations as possible, thus preserving Baxter's spirit and language. I have standardized biblical citations (placing them in the text rather than in the margins or footnotes) and have corrected several misprinted references, as well as updating the text to the English Standard Version (ESV).

As was common to seventeenth-century practice, Baxter used, by modern standards, frequent wordiness; when appropriate I have truncated these. Changes to the text, substantive and accidental, have been noted wherever possible. Most references to servants, more suited for prior centuries, have been removed. I have left, for the most part, Baxter's language of hierarchy alone (thus, he will often refer to fathers or parents as "governors"). Translations to Latin texts have been provided in parentheses. Several explanatory footnotes annotate the text, which, I hope, will facilitate a more enjoyable and informed reading. Words or phrases italicized in footnotes are those that have been removed from the original text and changed for a more common usage. Footnotes that are in quotations are from Baxter's own annotations. I have, when possible, traced the sources of these citations and provided brief biographical material. Readers may question the value of some of Baxter's prose (for example, his comments on the marriage of first cousins, or *cousin-germans*). I have decided to leave these alone as they are generally informative, provide insight into seventeenth-century marriage conflict, and may be of use in some missionary settings. Any remaining faults in the editing process, as always, are mine and mine alone.

I would like to thank Crossway for suggesting this project and for providing the impetus and support to carry it through. I am most grateful to Al Fisher for his constant support and unflagging enthusiasm and to Ted Griffin for his keen skills of observation that are reminiscent of the Lewis and Clark Expedition.

I am grateful to my *doctorvaters*, Richard A. Muller, Gijsbert van den Brink, and Jeffrey K. Jue, for their guidance and direction. I cannot express enough gratitude to Joel R. Beeke, Lyle D. Bierma, Crawford Gribben, Carl R. Trueman, Terreth Klaver, James Dolezal, Patrick R. Severson, and Peter A. Lillback for their influence on my life. "Iron sharpens iron, and one man sharpens another" (Prov. 27:17).

I also want to thank the staff at Westminster Bookstore—Chun Lai, Micah Bickford, Daniel Willson, Jim Weidenaar, and Mark Traphagen—for their chumminess.

I profoundly appreciate my wife, Sarah, my son, Tyler, and my parents, Gary and Rosa, for their selfless love and patience during countless hours of editing. Without your unflinching support and sacrificial love, this book would never have seen completion.

Finally, I wish to thank J. I. Packer for not only contributing the introduction but for his lifelong work as a lover and promoter of Puritan literature. It was his *A Quest for Godliness* (Crossway, 1994) that first opened my eyes to the beauties and usefulness of the Puritans. That book has been a constant bedside companion all these years, and I never tire flipping through its pages. May God bless your labors for years to come!

Randall J. Pederson
Cheltenham, Pennsylvania

Chapter One

Directions about Marriage

A s Christians in their private lives are holy, being dedicated and separated unto God, so also must their families be. HOLINESS TO THE LORD must be, as it were, written on their doors and on their relations, possessions, and affairs. To which it is necessary that there be a holy constitution of their families, a holy government of them, and discharge of the several duties of the members of the family.

To the right constituting of a family belongs the right contracting of marriage. . . .

Direction 1: Take heed that neither lust nor rashness thrust you into a married condition before you see reasons to invite you to it as may assure you of the call and approval of God. For, first, it is God whom you must serve in your married state, and therefore it is proper that you take his counsel before you rush upon it, for he knows best what belongs to his service. Second, it is God whom you must depend upon for the blessing and comforts of your relationship; therefore, there is great reason that you take his advice and consent as the chief things to the match. If the consent of parents is necessary, much more is the consent of God.

Question: But how shall a man know whether God calls him to marriage or consents to it? Has he not here left all men to their liberties, as in a thing indifferent?

Answer: God has not made any universal law commanding or forbidding marriage and in this regard has left it indifferent to mankind. Yet he does not allow all to marry (for to some it is unlawful), but he has by other general laws or rules directed men to know in what cases it is lawful and in what cases it is a sin. Every man is bound to choose that condition in which he may serve God with the best advantages and which tends most to his spiritual welfare and increase in holiness.

Now there is nothing in marriage itself that makes it commonly inconsistent with these benefits and the fulfilling of these laws. Therefore, it is said that "he who marries his betrothed does well" (1 Cor. 7:38a); that is, he does that which of itself is not unlawful and which to some is the most desirable state of life. But there is something in a single life that makes it, especially to preachers and persecuted Christians, to be the most advantageous state of life to these ends of Christianity; therefore, it is said that "he who refrains from marriage will do even better" (1 Cor. 7:38b). To individual persons it is hard to imagine how it can be either a duty or a sin, except in some unusual cases. For it is a thing of so great moment as to the ordering of our hearts and lives that it is hard to imagine that it should ever be indifferent as a means to our main end, but must either be a very great help or hindrance. If there are any persons whose case may be so equally poised with accidents[1] on both sides that to the most judicious man it is not discernible whether a single or married state of life is likely to conduce more to their personal holiness, public usefulness, or the good of others, to such persons marriage, in this circumstance,[2] is a thing indifferent.

By these conditions you may know what persons have a call from God to marry and who have not his call or approval. First, if there is the peremptory will or command of parents to children that are under their authority, and no greater matter on the contrary to hinder it, the command of parents signifies the command of God. But if parents do but persuade and not command, though their desires must not be causelessly refused, yet a smaller impediment may preponderate than in the case of a peremptory command. Second, they are called to marry who have not the gift of continence and cannot by the use of lawful means attain it and have no impediment that makes it unlawful to them to marry. "But if they cannot exercise self-control, they should marry. For it is better to marry than to

---

[1]Indifferences or non-essentials.
[2]*In the individual circumstantiated act.*

burn with passion" (1 Cor. 7:9). But here the diverse degrees of the urgent and the hindering causes must be compared, and the weightiest must prevail. For some who have very strong lusts may yet have stronger impediments; and though they cannot keep that chastity in their thoughts as they desire, yet in such a case they must abstain. There is no man but may keep his body in chastity if he will do his part. Yea, and thoughts themselves may be commonly and for the most part kept pure, and wanton imaginations quickly checked, if men are godly and will do what they can. But on the other side, there are some who have a more tamable measure of sexual desire[3] and yet have no considerable hindrance, whose duty it may be to marry, as the most certain and successful means against that small degree, as long as there is nothing to forbid it.

Third, another cause that warrants marriage is when upon a wise casting up of all accounts it is apparently most probable that in a married state one may be most serviceable to God and the public good, that there will be in it greater helps and fewer hindrances to the great ends of our lives: the glorifying of God and the saving of ourselves and others. It must be expected that every condition should be more helpful to us in one respect and hinder us more in another respect and that in one we have most helps for a contemplative life and in another we are better furnished for an active, serviceable life. The great skill, therefore, in the discerning of our duties lies in the prudent pondering and comparing of the advantages and disadvantages,[4] without the seduction of fantasy, lust, or passion, and in a true discerning which side it is that has the greatest weight.[5]

Here it must be carefully observed, first, that the two first reasons for marriages, sexual desire[6] and the will of parents, or any such like, have their strength but in subordination to the third, the final cause or interest of God and our salvation. This last reason (from the end) is of itself sufficient without any of the others, but none of the others are sufficient without this. If it is clear that in a married state

---

[3]*Concupiscence.*

[4]*Commodities and discommodities.*

[5]"Unmarried men are the best friends, the best masters, the best servants; but not always the best subjects: for they are light to run away and therefore venturous, &c." Lord Bacon, "Essay 8." Francis Bacon (1561–1626) was a prominent English philosopher, writer, and statesman and was generally regarded as one of the founders of the Scientific Revolution. His *Essays* (1597–1625), informal compositions, were among the earliest examples in English. For a general overview of Bacon's thought, see Perez Zagorin, *Francis Bacon* (Princeton, NJ: Princeton University Press, 1998).

[6]*Concupiscence.*

you have better advantages for the service of God and doing good to others and saving your own souls than you can have in a single state of life, then it is undoubtedly your duty to marry; for our obligation to seek our ultimate end is the most constant, indispensable obligation. Though parents command it not, though you have no physical[7] necessity, yet it is a duty if it certainly makes most for your ultimate end.

Second, observe that no pretense of your ultimate end will warrant you to marry when any other accident has first made it a thing unlawful while that accident continues. For we must not do evil that good may come by it. Our salvation is not furthered by sin; though we saw a probability that we might do more good to others if we did but commit such a sin to accomplish it, yet it is not to be done. For our lives and mercies being all in the hand of God, and the successes and acceptance of all our endeavors depending wholly upon him, it can never be a rational way to attain them by willfully offending him by our sin! It is a likely means to public good for able and good men to be magistrates and ministers; yet he that would lie or be perjured or commit any known sin that he may be a magistrate or that he may preach the gospel might better expect a curse on himself and his endeavors than God's acceptance or his blessing and success. So he that would sin to change his state for the better would find that he changed it for the worse, or if it does good to others, he may expect no good but ruin to himself, if repentance prevent it not.

Third, observe also that if the question is only which state of life it is (married or single) that best conduces to this ultimate end, then any one of the subordinate reasons will prove that we have a call, if there are no greater reasons on the contrary side. In the case you have no bodily[8] necessity, the will of parents alone may oblige you, if there is no greater thing against it. Or if parents oblige you not, physical necessity alone may do it. Or if neither of these invite you, a clear probability of the attaining of such an estate or opportunity as may make you more fit to relieve many others or be serviceable to the church, or the blessing of children who may be devoted to God, may warrant your marriage if no greater reasons lie against it. For when the scales are equal, any one of these may turn them.

By this also you may perceive those who have no call to marry

[7]*Corporal.*
[8]*Corporeal.*

and those to whom it is a sin. First, no man has a call to marry who, laying all the advantages and disadvantages[9] together, may clearly discern that a married state would be a greater hindrance to his salvation or to his serving or honoring God in the world, and so to disadvantage him as to his ultimate end.

Question: But what if parents command it or will set against me if I disobey?

Answer: Parents have no authority to command you anything against God or your salvation or your ultimate end. Therefore, here you owe them no formal obedience. But the will of parents, with all the consequents, must be put into the scales with all other considerations, and if they make the disadvantages[10] of a single life to become the greater as to your end, then they may bring you under a duty or obligation to marry; not a *necessitate praecepti* ("a necessary command or precept") as obedience to their command but a *necessitate medii* ("a necessary means") as a means to your ultimate end and in obedience to that general command of God that requires you to "seek first" your ultimate end, even "the kingdom of God and his righteousness" (Matt. 6:33).

Question: But what if I have a physical[11] necessity, and yet I can foresee that marriage will greatly disadvantage me to the service of God and my salvation?

Answer: First, you must understand that no physical[12] necessity is absolute. For there is no man so lustful but may possibly bridle his lust by other lawful means: by diet, labor, sober company, diverting business, solitude, watching the thoughts and senses, or at least by the physician's help, so that the necessity is *secundum quid*,[13] urgency rather than a simple necessity. Second, this measure of necessity must be itself laid in the balance with the other accidents; if this necessity will turn the scales by making a single life more disadvantageous to your ultimate end, your lust being a greater impediment to you than all the inconveniences of marriage will be, then the case is resolved: "it is better to marry than to burn with passion."

---

[9]*Commodities and discommodities.*
[10]*Discommodities.*
[11]*Corporal.*
[12]*Corporal.*
[13]More fully, *a dicto simpliciter ad dictum secundum quid*; that is, any argument arising from a general proposition without attention to qualifications that would invalidate it.

But if the hindrances in a married state are likely to be greater than the hindrances of your sexual desire,[14] then you must set yourself to the curbing and curing of that desire[15] and in the use of God's means expect his blessing.

Second, children are not ordinarily called of God to marry when their parents do absolutely and peremptorily[16] forbid it. For parents' commands cannot make it a duty when we are sure it would hinder the interest of God, our ultimate end; yet parents' prohibitions may make it a sin when there is a clear probability that it would most conduce to our ultimate end, were it not prohibited. Because, first, affirmatives are not *semper et ad semper* ("binding and governing always and on every occasion"), as negatives or prohibitions are, and because the sin of disobedience to parents will cross its tendency unto good and do more against our ultimate end than all the advantages of marriage can do for it. A duty is then to us no duty when it cannot be performed without a chosen, willful sin. In many cases we are bound to forbear what a governor[17] forbids when we are not bound to do the contrary if he commands it. It is easier to make a duty to be no duty than to make a sin to be no sin. One bad ingredient may turn a duty into a sin, when one good ingredient will not turn a sin into a duty, or into no sin.

Question: But may not a governor's prohibition be overweighed by some great degrees of disadvantage?[18] It is better to marry than to burn. What if parents forbid children to marry absolutely until death and so deprive them of the lawful remedy against lust? If they do not do this but forbid it when it is to children most seasonable and necessary, it seems little better. Or if they forbid them to marry where their affections are so engaged, so that they cannot be taken off without their mutual ruin? May not children marry in such cases of necessity as these, without and against the will of their parents?

Answer: I cannot deny that some cases may be imagined or fall out in which it is lawful to do what a governor forbids and to marry against the will of parents, for they have their power to edification

---

[14]*Concupiscence.*
[15]*Concupiscence.*
[16]*Resolutely.*
[17]Baxter uses the word "governor" to signify one who has authority over another, as parents have authority over their children, and so are said to be their "governors."
[18]*Incommodity.*

and not unto destruction. If a son is qualified with eminent gifts for the work of the ministry in a time and place that need much help, and a malignant parent, in hatred of that sacred office, should ever so peremptorily forbid him, yet may the son devote himself to the blessed work of saving souls. Even as a son may not forbear to relieve the poor (with that which is his own), though his parents should forbid him, nor forbear to put himself into a capacity to relieve them for the future, nor forbear his own necessary food and raiment though he is forbidden, as Daniel would not forbear praying openly in his house when he was forbidden by the king and law. When any inseparable accident makes a thing of itself indifferent become a duty, a governor's prohibition will not discharge us from that duty, unless the accident is smaller than the accident of the ruler's prohibition, and then it may be overweighed by it; but to determine what accidents are greater or less is a difficult task.

As to the particular questions, to the first I answer, if parents forbid their children to marry while they live, it is convenient and safe to obey them until death, if no greater obligation to the contrary forbid it. But it is necessary to obey them during the time that the children live under the government of their parents, as in their houses, in their younger years (except in some few extraordinary cases). But when parents are dead (though they leave commands in their wills), or when age or former marriage has removed children from under their government, a smaller matter will serve to justify their disobedience here than when the children in minority are less fit to govern themselves. For though we owe parents a limited obedience still, yet at full age the child is more at his own disposal than he was before. Nature has given us a hint of her intention in the instinct of animals[19] who are all taught to protect, lead, and provide for their young ones while the young are insufficient for themselves; but when they are grown to self-sufficiency they drive them away or neglect them. If a wise son who has a wife and many children and great affairs to manage in the world should be bound to absolute obedience to his aged parents, as he was in his childhood, it would ruin their affairs, and parents' government would pull down that in their old age which they built up in their middle age.

---

[19]*Brutes.*

To the second question, I answer that children who pretend to have unconquerable lust or love must do all they can to subdue such inordinate affections and bring their lusts to stoop to reason and their parents' wills. If they do their best, there are either none, or not one of many hundreds, but may maintain their chastity together with their obedience. If any say, "I have done my best and yet am under a necessity of marriage; am I not then bound to marry though my parents forbid me?" I answer it is not to be believed. Either you have not done your best or else you are not under a necessity. Your urgency being your own fault (seeing you should subdue it), God still obliges you both to subdue your vice and to obey your parents. But if there is anyone who has such an (incredible) necessity of marriage, he is to procure some others to solicit his parents for their consent, and if he cannot obtain it, some say, it is his duty to marry without it. I rather say that it is *minus malum* ("a lesser evil"), and that having cast himself into some necessity of sinning, it is still his duty to avoid both, and to choose neither; but it is the smaller sin to choose to disobey his parents rather than to live in the flames of lust and the filth of unchastity. Some divines say that in such a case a son should appeal to the magistrate, as a superior authority above the father. But others think this leaves it as difficult to resolve what he shall do if the magistrate also does not consent and that it resolves one difficulty by a greater, it being very doubtful whether in domestic cases the authority of the parent or the magistrate is the greater.

The same answer serves as to the third question, when parents forbid you to marry the person of whom you are most fond. For such fondness (whether you call it lust or love) as will not stoop to reason and your parents' wills is inordinate and sinful. Therefore, the thing that God binds you to is by his appointed means to subdue it and obey. If you cannot, the accidents and probable consequents must tell you which is the lesser evil.

Question: But what if the child has promised marriage and the parents are against it?

Answer: If the child was under the parents' government and short of years of discretion also, the promise is void for want of capacity. So too if the child was of age, yet the promise was a sinful promise as to the promising act and also as to the thing promised during the parents' dissent. If the *actus promittendi* ("promise making") only had been sinful, the promise might nevertheless oblige (unless it were null as well as sinful). But the *materia promissa* ("matter promised") being sinful, to marry while parents do dissent, such a child is bound to forbear the fulfilling of that promise until the parents consent or die. He is bound from marrying any other (unless he is disobliged by the person to whom he has made the promise), because he knows not but that his parents may consent hereafter; and whenever they consent or die, then the promise is obligatory and must be performed.

The thirtieth chapter of Numbers enables parents to disoblige a daughter who is in their house from a vow made to God, if they disallow it at the first hearing. Hence two doubts arise: first, whether this power extends to the disobliging of a promise or contract of matrimony; second, whether it extends to a son as well as a daughter. Most expositors are for the affirmative of both cases. But I have showed you before that it is upon uncertain grounds. First, it is uncertain whether God, who would thus give up his own right in case of vowing, will also give away the right of others, without their consent, in the case of promises or contracts. Second, it is uncertain whether this is not an indulgence only of the weaker sex, seeing many words in the text seem plainly to intimate so much. It is dangerous upon our own presumptions to stretch God's laws to everything we imagine there is the same reason for, seeing our imaginations may so easily be deceived; and God could have expressed such particulars if he would. Therefore (when there is not clear ground for our inferences in the text) it is but to say, "Thus and thus should God have said" when we cannot say, "Thus he has said." We must not make laws under the pretense of expounding them. Whatsoever God commands you, take heed that you do it: "You shall not add to it or take from it" (Deut. 12:32b).

Question: If the question therefore is not of the sinfulness but the nullity[20] of such promises of children because of the dissent of parents, for my part I am not able to prove any such nullity. It is said that they are not *sui juris* ("their own"), and therefore their promises are null; but if they have attained to years and use of discretion, they are naturally so far *sui juris* as to be capable of disposing even

---

[20]A nullity is the state or condition of being *legally* null and void.

of their souls, and therefore of their fidelity. They can oblige themselves to God or man, though they are not so far *sui juris* as to be
ungoverned; for so, no child, no subject, no man is *sui juris*, seeing
all are under the government of God. If a man promises to do a thing
sinful, it is not a nullity but a sin; not *no promise* but *a sinful promise*.
A nullity is when the *actus promittendi* is *reputative nullus vel non
actus* ("the promised act is regarded as nothing"). When no promise
is made, then none can be broken.

Question: But if the question is only how far such promises must
be kept, I answer by summing up what I have said: First, if the
child had not the use of reason, the want of natural capacity proves
the promise null: here *ignorantis non est consensus* ("ignorance is
not consent"). Second, if he was at the age and use of reason, then,
1. If the promising act only was sinful (as before I said of vows), the
promise must be both repented of and kept. It must be repented of
because it was a sin; it must be kept because it was a real promise
and the matter lawful. 2. If the promising act was not only a sin but
a nullity (by any other reason), then it is no obligation. 3. If not only
the promising act is sin but also the matter promised (as is marrying
without parents' consent), then it must be repented of and not performed until it becomes lawful, because an oath or promise cannot
bind a man to violate the laws of God.

Question: But what if the parties are actually married without
the parents' consent? Must they live together or be separated?

Answer: First, if marriage is consummated *per carnalem concubitum* ("by physical consummation"), by the carnal knowledge of
each other, I see no reason to imagine that parents can dissolve it or
prohibit their cohabitation; for the marriage (for aught I ever saw)
is not proved a nullity but only a sin, and their *concubitus* ("lying
together") is not fornication. Parents cannot forbid husband and
wife to live together; in marriage they do (really though sinfully)
forsake father and mother and cleave to each other and so are now
from under parents' government (though not disobliged from all
obedience).

Second, if marriage is only by verbal consensus,[21] divines are
disagreed what is to be done. Some think that it is no perfect mar-

---

[21]*Conjunction.*

riage *ante concubitum* ("before consummation") and also that their consent[22] has but the nature of a promise (to be faithful to each other as husband and wife), and therefore the matter promised is unlawful until parents consent and so not to be done. But I rather think (as most do) that it has all that is essential to marriage *ante concubitum* and that this marriage is more than a promise of fidelity *de futuro* ("in the future"), even an actual delivery of themselves to one another *de paesenti* ("in the present") also, and that the thing promised in marriage is lawful. For though it is a sin to marry without parents' consent, yet when that is past, it is lawful for married persons to come together though parents do not consent. Therefore, that marriage is valid and to be continued, though it was sinfully made.

A third sort who are not called of God to marry are they who have absolutely vowed not to marry. Such may not marry unless providence disobliges them by making it become an indispensable duty. I can remember but two ways by which this may be done.

1. In case there are any of so strong lust as no other lawful means but marriage can suffice to maintain their chastity. To such, marriage is as great a duty as to eat or drink or to cover one's nakedness or to hinder another from uncleanness, lying, stealing, or the like. If you should make a vow that you will never eat or drink or that you will go naked or that you will never hinder anyone from uncleanness, lying, or stealing, it is unlawful to fulfill this vow. But all the doubt is whether there are any such persons who cannot overcome or restrain their lust by any other lawful means. I suppose it is possible there are such, but I believe it is not one of a hundred. If they will but practice the directions before given,[23] I suppose their lust may be restrained. If that prevail not, the help of a physician may; and if that prevail not, some think the help of a surgeon may be lawful, to keep a vow, in case it is not an apparent hazard of life. For Christ seems to allow it, in mentioning it without reproof, if that text, Matthew 19:12, is to be understood of castration. Most expositors, however, think it is meant only of a *confirmed resolution* of chastity. Ordinarily, other means may make this needless; if it is either needless or perilous, it is unlawful without doubt.

---

[22]*Conjunction.*
[23]*Christian Directory,* "Christian Ethics," Tome 1, Chapter 8, Part 5, Titles 1 and 2. Baxter refers to directions against fornication, uncleanness, and inward lusts.

2. The second way by which God may dispense with a vow of chastity is by making the marriage of a person become of apparent necessity to the public safety. I am able to discern but one instance that will reach the case, and that is if a king has vowed chastity, and, if he does not marry, his next heir being a professed enemy of Christianity, the religion, safety, and happiness of the whole nation is apparently in danger to be overthrown. I think the case of such a king is like the case of a father who had vowed never to provide food or raiment for his children; or as if Ahab had vowed that no well should be dug in the land, and when the drought comes, it becomes necessary to the saving of the people's lives; or as if the shipmaster should vow that the ship shall not be pumped, and when it leaks it becomes necessary to save their lives. In these cases God disobliges you from your vow by changing circumstances.[24] A pastor may dispense with it declaratively. But for the pope, or any mortal man, to pretend to more is impiety and deceit.

Question: May the aged marry, who are frigid, impotent, and incapable of procreation?

Answer: Yea, God has not forbidden them. There are other lawful ends of marriage, such as mutual help and comfort and so on, which may make it lawful.[25]

Direction 2: To restrain your inordinate desire for marriage, keep the inconveniencies of it in memory. Do not rush into a state of life where you have never thought of the inconveniences. If you have a call to marry, knowledge of the difficulties and duties will be necessary to your preparation and will be a faithful undergoing. If you do not have a call, this knowledge is necessary to keep you from it. I shall first name the inconveniences common to all and then some that are proper to the ministers of the gospel, which have greater reason to avoid a married life than others have.

1. Marriage ordinarily plunges men into an excess of worldly cares; it multiplies their business and usually their wants. There are many things to mind and do; there are many to provide for. And many persons you will have to do with have a selfish disposition and interest and will judge you as you fit their ends. And among many

---

[24]*A mutation of the matter.*
[25]"Wives are young men's mistresses, companions for the middle age, and old men's nurses; so that a man may have a quarrel to marry when he will." Lord Bacon, *Essay 8.* See Clark Sutherland Northup, ed. *The Essays of Francis Bacon* (New York: Houghton Mifflin Company, 1908), 23–25.

persons and businesses, some things will frequently trouble you; you must look for many rubs and disappointments. Your natures are not so strong, content, and patient as to bear all these without frustration.[26]

2. Your needs in a married state are met scarcely more than in a single life. You will want so many things that before you never wanted and will have so many to provide for and content that all will seem little enough, if you had never so much. You will be often at your wit's end, taking thought for the future, what you shall eat and what you shall drink and with what you and yours shall be clothed.

3. Your needs in a married state are far more difficult to meet than when single. It is easier to bear personal wants ourselves than to see the wants of wife and children; affection will make their sufferings pinch you. And ingenuity will make it a trouble to your mind to need the help of servants and to want that which is fit for servants to expect. But especially the discontent and impatience of your family will more discontent you than all their wants. You cannot help your wife and children and servants to become content; oh, what a heart-cutting trial it is to hear them grumbling,[27] murmuring, and complaining; to hear them call for what you do not have and grieve at their condition and blame you or the providence of God because they do not have it! Do not think that riches will free you from these discontents; for as the rich are but few, so they that have much have much to do with it. A great foot must have a great shoe. When poor men want some small supplies, rich men may want great sums or larger provisions that the poor can go easily without. The condition of the rich, lifting them up to greater pride, torments them with greater discontents. How few in the world who have families are content with their estates!

4. A married life contains far more temptations to worldliness or covetousness than a single life. For when you think you need more, you will desire more; and when you find all too little to satisfy those you provide for, you will measure your estate by their desires and will be inclined to think that you never have enough. Birds and beasts that have young ones to provide for are most hungry and

---

[26]*Molestation.*
[27]*Repining.*

inordinately greedy.[28] You have so many now to scrape for that you will think you are still in want. It is not only till death that you must now lay up; you must provide for children who survive you. While you take them to be as yourselves, you have two generations now to make provisions for. Most men are as covetous for the well-being of their posterity as if it were theirs.

5. After this, you are hindered from works of charity to others; wife and children are the devouring gulf that swallows all. If you had but yourselves to provide for, a little would serve, and you could deny your own desires for unnecessary things and so might have plentiful provisions for good works. By the time wife and children are provided for and all their importunate desires satisfied, there is nothing considerable left for pious or charitable uses. Lamentable experience proclaims this.

6. Hereby it appears how much a married state ordinarily hinders men from honoring their profession. It is their vows of single life that have occasioned the papists to do so many works of public charity, as is boasted of for the honor of their sect. For when they have no children to bequeath their wealth to and cannot keep it for themselves, it is easy for them to leave it to such uses as will pacify their consciences most and advance their names. If it should prove as good a work and as acceptable to God to educate your own children piously for his service as to relieve the children of the poor, yet it is not so much regarded in the world, nor brings much honor to religion. One hundred pounds given to the poor shall more advance the reputation of your liberality and virtue than a thousand pounds given to your own children, though it is with as pious an end, to train them up for the service of the church. Though this is inconsiderable as your own honor is concerned in it, yet it is considerable as to the honor of religion and the good of souls.

7. There is a meeting of faults and imperfections on both sides that makes it much harder to bear the infirmities of others aright. If one party only were forward and impatient, the steadfastness of the other might make it the more tolerable; but we are all sick, in some measure, of the same disease. When weakness meets with weakness, and pride meets with pride, and passion with passion, it exasperates

---

[28]*Rapacious.*

the disease and doubles the suffering. Our corruption is such that though our intent is to help one another in our duties, we are more apt to stir up one another's distempers.

8. The business, care, and trouble of married life is a great temptation to call down our thoughts from God and to divert them from the "one thing . . . necessary" (Luke 10:42) and to distract the mind and make it unfit[29] for holy duty and to serve God with a divided heart, as if we did not serve him. How hard is it to pray or meditate with any serious fervency when you come out of a crowd of cares and business! Hear what Saint Paul said in 1 Corinthians 7:7–8, "I wish that all were as I myself am. . . . To the unmarried and the widows I say that it is good for them to remain single as I am," and in verses 26–28, "I think that in view of the present distress it is good for a person to remain as he is. . . . Yet those who marry will have worldly troubles, and I would spare you that," and in verses 32–33, "The unmarried man is anxious about the things of the Lord, how to please the Lord. But the married man is anxious about worldly things, how to please his wife," and in verses 34–35, "the unmarried . . . woman is anxious about the things of the Lord, how to be holy in body and spirit. But the married woman is anxious about worldly things, how to please her husband. I say this for your own benefit, not to lay any restraint upon you, but to promote good order and to secure your undivided devotion to the Lord," and in verses 37–38, "Whoever is firmly established in his heart, being under no necessity but having his desire under control, and has determined this in his heart, to keep her as his betrothed, he will do well. So then he who marries his betrothed does well, and he who refrains from marriage will do even better." And mark Christ's own words in Matthew 19:10–12: "The disciples said to him, 'If such is the case of a man with his wife, it is better not to marry.' But he said to them, 'Not everyone can receive this saying, but only those to whom it is given. . . . Let the one who is able to receive this receive it.'"

9. The business of a married state often devours almost all your time, so that little is left for holy contemplations or serious thoughts of the life to come. All God's service is contracted and thrust into a corner and done as it were on the by. The world will scarcely allow

---

[29]*Undisposed.*

you time to meditate or pray or read the Scripture; you think yourselves, like Martha, under a greater necessity of dispatching your
business than of sitting at Christ's feet to hear his Word. Oh, that
single persons knew (for the most part) the preciousness of their
leisure and how free they are to attend the service of God and learn
his Word in comparison to the married!

10. There is so great a diversity of temperaments and degrees of
understanding that there are scarce any two persons in the world
but there is some unsuitableness between them. Like stones that
have some unevenness that makes them lie crooked in the building,
there will be some crossness of opinion, disposition, interest, or will,
by nature or by custom and education, which will stir up frequent
discontents.

11. There is a great deal of duty that husband and wife owe to one
another, such as to instruct, admonish, pray, watch over one another,
and be continual helpers to each other in order to their everlasting
happiness; they must also patiently bear with the infirmities of each
other. To the weak and backward heart of man, the addition of so much
duty adds to their weariness, how good soever the work is in itself. Men
should feel their strength before they undertake more work.

12. The more they love each other, the more they participate
in each other's griefs, and one or the other will be frequently under
some sort of suffering. If one is sick or lame or pained or defamed or
wronged or disquieted in mind or by temptation falls into any wounding sin, the other bears the distress. Therefore, before you undertake
to bear all the burdens of another and share that one's hurts, it concerns you to observe your strength—how much more you have than
your own burdens require.

13. If you should marry one who proves to be ungodly, how
exceeding great would the affliction be! If you loved such persons,
your soul would be in continual danger by them; they would be the
most powerful instruments in the world to pervert your judgments,
to deaden your hearts, to divert you from a holy life, to kill your
prayers, to corrupt your lives, and to damn your souls. If you should
have the grace to escape the snare and save yourself, it would be by
so much the greater difficulty and suffering since the temptation is
greater. What a heartbreak it would be to converse so nearly with a

child of the Devil; it is like living forever in hell. The daily thoughts of it would be a daily death to you.

14. Women especially must expect so much suffering in a married life that if God had not put into them a natural inclination to it and so strong a love for their children (as will make them patient under the most annoying troubles), the world would have been at an end through their refusal of so calamitous a life. Their sickness in breeding, their pain in bringing forth, with the danger of their lives, the tedious trouble night and day that they have with nursing children in their childhood, all this is in addition to their subjection to their husbands and the continual care of family affairs—being forced to consume their lives in a multitude of troublesome business, this and more would have deterred women from marriage if nature had not inclined them to it.

15. And oh, what abundance of duty is incumbent upon both parents toward all children for the saving of their souls.[30] What incessant labor is necessary in teaching them the doctrine of salvation, which made God twice over charge them to teach his Word diligently, or sharpen them, "to your children, and shall talk of them when you sit in your house, and when you walk by the way, and when you lie down, and when you rise" (Deut. 6:7; 11:19). What abundance of obstinate, rooted corruptions are in the hearts of children, which parents must by all possible diligence root up. Oh, how great and hard a work it is to speak to them of their sins and Savior and of their God, their souls, and the life to come with that reverence, gravity, seriousness, and unwearied constancy as the weight of the matter requires! And to suit all their actions and conduct[31] to the same ends! Little do most parents know what abundance of care and labor God requires of them for the sanctifying and saving of their children's souls. Consider your fitness for so great a work before you undertake it.

16. It is abundance of affliction that is ordinarily to be expected in the disobedience[32] of children when you have done your best, and

---

[30]"Are you discontent with your childless estate, that your wife has given you no children? Only remember the kings of Rome, and how there was not one of them who left the crown to their son." *Plutarch.* A first-century biographer, essayist, and author, Plutarch's (46-c.119) works were revived from the sixteenth to the nineteenth centuries and influenced the evolution of the English essay. Here Baxter quotes from Plutarch's "On Tranquility and Contentment," which can be found in the latter's *Moralia*, or essays on moral teaching, which spans fifteen volumes in the Loeb Classical Library.
[31]*Carriage.*
[32]*Miscarriages.*

much more if you neglect your duty, as even godly parents too often do. After all your pains, care, and labor, you will see the foolishness of some and the obstinacy of others and the ingratitude[33] of those whom you have loved best pierce your hearts. You will see many vices spring up and trouble you and be the more grievous the dearer your children are to you. Oh, what a grief it is to breed up a child to be a servant of the Devil and an enemy of God and godliness and a persecutor of the church of God and to think of his lying forever in hell. Alas! How great is the number of such!

17. These marriage crosses are not for a year but for life; they deprive you of all hope of relief while you live together. There is no room for repentance or casting about for a way to escape them. Death only will be your relief. Therefore, such a change of your condition should be seriously thought on, and all the troubles foreseen and pondered.

18. If love makes you dear to one another, your parting at death will be more grievous. When you come together, you know that such a parting you must have; through all the course of your lives you may foresee it. One of you must see the body of your beloved turned into a cold and ghastly lump.[34] You must follow it weeping to the grave and leave it there in dust and darkness; there it must lie rotting as a loathsome lump whose sight or smell you cannot endure, until you shortly follow and lie down in the same condition. All these are the ordinary attendants[35] and consequents of marriage. They are easily and quickly spoken, but long and hard to be endured. Not fictions but realities, and less than most have reason to expect. And should such a life be rashly ventured upon in a pang of lust? Or such a burden undertaken without forethought?

The ministers of the gospel should, especially, think of what they do, and think again, before they enter upon a married life. Not that it is simply unlawful for them or that they are to be barred from it by a law, as they are in the kingdom of Rome, for carnal ends and with odious effects. But so great a hindrance is this troubled state of life to the sacred ministry that a very clear call should be expected for their satisfaction. That I am not tedious, consider well these four things: First, how well will a life of so much care and business agree

---

[33]*Unthankfulness.*
[34]*Clod.*
[35]*Concomitants.*

to you who have little time for the greater work that you have undertaken? Do you know what you have to do in public and private, in
reading, meditating, praying, preaching, instructing personally, and
from house to house? Do you know how great importance it is, even
for the saving of men's souls? Have you time to spare for so much
worldly care and business? Are you not charged, "Practice these
things, immerse yourself in them" (1 Tim. 4:15), and, "No soldier gets
entangled in civilian pursuits, since his aim is to please the one who
enlisted him" (2 Tim. 2:4)? Is this not plain? At one time soldiers did
not look after farms and servants. If you are faithful ministers, I dare
confidently say, you will find all your time so little for your proper
work that many a time you will groan and say, "Oh, how short and
swift time is!" and "Oh, how great and slow is my work and duty!"

Second, consider how well a life of so great diversions and dis-
tractions suits a mind devoted to God, which should be always free
and ready for service. Your studies are on such great and mysteri-
ous subjects that they require the whole mind. To resolve the many
difficulties that are before you, to prepare those suitable convincing
words that may pierce and persuade the hearers' hearts, to get within
the bosom of a hypocrite, to follow on the Word till it attains its effect,
and to deal with poor souls according to their great necessity and
to handle God's Word according to its holiness and majesty—these
are things that require a whole man and are not employments for
a divided or distracted mind. The talking of women and crying of
children and the cares and business of the world are ill preparations
or attendants on these studies. *Non bene fit, quod occupato animo
fit* ("Nothing is well done that is done with a preoccupied mind").[36]

Third, consider well whether a life of so great disturbance is
agreeable to one whose affections should be taken up for God and
whose work must be done not formally and affectedly with the lips
alone but seriously with all the heart. If your heart and warm affections are at any time left behind, the life and power, beauty and glory
of your work are lost. How dead will your studies, praying, preach-

---

[36]This quote is from Jerome's (c.347–419) *Epistles on Saint Paul* (Epistle 5.3). Saint Jerome, as he
is called, was a biblical translator, early church leader, and the most regarded of the Latin Fathers.
His theological writings profoundly affected the development of the early Middle Ages, and he is best
known for his Latin translation of the Bible, the Vulgate. For an introduction to Jerome's life and
thought, see J.N.D. Kelly, *Jerome: His Life, Writings, and Controversies* (Peabody, MA: Hendrickson
Publishers, 1998).

ing, and conversation[37] be! Can you keep these affections warm and vigorous for God and taken up with heaven and heavenly things that are disturbed with the cares and the crosses of the world and taken up with carnal matters?

Fourth, consider also how well that ingredient life will agree to one who by charity and good works should second his doctrine and win men's souls to the love of holiness.[38] If you do not feed the bodies of the poor, they will less relish food for the soul. Nay, if you abound not above others in good works, the blind, malicious world will see nothing that is good in you but will say, "You have good words, but where are your good works?" What abundance have I known hardened against the gospel and religion by a common fame, that these preachers are as covetous, worldly, and uncharitable as any others, and it must be something extraordinary that will confute such fame. What abundance of success have I seen of the labors of those ministers who give all they have in works of charity! Though a rich and resolved man may do some good in a married state, yet often it is next to nothing, as to the ends now mentioned; wife and children and family necessities devour all if you have never so much. Some provision must be made for them when you are dead; and the maintenance of the ministry is not so great as to suffice for all this, much less for any eminent works of charity! Never reckon upon the doing of much good to the poor if you have wives and children of your own! Such instances are rarities and wonders. All will be too little for yourselves. Whereas if all that were given to the poor goes to the maintenance of your families, you little know how much it would reconcile the minds of the ungodly and further the success of your ministerial work.

Direction 3: If God calls you to a married life, expect all these troubles or most of them and make particular preparation for each temptation, cross, and duty that you must expect. Do not think that you are entering into a state of mere delight, lest it prove a fool's paradise to you. See that you are furnished with marriage strength

---

[37]*Conference.*
[38]"A single life doth well with churchmen: for charity will hardly water the ground, where it must fill a pool." Lord Bacon, *Essay 8.* "The greatest works and foundations have been from childless men, who have sought to express the image of their minds that have none of their body: so the care of posterity hath been most in them that had no posterity." Bacon, *Essay 7.* "He that hath a wife and children hath given hostages to fortune. For they are impediments to great enterprises. The best works, and of greatest merit, for the public, have proceeded from unmarried and childless men." Bacon, *Essay 8.*

and patience for the duties and sufferings of a married state before you venture on it. First, be well provided against temptations to a worldly mind and life; for here you are like to be most violently and dangerously assaulted. Second, see that you are well provided with marital[39] affections, for they are necessary both to the duties and sufferings of married life. You should not enter upon the state without the necessary preparations. Third, see that you are well provided with marriage prudence and understanding, that you may be able to instruct and edify your families and may live with them as men of knowledge (1 Pet. 3:7) and may manage all your business with discretion (Ps. 112:1–5). Fourth, see that you are provided with resolve and constancy, that you do not vex yourself and your family by repenting too late. Do not say, "Had I but known" or *non putaram*, "I never thought of that." Levity and mutability are no fit preparatives for a state that only death can change. Let the love and resolutions that brought you into that state continue with you to the last.

Fifth, see that you are provided with a diligence answerable to the greatness of your undertaken duties. A slothful mind is unfit for one who enters himself voluntarily upon so much business, as a cowardly mind is unfit for him who considers[40] himself a soldier for the wars. Sixth, see that you are provided with marriage patience, to bear with the infirmities of others and undergo the daily crosses of your life that your business and your necessities and your own infirmities will unavoidably infer. To marry without this preparation is as foolish as to go to sea without the necessary preparations for your voyage or to go to war without armor or ammunition or to go to work without tools or strength or to seek to buy meat in the market when you have no money.

Direction 4: Take special care that fancy and passion do not overrule reason and friends' advice in the choice of your condition or of the person. I know you must have love to those with whom you match, but that love must be rational and such as you can justify in the severest trial by the evidences of worth and fitness in the person whom you love. To say you love but that you do not know why is more beseeming children or the insane[41] than those who are soberly

---

[39]*Conjugal.*
[40]*Listeth.*
[41]*Mad folks.*

entering upon a change of life of so great importance to them. A blind love that makes you think a person excellent and amiable who, in the eyes of the wisest who are impartial, is nothing so or that makes you overvalue the person whom you fancy (and be fond of one as some admirable creature) who in the eyes of others is next to contemptible—this is but the index and evidence of your folly.

And though you please yourselves and honor it with the name of love, there is none who is acquainted who will give it any better name than lust or fancy. The marriage that is made by lust or fancy will never tend to solid contentment or true happiness.[42] Rather it will feed till death on the fuel that kindled it and then go out in everlasting shame, or else it proves but a blaze and turns into loathing and weariness of each other. And because this passion of lust (called "love") is such an infatuating,[43] blinding thing (like the longing of a woman with child), it is the duty of all who feel any touch of it to kindle their hearts to call it presently to the trial and to quench it effectually. Till that is done (if they have any relics of wit or reason) they are to suspect their own apprehensions and much more to trust the judgment and advice of others.

The means to quench this lust (called "love"), I have largely opened before. I shall now only remind you of these few: First, separate yourself and keep a sufficient distance from the person to whom you are attracted.[44] The nearness of the fire and fuel causes the combustion, since fancy and lust are inflamed by the senses. Keep out of sight, and in time the fever may abate. Second, do not overvalue vanity or think highly of a silken coat, the great names of ancestors, money, lands, a painted or spotted face, or that natural comeliness called "beauty." Do not judge of things as children but as men, and do not be fools in magnifying trifles and overlooking inward, real worth. Would you thus fall in love with a flower or picture? Bear in mind[45] what work the pox or any other withering sickness[46] will make with that silly beauty that you so admire. Think what a spectacle death will make it and how many thousands once beautiful are turned now to common earth! Think about how many thousands of

---

[42]*Felicity.*
[43]*Besotting.*
[44]*Keep asunder and at a sufficient distance from the person that you dote upon.*
[45]*Bethink.*
[46]E.g., smallpox, cowpox, or chicken pox.

souls are now in hell that by a beautiful body were drowned in lust and tempted to neglect themselves, and how few in the world were ever better for it! What a childish thing it is to be ravished[47] with a book of tales and lies because it has a beautiful, gilded cover and to undervalue the writings of the wise because they have a plain and homely outside.

Third, rule your thoughts and do not let them run wild[48] as fancy shall command them. If reason cannot call off your thoughts from following a lustful desire and imagination, no wonder if one who rides on such an unbridled colt is cast into the dirt. Fourth, do not live idly, but let the business of your callings take up your time and employ your thoughts. An idle, fleshly mind is the carcass where the vermin of lust crawls and the nest where the Devil hatches both this and many other sins. Fifth, lastly and chiefly, do not forget the concerns of your souls. Remember how near you are to eternity and what work you have to do for your salvation. Do not forget the presence of God or the approach of death. Look often by faith into heaven and hell, and keep your conscience tender. Then I promise[49] you, you will find something else to mind than lust, and greater matters than a silly carcass to take up your thoughts, and you will feel that heavenly love within you that will extinguish earthly, sensual[50] love.

Direction 5: Do not be too hasty in your choice or resolution, but deliberate well, and thoroughly know the person on whom so much of the comfort or sorrow of your life will depend. Where repentance has no place, there is the greater care to be used to prevent it. Reason requires you to be well acquainted with those whom you trust with an important secret, much more with all your honor or estates, and most of all with one to whom you must entrust so much of the comfort of your lives and your advantages for a better life. No care and caution can be too great in a matter of so great importance.

Direction 6: Do not let carnal motives persuade you to join yourself to an ungodly person. Rather, let the holy fear of God be preferred in your choice before all worldly excellence whatsoever. Do not marry a swine for a golden trough, or an ugly soul for a beautiful[51]

[47]*Doted upon.*
[48]*Masterless.*
[49]*Warrant.*
[50]*Carnal.*
[51]*Comely.*

body. Otherwise, first, you will give cause of great suspicion that you are yourself ungodly; for those who know the misery of an unrenewed soul and the excellency of the image of God can never be indifferent whether they are joined to the godly or the ungodly. To habitually prefer things temporal before things spiritual in the predominant acts of heart and life is the certain character of a graceless soul. He who deliberately prefers riches and beauty[52] in another, before the image and fear of God, gives a very dangerous sign of a graceless heart and will. If you value beauty and riches more than godliness, you have the surest mark that you are ungodly; if you claim not to value them, then why do you prefer them? How could you do a thing that detects your ungodliness and condemns you more clearly? Does this not show that you either do not believe the Word of God, or else that you do not love God and regard his interest? Otherwise, you would take his friends as your friends and his enemies as your enemies.

Tell me, would you marry an enemy as your own, before any change or reconciliation? I am confident that you would not. Can you so easily marry an enemy of God? If you do not know that all the ungodly and unsanctified are his enemies, you do not believe or know the Word of God, which tells you that "the mind that is set on the flesh is hostile to God, for it does not submit to God's law; indeed, it cannot. Those who are in the flesh cannot please God" (Rom. 8:7–8). If you fear God, your chief end in marriage will be to have one who will be a helper to your soul and further you in the way to heaven. If you marry a person who is ungodly, either you have no such end or else you must know that you have not chosen anything wiser than if you chose water to kindle the fire or a bed of snow to keep you warm. Will an ignorant or ungodly person assist you in prayer and holy watchfulness and stir you up to the love of God and a heavenly mind? Can you so willingly lose all the spiritual benefit that you should principally desire and intend? Third, nay, instead of a helper, you will have a continual hinderer. When you should go to prayer, you will have one to pull you back or fill your mind with diversions or disquietness![53] When you should keep close to God in holy medita-tions, you will have one to cast in worldly thoughts or trouble your

---

[52]*Comeliness.*
[53]*Disquietments.*

mind with vanity or vexation. When you should speak of God and heavenly things, you will have one to stifle such discourse and fill your ears with idle, impertinent, or worldly talk. One such hindrance so near you, in your bosom, will be worse than a thousand further off. As an ungodly heart that is next to us is our greatest hindrance, so an ungodly husband or wife is worse to us than many ungodly neighbors. If you think that you can overcome such hindrances and that your heart is so good that no such obstruction[54] can keep it down, you show that you have a proud, arrogant[55] heart that is prepared for a fall. If you know yourselves and the badness of your hearts, you will know that you have no need of hindrances in any holy work and that all the helps in the world are little enough, and too little, to keep your souls in the love of God.

Fourth, such an ungodly companion will be to you a continual temptation to sin. Instead of stirring you up to good, you will have one to stir you up to evil—passion or discontent or covetousness or pride or revenge or sensuality. Can you not sin enough without such a tempter? Fifth, what a continual grief will it be to you, if you are a believer, to have a child of the Devil in your bosom and to think how far you must be separated at death! And in what torments those must lie forever who are so dear unto you you know! Sixth, yea, such companions will be incapable of the principal part of your love. You may love them as husbands or wives, but you cannot love them as saints and members of Christ. And how great an absence[56] this will be in your love those know who know what this holy love is.

Question: But how can I tell who are godly when there is so much hypocrisy in the world?

Answer: You may know who is ungodly if it is clearly[57] discovered. I do not take a barren knowledge for ungodliness or a clever[58] tongue for godliness. Judge them by their love; as their love is, so they are. If they love the Word and the servants and worship of God and love a holy life and hate the contrary, you may embrace[59] such, though their knowledge is small and abilities weak.[60] But if they

---

[54]*Clogs.*
[55]*Unhumbled.*
[56]*Want.*
[57]*Palpably.*
[58]*Nimble.*
[59]*Close.*
[60]*Parts are weak.*

have no love to these and live a common, careless, sensual[61] life, you may avoid them as ungodly.

Question: But if ungodly persons may marry, why may I not marry one who is ungodly?

Answer: Though dogs and swine may reproduce,[62] it does not follow that men or women may join with them. Pardon the comparison (while Christ calls the wicked "dogs" and "pigs," Matt. 7:6), but it shows the badness of your conclusion.[63] Unbelievers may marry, and yet we may not marry unbelievers. "Do not be unequally yoked with unbelievers. For what partnership has righteousness with lawlessness? Or what fellowship has light with darkness? What accord has Christ with Belial? Or what portion does a believer share with an unbeliever? What agreement has the temple of God with idols? For we are the temple of the living God. . . . Therefore go out from their midst, and be separate from them, says the Lord, and touch no unclean thing" (2 Cor. 6:14–17).

Question: But I make no doubt that they may be converted. God can call them when he will; if there is but love, will they not easily be won to be of the same mind as those they love are?

Answer: First, then, it seems because you love an ungodly person, you will be easily turned to be ungodly. If so, you are not much better already. If love will not draw you to their mind to be ungodly, why should you think love will draw them to your mind to be godly? Are you stronger in grace than they are in sin? Second, if you know well what grace is and what a sinful, unrenewed soul is, you would not think it so easy a matter to convert a soul. Why are so few converted if it is so easy a thing? You cannot make yourselves better by adding higher degrees to the grace you have; much less can you make others better by giving them the grace that they do not have. Third, it is true that God is able to convert them when he will; and it is true that for aught I know it may be done. What of it? Will you, in so weighty a case, take up with a mere possibility? God can make a beggar rich, and for aught you know to the contrary, he will do it; and yet you will not, therefore, marry a beggar; nor will you marry a leper because God can heal him. Why then should you marry an ungodly person

---

[61]*Carnal.*
[62]*Join in generating.*
[63]*Consequence.*

because God can convert him? See it done first, if you love your peace and safety.

Question: What if my parents command me to marry an ungodly person?

Answer: God having forbidden it, no parent has authority to command you to do so great a mischief to yourself, no more than to cut your own throats or to dismember your bodies.

Question: What if I have a necessity of marrying and can find no one but an ungodly person?

Answer: If that is really your case, and your necessity is real and you can find no other, I think it is lawful.

Question: Is it not better to have a good-natured person who is ungodly than an ill-natured person who is religious, as many are? And may not a bad man be a good husband?

Answer: First, a bad man may be a good tailor or shoemaker or carpenter or seaman because there is no moral virtue necessary to the well-doing of his work. But a bad man cannot be a good magistrate or minister or husband or parent because there is much moral virtue necessary to his duties. Second, a bad nature not spiritually mortified or subdued[64] is inconsistent with true godliness; such persons may talk and profess what they please, but "If anyone thinks he is religious and does not bridle his tongue but deceives his heart, this person's religion is worthless" (James 1:26). Third, I did not say that godliness alone is all that you must look after; though this is the first, more is necessary.

Direction 7: Next to the fear of God, make the choice of a nature or temperament that is not too much unsuitable to you. A crossness of dispositions will be a continual vexation, and you will have a domestic war instead of love. Especially make sure of these qualities: First, that there is a loving and not a selfish nature that has no regard to another but for that person's own end. Second, that there is a nature competently quiet and patient and not hard to please.[65] Third, that there is a competency of wit,[66] for no one can live lovingly and comfortably with a fool. Fourth, that there is a competent humility; for there is no quietness to be expected with the proud. Fifth, that

---

[64]*Unmortified and untamed.*
[65]*Intolerably froward and unpleasable.*
[66]That is, intelligence.

there is a power to be silent as well as to speak; for a babbling tongue is a continual vexation.

Direction 8: Next to grace and nature, have a due and moderate respect to person, education, and estate. So far have respect to the person as there is no sickness[67] to make your condition overburdensome, nor any such deformity that may hinder your affections. And have respect to parentage and education so there is no great unsuitableness of mind or any preconceived[68] opinions in religion that may make you too unequal. Differing opinions in religion are much more tolerable in persons more distant than in near relations. Those who are bred too high in idleness and luxury must have a thorough work of grace to make them fit for a low condition and cure the pride and sensuality that are taken for the honorable badges of their gentility. It is scarcely considerable how rich such are—for their pride and luxury will make them even with all and to be in greater want than honest, contented, temperate poverty.

Direction 9: If God calls you to marriage, take notice of the helps and comforts of that condition as well as the hindrances and troubles, that you may cheerfully serve God in it, in the expectation of his blessing. Though man's corruption has filled that and every state of life with snares and troubles, yet from the beginning it was not so. God appointed it for mutual help, and as such it may be used.

As a married life has its temptations and afflictions, so it has its benefits, which you are thankfully to accept and acknowledge to God (see Eccles. 4:10–12). First, it is a mercy for the propagating of a people on earth to love and honor their Creator and to serve God in the world and enjoy him forever. It is no small mercy to be the parents of a godly seed; and this is the purpose[69] of the institution of marriage (Mal. 2:15). This parents may expect, if they are not wanting on their part; however, sometimes their children prove ungodly. Second, it is a mercy to have a faithful friend who loves you entirely and is as true to you as yourself, to whom you may open your mind and communicate your affairs and who would be ready to strengthen you and to divide the cares of your affairs and family with you and to help you bear your burdens and comfort you in your sorrows and

---

[67]*Unhealthfulness.*
[68]*Prejudicate.*
[69]*End.*

be the daily companion of your lives and partaker of your joys and sorrows. Third, it is a mercy to have so near a friend to be a helper to your soul, to join with you in prayer and other holy exercises, to watch over you and tell you of your sins and dangers and to stir up the grace of God and remind you[70] of the life to come and cheerfully accompany you in the ways of holiness. "House and wealth are inherited from fathers, but a prudent wife is from the LORD" (Prov. 19:14). Thus it is said in Proverbs 18:22, "He who finds a wife finds a good thing and obtains favor from the LORD." See also Proverbs 31:10–12.

Direction 10: Let your marriage covenant be made understandingly, deliberately, heartily, in the fear of God, with a fixed resolution to perform it. Understand well all the duties of your relation before you enter into it. Do not run upon it as boys to a play, but with the sense of your duty, as those who engage themselves in a great deal of work of great importance toward God and toward each other. Address yourselves beforehand to God for counsel, and earnestly beg his guidance and blessing, and do not run without or before him. Reckon upon the worst, and foresee all temptations that would diminish your affections or make you unfaithful to each other. See that you are fortified against them all.

Direction 11: Be sure that God is the ultimate end of your marriage and that you choose that state of life in which you may be most serviceable to him and that you heartily devote yourselves and your families unto God, so that it may be to you a sanctified condition. It is nothing but making God our guide and end that can sanctify our state of life. Those who sincerely[71] follow God's counsel and aim at his glory and do it to please him will find God owning and blessing their relation; but those who do it to please the flesh, to satisfy lust, and to increase their estates and to have children surviving them to receive the fruits of their pride and covetousness can expect to reap no better than they sow; and so they will have the flesh, the world, and the Devil as the masters of their family, according to their own desire and choice.

Direction 12: When you are first joined together[72] (and through the rest of your lives), remember the day of your separation. Do not

---

[70]*Remember you.*
[71]*Unfeignedly.*
[72]*At your first conjunction.*

think that you are settling yourselves in a state of rest or happiness[73] or continuance, but only assuming a companion in your travels. Whether you live in a married or an unmarried life, remember that you are hasting to the everlasting life, where there is neither "marrying [nor] giving in marriage" (Matt. 24:38; 1 Cor. 7:29–30). You are going as fast to another world in one state of life as in the other. You are to help each other in your way, that your journey may be the easier to you and that you may happily meet again in the heavenly Jerusalem. When worldly people[74] marry, they take it for a settling themselves in the world; and as regenerate persons begin the world anew, by beginning to lay up a treasure in heaven, so worldly people[75] call their marriage their beginning in the world, because then, as engaged servants to the world, they set themselves to seek it with greater diligence than ever before. They do but in marriage begin, as seekers, that life of being foolish[76] that when he had found what he sought, that rich man ended with "'I will do this: I will tear down my barns and build larger ones, and there I will store all my grain and my goods. And I will say to my soul, Soul, you have ample goods laid up for many years; relax, eat, drink, be merry.' But God said to him, 'Fool! This night your soul is required of you, and the things you have prepared, whose will they be?'" (Luke 12:18–20). If you would not die as fools, do not marry and live as the worldly.

Cases of Marriage

Question 1: What should one follow as a certain rule about the prohibited degrees of blood-relatedness[77] or affinity? See, first, that the Law of Moses is not in force to us. Second, if it were, it is very dark whether it may by likeness[78] be extended to more degrees than are named in the text. Third, seeing the law of nature is hardly legible in this case.[79]

Answer: First, it is certain that the prohibited degrees are not so constantly[80] and universally unlawful, since such marriage may

---

[73]*Felicity.*
[74]*Worldlings.*
[75]*Worldlings.*
[76]*Foolery.*
[77]*Consanguinity.*
[78]*Parity of reason.*
[79]In contrast, "The case of polygamy is so fully and plainly resolved by Christ that it is not necessary to write against it, especially while the law of [England] makes it death."
[80]*Statedly.*

not be lawful by any necessity. For Adam's sons did lawfully marry their own sisters.

Second, now that the world is peopled, such necessities as will warrant such marriages need to be rare, and such as we are never likely to meet with.

Third, the law of nature prohibits the degrees that are now unlawful, and though this law is dark as to some degrees, it is not so as to others.

Fourth, the law of God to the Jews, Leviticus 18, does not prohibit those degrees there named because of any reason proper to the Jews, but as an exposition of the law of nature and so for reasons common to all.

Fifth, therefore, though the Jewish law cease (yea, never bound other nations) formally as that political national law, yet it was God's exposition of his own law of nature, of its use and consequential obligation to all men, even to this day; for if God once had told but one man, "This is the sense of the law of nature," it remains true and all must believe it. Then the law of nature itself, so expounded, will still oblige.

Sixth, the world is so wide for choice, and a necessity of doubtful marriage so rare, and the trouble so great, that prudence tells everyone that it is sin, without flat necessity, to marry in a doubtful degree. Therefore, it is thus safest to avoid all degrees that seem to be equal to those named (Leviticus 18) and to have the same reason, though they are not named.

Seventh, because it is not certain that the unnamed cases have the same reason (since God does not acquaint us with all the reasons of his law), therefore, when the thing is done, we must not censure others too deeply nor trouble ourselves too much about those unnamed, doubtful cases. We must avoid them beforehand because otherwise we shall cast ourselves into doubts and troubles unnecessarily. But when it is past, the case must be considered, as I shall afterward show.

Question 2: What if the law of the land forbids more or fewer degrees than Leviticus 18?

Answer: If it forbids fewer, the rest are nevertheless to be avoided as forbidden by God. If it forbids more, the forbidden ones must be avoided in obedience to our rulers.

Question 3: Is the marriage of first cousins[81] unlawful?

Answer: I do not think so. First, this is not forbidden by God. Second, none of that same rank are forbidden—that is, no one who is two degrees from the root on both sides. For my reasons, I refer the reader to the Latin treatise of Charles Butler on this subject, [82] for in those reasons I rest. As all the children of Noah's sons did marry their first cousins (for they could not marry in any remoter degree), so have others since without reproof, and none are forbidden. Third, it is safest to do otherwise because there are enough choices, and many divines, being of the contrary opinion, may make it a matter of conscience[83] and trouble afterward to those who venture upon it without need.

Question 4: What would you have those do who have married first cousins[84] and now doubt whether it is lawful to do so?

Answer: I would have them cast away any such doubts or at least conclude that it is now their duty to live peaceably in the state in which they are, and a great sin for them to be separated on such scruples. The reason is, if it is not certain that the degree is lawful, at least no man can be sure that it is unlawful. For husband and wife to break their covenant and part without a necessary cause is a great sin; and that which no man can prove to be a sin is no necessary and lawful cause for divorce.

Marriage duties are certainly commanded to the married, but the marriage of first cousins[85] is not certainly forbidden. Therefore, if it were a sin to marry for those who doubted, or if they have since fallen into doubt whether it was not a sin, yet may they be sure that the continuance of it is a duty and that all they have to do is repent of doing a doubtful thing but not part or forbear their covenanted duties. No, nor to indulge or suffer those troublesome scruples, which would hinder the cheerful discharge of their duties and the comfortable serving of God in their relations.

Question 5: What should those do who are married in those

---

[81]*Cousin-germans*, that is, an uncle's children or an aunt's children.

[82]Baxter refers to Butler's (c. 1559–1647) work on the marriage of first cousins, *Syngeneia: De propinquitate matrimonium impendiente, regula,* published in 1625. Butler, vicar of Wotton, is best known for beekeeping and writing one of the first English books on insects, *Feminine Monarchie; Or, A Treatise Concerning Bees and the Due Order of Them* (1609).

[83]*Scruple.*

[84]*Cousin-germans.*

[85]*Cousin-germans.*

degrees that are not forbidden by name in Leviticus 18 and yet are at the same distance from the root with those that are named and seem to have the same reason of unlawfulness?

Answer: If there is clearly closeness[86] of degree, and also the reason of prohibition, then no doubt they must part as incestuous and not continue in a forbidden state. But divines are disagreed whether there is in all instances a likeness[87] of the prohibition where there is an equal distance as to degrees; and so in those cases some think it is a duty to be separated, and others think it is enough to repent of their union[88] and not to be separated, because the case is doubtful (as the controversy shows). I shall not venture to cast in my judgment in a case where so many such men are disagreed; instead, I shall only advise all to prevent such troublesome doubts beforehand and not by rashness to run themselves into perplexities when there is no necessity, unless they will call their fleshly[89] ends or sinful passions a necessity.

Question 6: But if a man marries in a degree there forbidden, is it in all cases a sin to continue in that state? If necessity made such marriage a duty to Adam's children, why may not necessity make the continuance lawful to others? And suppose parents command it? Suppose the woman will die or be distracted with grief? Suppose one has made a vow to marry no other and yet cannot live single? Here I shall suppose that if a lustful person marries a relative,[90] he may have a change, knowing beforehand that he must be divorced, punished, and not continue in the sin. If one has married a relative,[91] one should be glad to be divorced because he does not love her; therefore, punishment must rebuke him, and he is not to continue in incest.

Answer: First, natural necessity justified Adam's children, and such would now justify you. Yea, the benediction "be fruitful and multiply" did not only allow but obliged them to marry, to replenish the earth (or else mankind would soon have ceased); but it is not now so, when the earth is replenished. Yet I do not deny that if a man and his sister were cast alone upon a foreign wilderness, where they

---

[86]*Parity of the reason.*
[87]*Parity.*
[88]*Conjunction.*
[89]*Carnal.*
[90]*Kinswoman.*
[91]*Kinswoman.*

justly despaired of any other company, if God should bid them to "be fruitful and multiply," it would warrant them to marry. But otherwise there is no necessity for it, and therefore no lawfulness. Second, a vicious necessity does not justify the sin. If the man or woman who abstain will be mad or dead with passion rather than obey God and deny and mortify their lust, one sin will not justify them in another. The thing that is necessary is to conform their wills to the law of God; and if they will not, and then say that they cannot, then they must bear what they get by it. Third, it is no necessity that is imposed by the command of parents when it is against the law of God. Fourth, not by a vow either; for a vow to break God's law is not an obligation to be kept but to be repented of; nor is the necessity remediless when one brings it on himself by vowing never to marry any other, seeing chastity may be kept.

Question 7: Is it lawful for one to marry who has vowed chastity during life and not to marry and afterward finds a necessity of marrying, for the avoiding of lust and fornication?

Answer: I know that many great divines have easily absolved those who under popery vowed chastity. The principal part of the solution of the question, you must fetch from my solution of the "Case of Vows."[92] At present, this shall suffice to be added to it: first, such vows of chastity that are absolute, without any exceptions of after alterations or difficulties that may arise, are sinfully made or are unlawful *quoad actum jurandi* ("as long as the oath stands").[93]

Second, if parents or others impose such oaths and vows on their children or subjects or induce them to it, it is sinfully done; therefore, the *actus imperantium* ("act of commanding") is unlawful.

Third, as long as the *materia jurata* ("the matter vowed") remains lawful, the vow does bind, and it is treachery[94] to break it because the sinfulness of the imposer's act proves no more than such a command did not oblige you to vow. A vow made arbitrarily without any command nevertheless binds. The sinfulness of making the vow only calls for repentance (if you made it carelessly,[95] rashly, upon

---

[92]Baxter's "Case of Vows" can be found in the fourth part of *A Christian Directory*, "Christian Ecclesiastics, or Church Duties," Chapter 5, the second section.
[93]"By this you may see how to resolve the cases about vows and covenants which are the great controversies of this time among us."
[94]*Perfidiousness.*
[95]*Causelessly.*

ill motives, and to ill ends or in ill circumstances). The vow that you repent you ever made must nevertheless be kept if the thing vowed is lawful and the act of vowing is not made a nullity (though it was a sin). And when it is a nullity, I have showed in the before-cited place.

Fourth, a vow of celibacy or chastity during life, which has this condition or exception expressed or implied in the true intent of the votary[96] (unless anything falls out that shall make it a sin for one not to marry), may in some cases be a lawful vow, as to one who foresees great inconveniences in marriage and would by firm resolution fortify himself against temptations and mutability.

Fifth, if there were no such excepting thought in the person vowing, yet when the thing becomes unlawful, the vow is not to be kept; though it obliges us under guilt for sinfully making it, yet God commands us not to keep it because we vowed that which he forbade us, not only to vow but to do.

Sixth, either the papists suppose such exceptions to be always implied by their votaries or at least they are contained in the law of God, or else they would never dare pretend that the pope has power to dispense with such vows (as they have often done for princes, men and women, that they might be taken from a monastery to a crown). For if they suppose that the persons before the dispensation are under the obligation of their vow and bound by God to keep it, then it would be too gross and odious a blasphemy for the pope to claim a power of disobliging them and dissolving God's commands. This is not only against Christianity but against theism[97] itself, a setting of himself above God Almighty, under the pretense of his own commission. But if they only pretend to dissolve such vows judicially or decisively, by judging when the person is no longer obliged to keep them by God's law, then they suppose that the obligation of God's law is ceased before they judicially declare it to be ceased. (And if that were all that the pope undertook, he had no power to do it out of his own parish, no more than any lawful bishop has in his proper charge.)

Seventh, the matter of a vow of celibacy or chastity is then unlawful when it cannot be kept without greater sin than that life of chastity escapes and that would be escaped if it were forsaken or without the omission of greater duty and omission of greater good

---

[96]One who is bound by vows to a religious life, such as a monk or nun.
[97]*Anti-theistical.*

than a life of chastity contains or attains. For the further opening of
this, let it be noted, that,

Eighth, not every degree of sin that marriage would cure will
warrant the breach of a vow of chastity, as if I had some more lustful
thoughts or instigations and irritations in a single life than I should
have if I married, because no man lives without some sin, and it is
supposed that there are greater sins of another kind that by a life of
chastity I avoid. The breach of the vow itself is a greater matter than
a lustful thought.

Ninth, so it is not every degree of good, which by marriage I may
attain or do, that will warrant it against a vow of chastity. Though I
may do and get a greater good by chastity, and though the evil of per-
jury is not to be done that good may be done by it, I must prove that
it is not only good in itself but a duty *hic et nunc* ("here and now").

Tenth, a man should rather break his vow of celibacy than commit
fornication, if there were a necessity that he must do the one, because
fornication is a sin that no vow will warrant any man to commit.

Eleventh, a man should rather break his vow of celibacy than live
in such constant or ordinary lust as unfits him for prayer and a holy
life and keeps him in danger of fornication, if there were a necessity
that he must do the one. The reason is also because now the matter
vowed is become unlawful, and no vow can warrant a man to live in
so great sin (unless there were some greater sin on the other side
that could not be avoided in a married life, which is hardly to be supposed, however much popish priests think disobedience to the pope
and the disadvantage[98] and disgrace of a married life to be a greater
sin than fornication itself).

Twelfth, if a prince vows chastity, when it is likely to endanger
the kingdom for want of a safe and sure succession, he is bound to
break that vow because he may not lawfully give away the people's
right or do that which is injurious to so many.

Thirteenth, whether the command of a parent may dissolve the
obligation of a vow of celibacy I have answered already. I now say
but this: first, when parents may justly command it, we may justly
obey them. But this is not one of those accidental evils that may be
lawfully done, though unlawfully commanded. Second, it is to par-

---

[98]*Incommodity.*

ents that God has committed this care and power about children's marriage, more than to princes. Third, parents, not princes, may not lawfully command the breach of such a vow, not nullified at first, except in such cases as disoblige them whether they do it or not, so that the resolving of the main case suffices for all.

Fourteenth, he who by lawful means can overcome his lust, to the measure before mentioned, is under no necessity of violating his vow of single life.

Fifteenth, I think that it is not one of twenty who have bodies so unavoidably prone to lust, but that by due means it might be so far, though not totally, overcome without marriage, fornication, willful self-pollution,[99] or violent, vexatious, lustful thoughts. That is, 1. If they employ themselves constantly and diligently in a lawful calling and are not guilty of idleness, as leaves room in their minds and imaginations for vain and filthy thoughts; if they follow such a calling as shall lay a necessity upon them to keep their thoughts closely employed about it. 2. If they use such abstinence and coarseness in their diet as is meet to tame inordinate lusts without destroying health, and not only avoid fullness and gluttony[100] and vain sports and pleasures but also use convenient fasting and tame the body by necessary austerities. 3. If they sufficiently avoid all tempting company and sights and keep at a meet distance from them. 4. If they set such a restraint upon their thoughts as they may do. 5. If they use such a quality of diet and medicine[101] as is fittest[102] for the altering of those bodily distempers that are the cause. 6. And lastly, if they are earnest in prayer to God and live in mortifying meditations, especially in a constant familiarity with a crucified Christ and with the grave and with the heavenly society. He who breaks his vow to save himself the labor and suffering of these ungrateful means, I take to be devious,[103] though perhaps he sinfully made that vow. No greater numbers are excusable for continence after such a vow than those who have bodies so extraordinarily lustful that no other means can tame and those mentioned before who have extraordinary qualities[104] to make a single life unlawful.

---

[99]That is, masturbation.
[100]*Gulosity.*
[101]*Physic.*
[102]*Aptest.*
[103]*Perfidious.*
[104]*Accidents.*

Sixteenth, it must not be forgotten that if men trust marriage alone as the cure for their lust, without other means, such violent lusts as nothing else will cure may be much uncured afterward. For adulterers are as violent in their lusts as the unmarried and often find it as hard to restrain them. Therefore, the married, as well as others, need to be careful to overcome their lust because it is in them a double sin if they do otherwise.

Seventeenth, when all other means fail, marriage is God's appointed means to quench those flames that men's vows cannot; in cases of true necessity, this disobliges them.

Chapter Two

Worship of God in Families:
Is It by Divine Appointment?

That excellent speech of Mirandula is often in mind, *Veritatem philosophia quaerit, theologia invenit, religio possidet* ("Philosophy seeks truth, theology discovers it, and religion possesses it").[1] I do, therefore, with greater alacrity and delight dispute these points that are directly religious, that is, immediately practical, rather than those that are only remotely such. Though I am loath we should see among us any wider division *inter philosophum theologum et religiosum* ("between philosophy, theology, and religion") than between the fantasy, the intellect, and the will, which never are found disjoined[2] in any act, or rather than between the habits of practical natural knowledge and the habits of practical supernatural knowledge and the practical resolutions, affections, and endeavors into which both the former are devolved, yet may we safely and profitably distinguish where it would be mortal to divide. If disputing our present case do but tend to, and end in, a religious performance, we shall then be able to say, "We disputed not in vain" when, by experience of the delight and profit of God's work, we perceive that we do not worship him in vain. Otherwise, to evince by a dispute that God should be worshipped, and not to worship him when we are done, is but to draw forth our learning and sharpen our wits to plead for our condemnation, as if the accuser wanted our help

---

[1]John Picus of Mirandula (1463–1494) was a learned linguist and Christian philosopher whose *Epistles* (lib. i.6) Baxter here quotes.
[2]*Disjunct.*

or the Judge of all the world did lack evidence or arguments against us unless he had it from our own mouth. Concerning the sense of the terms, I shall say somewhat, both as to the subject and the predicate, so that we contend not in the dark.

First, by "worship of God" we mean not only, nor principally obedience as such or service in common things, called Δελεια; but we mean a religious performance of some sacred actions, with an intention of honoring God as God, and that more directly than in common works of obedience. This is commonly called Λατρεια by Augustine, and since him by all the orthodox, appropriated to God alone; and indeed to give it to any other is contrary to its definition.

This worship is of two sorts, whereof the first is by an excellence called "worship," that is, when the honoring of God is so directly the end and whole business of the work that our own advantage falls in but impliedly and in evident subordination. Such are the blessed works of praise and thanksgiving that we here begin and shall in heaven perpetuate. Yet we see a more admirable mystery of true religion—we indeed receive more largely from God and enjoy more fully our own happiness[3] in him in these acts of worship that give all to God than in the other, wherein we more directly seek something from him. And those are the second sort of worship actions, when the substance or matter of the work is a seeking or receiving something from God or delivering something religiously in his name, and so is more directly for ourselves, though it is God who should be our ultimate end in this too. You may perceive I make of this three sorts: The first consists in our religious addresses to God for something that we want and is called "prayer." The second consists in our religious addresses to God to receive from him, that is, instructions, precepts, promises, and threatenings from his mouth, messengers, and so on and the sacramental signs of his grace in baptism and the Lord's Supper. The third is when the officers of Christ do in his name solemnly deliver either his laws or sacraments, his laws either in general by ordinary preaching or by a more particular application in acts of discipline.

Second, the word "solemn" signifies sometimes anything usual, and so some derive it *Solenne est quod fieri solet* ("as certain as that which occurs habitually"), sometimes that which is done on one set

---

[3]*Felicity.*

day in the year, and so some make *solenne* to be *quasi solum semel in anno* ("as if only at set times in the year"). But commonly[4] it is taken, and so we take it here, for both *celebre et usitatum* ("frequent and common"), that is, a thing that is not accidentally and seldom but statedly and ordinarily to be done, and that with such gravity and honorable seriousness as beseems a business of such weight.

Third, by "family" we do not mean a tribe or stock of kindred, dwelling in many houses, as the word is often taken in Scripture but a household—*Domus et familia*. "A household and family" are indeed in economics[5] somewhat different notions but one thing. *Domus* is to *familia* as *civitas* is to *respublica* ("a household is to family as citizenship is to a commonwealth"). The former is made the subject of the latter, the latter the *finis internus* ("final end") of the former. And so, *Domus est societas naturae consentanea, e personis domesticis, vitae in dies omnes commode sustentandae causa, collecta. Familia est ordo domus per regimen patris-familias in personas sibi subjectas* ("A home is a natural and agreeable society, living suitably every day. Family is a household ordained for the ruling of fathers over subordinates").

Note that to a complete family there must be four integral parts, *pater-familias, mater-familias, filius, servus*; that is, "father, mother, son, and servant." But as to the essence of a family it suffices if there is but the *pars imperans, et pars subdita* ("role of a leader, and role of a subordinate"), one head or governor, either father, mother, master, or mistress, and one or more governed under this head.

Note, therefore, that the governor is an essential part of the family, and so are some of the governed (whatever such there be), but not each member. If, therefore, twenty children or servants shall worship God without the father or master of the family either presenting himself or in some representative, it is not a family worship in the strict sense. But if the head of the family in himself (or in a delegate or representative) is present with any of his children or servants though all the rest be absent, it is yet a family duty, though the family is incomplete and maimed (and so is the duty, therefore, if culpably so performed).

Fourth, when I say "in and by" family, I mean not that each

[4]*Vulgarly.*
[5]That is, the study of family life.

must do the same parts of the work, but that one (either the head or someone designated[6] by him and representing him) be the mouth, the rest performing their parts by receiving instructions or mentally concurring in the prayers and praise put up by him. Lastly, by "divine appointment" I mean any signification of God's will, that it is men's duty to perform this; whether a signification by natural means or supernatural, directly or by consequence, we may be sure it is God's will. The sum of the question, then, is, "Whether any sacred actions religiously and ordinarily to be performed to God's honor by the head of the family, with the rest, is by God's appointment made our duty?" My thoughts I shall reduce to these heads and propound in this order: first, of family worship in general; second, of the sorts of that worship in special; and third, of the time.

Concerning the first, I lay down my thoughts in these propositions, for limitation and caution, and then prove the main conclusion.

Proposition 1: First, it is not all sorts of God's worship that he has appointed to be performed by families as such, there being some proper to more public assemblies.

Second, more particularly the administration of the sacraments of baptism and the Lord's Supper are proper to the ministerial or organized churches and are not common to families; for as they are both committed only to ministers of the gospel and have been only used by them for many hundreds of years in the church (except that some permitted others to baptize in cases of necessity), so the Lord's Supper was appointed for a symbol and means of a more public communion than that of families. Though some conjecture the contrary, from its first institution, and think that as there is family prayer and church prayer, family teaching and church teaching, so there should be family sacraments and church sacraments, this is a mistake. For though Christ administered it to his family, yet it was not as a family but as a church. For that which is but one family may possibly be a church also. This exposition we have from the doctrine and practice of the apostles and constant custom of all the churches, which have never thought the Lord's Supper to be a family duty, but proper to larger assemblies and administrable only by ordained ministers. Nor will the reasons drawn from circumcision and the Passover prove the

---

[6]*Deputed.*

contrary: both because particular churches were not then instituted as now, and therefore families had the more to do, and because there were some duties proper to families in the very institution of those sacraments, and because God gave them a power in those that he has not given to masters of families now in our sacraments.

Third, many thousands do, by their own viciousness and negligence, disable themselves, so that they cannot perform what God has made their duty; yet it remains their duty still. Some disability may excuse them in part, but not in whole.

I shall now prove that the solemn worship of God in and by families as such is of divine appointment.

Argument 1: If families are societies of God's institution, furnished with special advantages and opportunities for God's solemn worship, having no prohibition not to use them, then the solemn worship of God in and by families as such is of divine appointment. The antecedent is true; therefore, so is the consequent.

For the parts of the antecedent: first, that families are societies of God's institution needs no proof.

Second, that they are furnished with special advantages and opportunities may appear by an enumeration of particulars: 1. There is the advantage of authority in the ruler of the family, whereby he may command all who are under him in God's worship; yea, and may inflict penalties on children and servants who refuse; yea, may cast some out of the family if they are obstinate. 2. He has the advantage of a singular interest in wife and children, by which he may bring them to it willingly, so that they may perform a right evangelical worship. 3. He has the advantage of a singular dependence of all upon him for daily provisions and of his children for their portions for livelihood in the world, whereby he may yet further prevail with them for obedience, he having a power to reward, as well as to punish and command. 4. They have the opportunity of cohabitation and so are still at hand and more together and so in readiness for such employments. 5. Being nearest in relation, they are strongly obliged to further each other's salvation and help each other in serving God. 6. They have hereby an advantage against all prejudices and jealousies that strangeness and mistakes may raise and cherish among those who live at a greater distance and so may close more heartily in God's worship. Their nearness of relation and natural affections do singularly advantage them for a more affectionate bond[7] and so for a more forcible and acceptable worship of God when they are in it as of one heart and soul. 7. If any misunderstanding or other impediment arise, they, being still at hand, have opportunity to remove them and to satisfy each other; and if any distempers of understanding, heart, or life be in the family, the ruler, by familiarity and daily converse, is enabled more particularly to fit his reproofs and exhortations, confessions and petitions accordingly, which even ministers in the congregations cannot so well do. Thus, I have made it evident in this enumeration that families have advantages, yea, special and most excellent advantages and opportunities, for the solemn worship of God.

Third, the last part of the antecedent was that they have no prohibition to use these advantages and opportunities for God's solemn worship. I add this lest any should say, though they have such advantages, yet God may restrain them to avoid some greater inconveniencies another way, as he has restrained women from speaking in the assemblies. But, 1. God has neither restrained them in the law of nature, nor in the written law; therefore not at all. He who can show it in either, let him do it. 2. I never yet read or heard any knowing Christian once affirm that God has forbidden families solemnly to worship him, and therefore I think it needless to prove a negative when no man is known to hold the affirmative. Indeed, for some kinds of worship, as preaching and expounding Scripture, some have prohibited them; but not reading, catechizing, all instructing, praying, praises, singing psalms, much less all solemn worship wholly. So much for the antecedent.

I now come to prove the consequence. The foresaid advantages and opportunities are talents given by God, which they who receive them are obliged faithfully to improve for God. Therefore, families having such advantages and opportunities for God's solemn worship are bound to improve them faithfully for God in the solemn worshipping of him. For the antecedent, 1. It is unquestionable that these are talents, that is, improvable mercies given by God. For as none dare deny them to be mercies, so none dare, I hope, say that

---

[7]*Conjunction.*

God is not the giver of them. And then, 2. That such talents must be improved faithfully for God, from whom they are received, is plain from Matthew 25 throughout, especially verses 14–30. And in Luke 20:10 he requires the fruits of his vineyard; and in Matthew 10:42, if he entrusts us with a cup of cold water, he expects it for a prophet when he calls for it. If he entrusts us with outward riches, he expects that we "give to the one who begs from you" (Matt. 5:42; Luke 6:30, 38; 11:41; 12:33). His stewards must give an account of their stewardships (Luke 16:2). Christ tells us of all our talents in general, "Everyone to whom much was given, of him much will be required, and from him to whom they entrusted much, they will demand the more" (Luke 12:48). And of our words in particular, Christ tells us, "On the day of judgment people will give account for every careless word they speak" (Matt. 12:36), and much more for denying to use both our tongues and hearts in God's worship when he gives us such opportunities. "Moreover, it is required of stewards that they be found trustworthy" (1 Cor. 4:2). "As each has received a gift, use it to serve one another, as good stewards of God's varied grace: whoever speaks, as one who speaks oracles of God" (1 Pet. 4:10–11). Many more similar Scriptures prove the antecedent of the enthymeme,[8] and the consequent needs no proof.

Argument 2: The solemn worship of God in and by families as such is required by the law of nature; therefore, it is of divine institution. The consequence can be denied by no man who renounces not reason and nature itself, not denying the law of nature to be God's law, which is indeed partly presupposed in the law supernatural and partly rehearsed in it but never subverted by it. Positives are more mutable than naturals are.

The antecedent is thus manifested: first, natural reason (or the law of nature) requires that all men faithfully improve all the talents that God has entrusted them with to his honor; therefore, natural reason (or the law of nature) requires that God is solemnly worshipped in families, having given them such advantages as before mentioned. Second, the law of nature requires that all societies that have God for their founder or instituter should, to their utmost

---

[8]Maintaining the truth of a proposition from the assumed truth of its contrary, as in, "If it is great praise to please good men, surely to please evil men is a great shame." For an introduction to rhetorical terms, see Richard A. Lanham, *A Handlist of Rhetorical Terms*, second edition (Berkeley, CA: University of California Press, 1991).

capacities, be devoted to him who founded and instituted them. That God is the founder and instituter of families is known by the light of nature itself; therefore, the law of nature requires that families are to the utmost of their capacities devoted to God, and consequently that they solemnly worship him, being capable of so doing. I do not need to prove the major thesis because I speak only to men who are possessed of the law of nature mentioned in it. Therefore, they know it themselves to be true. Yet let me so far stay on the illustration as to tell you the grounds of it: 1. God is the Alpha and Omega, the first and the last, the principal efficient and ultimate end of all, and therefore of families. And, therefore, they should be *for* him as well as they are *from* him: for "from him and through him and to him are all things" (Rom. 11:36). This argument I draw from nature, which can have no beginning but God, nor any end but God. 2. I draw from the divine intention in the fabrication and ordination of all things. God made all things for himself and can have no ultimate end below himself. 3. I draw from his *jus dominii*, his "right of ownership," which he has over all things, and so over families as such; they are all absolutely his alone. That which is solely or absolutely a man's own should be for his use and employed to his honor and ends: much more that which is God's, seeing man is not capable of such a plenary propriety of anything in the world as God has in all things. 4. I argue *jure imperii,* from God's "just command." If he has a full right of government of families as families, they must honor and worship him according to their utmost capacities. Indeed he has a full right of absolute government over families as families; therefore, the consequent of the major is grounded on these two things: 1. That God himself is the end of his own government; this is proper to his regimen. All human government is said by politicians to be terminated ultimately in the public good of the society. But God's pleasure and glory is the end of his government and is, as it were, the public or universal good. 2. Nature teaches us that supreme honor is due to all who are supreme governors; therefore, they are to have the most honorable titles of majesty, highness, excellency, and so on and actions answerable to those titles (see Mal. 1:6, "If then I am a father, where is my honor? And if I am a master, where is my fear?"). Fear is often put for all God's worship.

READ ALOUD

[If then there is no family whereof God is not the Father or Founder and the Master or Owner and Governor, then there is none but should honor and fear him or worship him, and that not only as single men but as families, because he is not only the Father and Master, the Lord and Ruler of them as men but also as families. Honor is as due to the rector, as protection to the subjects, and in our case much more. God is not Governor in name only[9] but is a real Governor. All powers on earth are derived from him and are indeed his power. All lawful governors are his officers and hold their places under him and act by him. As God is the proper Sovereign of every commonwealth and the Head of the church, so he is the Head of every family.] Therefore, as every commonwealth should perform such worship or honor to their earthly sovereign as is due to man, so each society should, according to its capacities, offer divine worship and honor to God. If any object that by this rule, commonwealths as such must meet together to worship God, which is impossible, I answer, they must worship him according to their natural capacities; so must families according to theirs. The same general precept obliges a diverse manner of duty according to the diverse capacities of the subject. Commonwealths must, in their representatives at least, engage themselves to God as commonwealths and worship him in the most convenient way of which they are capable. Families may meet together for prayer, though a nation cannot. An association of churches, called a provincial or national church, is obliged to worship God as well as particular congregations, yet not in one place; it is impossible—nature limits and makes the difference.

That the obligation of families to honor and worship God may yet appear more evidently, consider that God's right of sovereignty[10] and rule is twofold, yet each title is plenary alone: 1. He is our Owner and Ruler upon his title of creation. 2. So he is by his right of redemption. By both of these he is not only Lord and Ruler of persons but of families. All societies are his, the regimen of persons being chiefly exercised over them in societies. All power in heaven and earth is given unto Christ (Matt. 18:18), "all judgment to the Son" (John 5:22), "all things into his hands" (John 13:3), "so that at the name of Jesus every knee should bow, in heaven and on earth and under the

---

[9]*Mere titular.*
[10]*Propriety.*

earth" (either with a bowing of worship or of forced acknowledgment) and "every tongue confess that Jesus Christ is Lord, to the glory of God the Father" (Phil. 2:10–11). Bowing to and confessing Christ voluntarily to God's glory is true worship. All must do this according to their capacities; therefore, families must do this according to theirs.

Brsant?   A third consideration, which I thought to have added for illustration, may well stand as an argument itself and is this:

Argument 3: If besides all the opportunities and obligations mentioned before, families do live in the presence of God, they should, by faith, apprehend that presence. It is God's will that families as such should solemnly worship him. The former is true, and so therefore the latter.

The consequence of the major, which alone requires proof, I prove by an argument *a fortiori*,[11] from the honor due to all earthly governors. When a king, a father, a master are absent, actual honor to be presented to them is not due because they are not capable of receiving it (further than *mediante aliqua persona, vel re*, which bears some representation of the superior or relation to him); yet when they stand near, it is a contemptuous subject, a disobedient child, who will not offer actual honor to them. Now God is ever present not only with each person as such but also with every family. As he is said to walk among the golden candlesticks in his churches, so does he in the families of all by his common presence and of his servants by his gracious presence. This they easily find by his directing them, blessing the affairs of their families. If any say, "We do not see God, otherwise we would worship him daily in our families," I answer, faith sees him who is invisible. If one of you had a son who was blind and could not see his own father, would you think him excusable if he did not honor his father when he knew him to be present? We know God to be present, though flesh is blind and cannot see him.

Argument 4: If Christian families (besides all the before mentioned advantages and obligations) are also societies sanctified to God, then it is God's will that families as such should solemnly worship him. Christian families are societies sanctified to God.

The reason of the consequence is because things sanctified must in the most eminent sort of which they are capable be used for God.

---

[11]An *a fortiori* argument is drawn from a stronger or more convincing corollary, as in, "The man of prejudice is, *a fortiori*, a man of limited mental vision."

To sanctify a person or thing is to set it apart, to separate it from common or unclean use, and to devote it to God, to be employed in his service. To alienate this from God, or not to use it for God, when it is dedicated to him or sanctified by his own election and separation from common use is sacrilege. God has a double right (of creation and redemption) to all persons, but he has a third right to the sanctified. Ananias was a sad example of God's wrath on those who withhold from him what was devoted to him. If Christian families are sanctified to God, they must worship him in their best capacity.

That Christian families are sanctified to God I prove thus: first, a society of holy persons must needs be a holy society. A family of Christians is a society of holy persons; therefore, etc. Second, we find in Scripture not only single persons but the societies of such sanctified to God. "For you are a people holy to the LORD your God. The LORD your God has chosen you to be a people for his treasured possession, out of all the peoples who are on the face of the earth" (Deut. 7:6). So also Deuteronomy 14:20–21. So the body of that commonwealth did all jointly enter into covenant with God, and God to them: "You have declared today that the LORD is your God, and that you will walk in his ways, and keep his statutes and his commandments and his rules, and will obey his voice" (Deut. 26:17–19; 29; 30). So 28:9; Daniel 8:24; 12:7. Joshua devotes his whole house to the Lord: "Therefore we also will serve the LORD" (Josh. 24:18). And Abraham by circumcision (the covenant or seal of the covenant of God) consecrated his whole household to God; and so were all families after him to do (the males, in whom the whole was consecrated). It may be questioned whether besides the typifying intent, there was intended the sanctifying of all the firstborn to God who, if they lived, were to be the heads of the families.

The Passover was a family duty, by which they were yet further sanctified to God. Yea, it is especially to be observed how in the New Testament the Holy Spirit imitates the language of the Old and speaks of God's people as holy societies, as the Jews were. In many prophecies it was foretold that nations and kingdoms should serve him (of which I have spoken more in my book on "Baptism"); and among those who would "mourn for him . . . whom they have pierced" (Zech. 12:10) in gospel times, when the spirit of grace and supplication was poured forth, are "the family of the house of David by itself, and their wives by themselves; the family of the house of Nathan by itself, and their wives by themselves" (Zech. 12:12). So Christ sends his disciples to "baptize nations," having discipled them; and "the kingdom of the world has become the kingdom of our Lord and of his Christ." And as God says of the Jews, "Now therefore, if you will indeed obey my voice and keep my covenant, you shall be my treasured possession among all peoples, for all the earth is mine; and you shall be to me a kingdom of priests and a holy nation" (Ex. 19:5–6), so Peter says of all Christians, "you yourselves like living stones are being built up as a spiritual house, to be a holy priesthood, to offer spiritual sacrifices acceptable to God through Jesus Christ. . . . But you are a chosen race, a royal priesthood, a holy nation, a people for his own possession, that you may proclaim the excellencies of him who called you out of darkness into his marvelous light" (1 Pet. 2:5–7, 9).

Mark how fully this text proves all that we are about. It speaks of Christians collectively, as in societies, and in societies of all the most eminent sorts, "a spiritual house," which seems especially to refer to tribes and families; "a priesthood, nation, people," which comprehends all the orders in the nation. And in all these respects they are holy and peculiar and chosen, to show that God's people are sanctified in these relations and societies. And then mark the end of this sanctification: "to offer spiritual sacrifices acceptable to God through Jesus Christ" (v. 5), "that you may proclaim the excellencies of him who called you" (v. 9).

Yea, it seems that there was a special dedication of families to God. Therefore, we read so frequently of households converted and baptized, though none at age were baptized but only such as seemed believers; yet when they professed faith, they were all together initiated as a household. It seems the master's interest and duty were taken to be so great for the conversion of the rest that he was not content himself with his own conversion but labored presently, even before his baptism, that his household should join with him, so that the whole family at once might be devoted to God. So God did bless his own order and ordinance to that end. Where he imposed duty on masters, he usually gave success, so that commonly the whole family was converted and baptized with the ruler of the family. So Acts 18:8, "Crispus, the ruler of the synagogue, believed in the Lord, together with his entire household. And many of the Corinthians hearing Paul believed and were baptized." And so Paul promised the jailer, "'Believe in the Lord Jesus, and you will be saved, you and your household.' And they spoke the word of the Lord to him and to all who were in his house" (Acts 16:31–32). Lydia is described as "a worshiper of God" (Acts 16:14), and "she was baptized, and her household as well" (v. 15). The angel told Cornelius that Peter would tell him "a message by which [he] will be saved, [he] and all [his] household" (Acts 11:14), who were then baptized accordingly. Paul baptized the household of Stephanas (1 Cor. 1:16). Christ told Zacchaeus that salvation had come that day to his house (Luke 19:1–10). So a nobleman (and his entire household) believed in John 4:53. Therefore, when Christ sent forth his disciples, he said, "And if the house is worthy, let your peace come upon it, but if it is not worthy, let your peace return to you" (Matt. 10:13).

So it is apparently the duty of every Christian sovereign to do what he is able to make all his people God's people and so to dedicate them to God as a holy nation, in a national covenant, as the Israelites were. It is the unquestionable duty of every Christian ruler of a family to improve his interest, power, and parts to the uttermost, to bring all his family to be people of Christ in the baptismal covenant, and so to dedicate all his family to Christ. I further prove this in that believers themselves being all sanctified to God, it therefore follows that all their lawful relations (and especially all commanded states of relation) are also sanctified to God; for when they are themselves dedicated to God, it is absolutely without reserve to serve him with all that they have and in every relation and capacity in which he shall set them. It would be madness to think that a Christian totally devoted to God, when he is a private man, if he is afterward made a soldier, minister, magistrate, or king, is not bound by his dedication now to serve God as soldier, minister, magistrate, or king. So he who is devoted to God in a single state is bound to serve him as husband, father, and master when he comes into that state. We devote all that we have to God when we devote ourselves to him.

Moreover, the Scripture tells us, "To the pure, all things are pure" (Titus 1:15). And everything "is made holy by the word of God and prayer" (1 Tim. 4:5), in that they are made the goods and enjoyments, actions and relations of a sanctified people, who are themselves devoted or sanctified to God. So all sanctification refers ultimately and principally to God (*Quod sanctum Deo sanctum est*, "As far as it is sanctified to God, it is sanctified"), though it may be said to be subordinately sanctified to us. Seeing then it is past all doubt that every Christian is a man sanctified and devoted to God, and that whenever any man is so devoted to God, he is devoted to serve him to the utmost capacity in every state, relation, or condition that he is in and with all the faculties he possesses, it follows that those relations are sanctified to God, and in them he ought to worship him and honor him.

Yet further, we find in Scripture that particular family relations are expressly sanctified. Family consists of two pairs of relations: husband and wife, and parents and children. Husbands must love their wives with a holy love in the Lord, even as "Christ loved the church and gave himself up for her, that he might sanctify her, having cleansed her by the washing of water with the word, so that he might present the church to himself in splendor, without spot or wrinkle or any such thing, that she might be holy and without blemish" (Eph. 5:25–27). "Wives, submit to your own husbands, as to the Lord" (Eph. 5:22). "Children, obey your parents in the Lord, for this is right" (Eph. 6:1). Parents must bring up their children "in the discipline and instruction of the Lord" (Eph. 6:4). Thus it is evident that every distinct family relation should be dedicated or holy to God and should be used to the utmost for God. I shall have occasion to make further use later[12] of these texts for the particular sorts of worship, though I now make use of them for worship in general.

Argument 5: Several sorts of solemn worship in and by Christian families are found, appointed, used, and commanded in the Scripture. Therefore, it may well be concluded of worship in the general, seeing the genus is in each species. This argument brings me to the second part of my undertaking; that is, to prove the point as to some special kinds of worship.

---

[12]*Anon.*

Concerning God's worship in special, I shall speak to two or three of the chief parts of it that belong to families.

First is teaching, under which I comprise:

1. Teaching the letter of the Scripture by reading it, teaching others to read it, and causing them to learn it by memory, which is a kind of catechizing.

2. Teaching the sense of it.

3. Applying what is so taught by familiar reproofs, admonitions, and exhortations.

Proposition 2: It is the will of God that the rulers of families should teach those who are under them the doctrine of salvation; that is, the doctrine of God concerning salvation and the terms on which it is to be had, the means to be used for attaining it, and all the duties requisite on our parts in order to do it.

Before I come to the proof, take these cautions: First, when I say men must thus teach, I imply they must be able to teach, and not teach before they are able; and if they are not able, it is their own sin, God having given[13] means for enablement. Second, men must measure their teaching according to their abilities, and not pretend to more than they have, nor attempt that which they cannot perform, thereby incurring the guilt of proud self-conceitedness, profanation, or other abuse of holy things. For example, men who are not able judiciously to do it must not presume to interpret the original or to give the sense of dark prophecies and other obscure texts of Scripture or to determine controversies beyond their reach.

Third, yet may such conveniently study what more learned, able men say to such cases and tell their families, "This is the judgment of fathers or councils or such and such learned divines." Fourth, ordinarily it is the safest, humblest, wisest, and most orderly way for the master of the family to leave controversies and obscure Scriptures alone and to teach the plain, few necessary doctrines commonly contained in catechisms and to direct in matters of necessary practice. Fifth, family teaching must stand in subordination to ministerial teaching, as families are subordinate to churches. Therefore, 1. Family teaching must give place to ministerial teaching and never be set against it. You should not be listening to the

---

[13]*Vouchsafed.*

head of the master when you should be in church hearing the pastor. If the pastor sends for children to be catechized at an appropriate place and time, the master is not then to be doing it himself or to hinder them, but they must go first to the pastor to be taught; also, if a pastor comes into a family, the master is to give place, and the family to hear him first. 2. Therefore, when any hard text or controversies fall in, the head should consult with the pastor for their exposition, unless, of course, the master of the family is better learned in the Scriptures than the pastor is, which is rare, and rarer should be seeing unworthy ministers removed and private men who are worthy made ministers. The pastors should be the ablest men in the congregation. Now to the proof (remembering still that whatsoever proves the ruler's duty to teach must also prove the family's duty to learn and to hearken to his teaching so they may learn).

Argument 1: From Deuteronomy 11:18–21, "You shall therefore lay up these words of mine in your heart and in your soul, and you shall bind them as a sign on your hand, and they shall be as frontlets between your eyes. You shall teach them to your children, talking of them when you are sitting in your house, and when you are walking by the way, and when you lie down, and when you rise. You shall write them on the doorposts of your house and on your gates, that your days and the days of your children may be multiplied in the land that the LORD swore to your fathers to give them, as long as the heavens are above the earth." Similar words are in Deuteronomy 6:7, where we read, "You shall teach them diligently to your children." So Deuteronomy 4:9, "Make them known to your children and your children's children." Here is one part of family duty, which is teaching children the laws of God, as plainly commanded as words can express it.

Argument 2: From these texts that commend this: "All the nations of the earth shall be blessed in him. For I have chosen him, that he may command his children and his household after him to keep the way of the LORD" (Gen. 18:18–19). And it was not only a command at his death as to what they should do when he was dead; for, first, it cannot be imagined that so holy a man should neglect a duty all his lifetime and perform it but at death and be commended for that. Second, he might then have great cause to question the efficacy. Third, as God commands diligent teaching[14] of precepts to children, so, no doubt, it is a practice answerable to such precepts that is here commended; and it is not bare teaching but commanding that is here mentioned, to show that it must be an improvement of authority as well as of knowledge and elocution. So 2 Timothy 3:15. From a child Timothy knew the Scripture by the teaching of his parents, as appears from 2 Timothy 1:5.

Argument 3: Ephesians 6:4, "but bring them up in the discipline and instruction of the Lord"; παιδεία, translated "discipline," signifies both instruction and correction, showing that parents must use both doctrine and authority, or force, with their children for the matters of the Lord; and νουθεσία, translated "instruction," signifies such instruction as puts doctrine into the mind and charges it on them and fully stores their minds therewith; and it also signifies chiding, and sometimes correction. It is to be noted that children must be brought up in this; the word ἐκτρέφετε, signifying "carefully to nourish," imports that as you feed them with milk and bodily food, so you must as carefully and constantly feed and nourish them with the discipline and instruction of the Lord. It is called the discipline and instruction and admonition of the Lord because the Lord commands it and because it is the doctrine concerning the Lord, the doctrine of his teaching, and the doctrine that leads to him.

Argument 4: Proverbs 22:6, "Train up a child in the way he should go; even when he is old he will not depart from it."

Argument 5: From all those places that charge children to hearken to the instructions of their parents, "Hear, my son, your father's instruction, and forsake not your mother's teaching" (Prov. 1:8). Proverbs 6:20 is similar along with 23:22, with many the like. Yea, the son who was stubborn and rebellious against the instruction and correction of a father or mother in gluttony, drunkenness, and so on was to be brought forth to the magistrate and stoned to death (Deut. 21:18–21). Now all the Scriptures that require children to hear their parents imply that the parents must teach their children, for there is no hearing and learning without teaching. Lest you say that parents and children are not the whole family (though they may be, and in Abraham's case before mentioned, the

---

[14]*Inculcating.*

whole household is mentioned), the next argument shall speak to other relations.

Argument 6: First Peter 3:7, "Likewise, husbands, live with your wives in an understanding way, showing honor to the woman as the weaker vessel, since they are heirs with you of the grace of life, so that your prayers may not be hindered"; and Ephesians 5:25–26, "Husbands, love your wives, as Christ loved the church and gave himself up for her, that he might sanctify her, having cleansed her by the washing of water with the word." This plainly implies that this knowledge must be used for the instruction and sanctification of the wife. In 1 Corinthians 14:34–35, women must "keep silent in the churches. For they are not permitted to speak, but should be in submission, as the Law also says. If there is anything they desire to learn, let them ask their husbands at home." This shows that at home their husbands must teach them.

Argument 7: A fortiori, fellow-Christians must "exhort one another every day, as long as it is called 'today,' that none of you may be hardened by the deceitfulness of sin" (Heb. 3:13). Much more must the rulers of families do to wives, children, and servants; "whoever speaks, as one who speaks oracles of God" (1 Pet. 4:11), and much more to our own families. "Let the word of Christ dwell in you richly, teaching and admonishing one another in all wisdom, singing psalms and hymns and spiritual songs, with thankfulness in your hearts to God" (Col. 3:16); and much more must a man do to wife and children than to those more remote.

Argument 8: Those who are chosen to be deacons or bishops must be such as rule their own children and their own household well (1 Tim. 3:4, 12). Now mark, first, that this is one of those Christian virtues that they were to have before they were made officers; therefore, other Christians must have and perform it as well as they. Second, it is a religious, holy governing, such as a minister is to exercise over his flock, that is here mentioned, which is in the things of God and salvation, or else the comparison or argument would not suit (verse 5, "if someone does not know how to manage his own household, how will he care for God's church?"). I would say more on this point, but I think it is so clear in Scripture as to make further comment needless.

Proposition 3: Family discipline is part of God's solemn worship or service appointed in his Word. This is not called worship in so near a sense as some of the rest, but more remotely; yet so it may well be called in that, first, it is an authoritative act done by commission from God; second, upon such as disobey him and as such; third, to his glory; yea, and it should be done with as great solemnity and reverence as other parts of worship.

The acts of this discipline are, first, denying the ungodly entrance into the family; second, correcting; and third, casting out those who are in.

1. The first you have in 2 John 10–11, "If anyone comes to you and does not bring this teaching, do not receive him into your house or give him any greeting, for whoever greets him takes part in his wicked works."

2. The duty of correcting, either by corporal, sensible punishment or by withdrawing some benefit, is so commonly required in Scripture, especially toward children, that I will not dwell on it, lest I speak in vain what you all know already. How Eli suffered for neglecting it, you know.

3. The discipline of casting the wicked out of the family (servants, I mean, who are separable members) you may find in Psalm 101:2, 7: "I will walk with integrity of heart within my house. . . . No one who practices deceit shall dwell in my house; no one who utters lies shall continue before my eyes."

Proposition 4: Solemn prayer and praises of God in and by Christian families is of divine appointment.

For proof of this, I desire you to look back to all the arguments that proved the obligation[15] of worship in general, for they will prove this sort of worship, seeing prayer and praise are most immediately and eminently called God's worship (under praises I comprehend psalms of praise, and under prayer, psalms of prayer); yet let us add some more.

Argument 1: It is God's will that Christians who have fit occasions and opportunities for prayer and praises should improve[16] them. Christian families have fit occasions and opportunities for prayer and praise; therefore, it is God's will they should improve them.

---

[15]*Dueness.*
[16]That is, to turn a thing to profit or a good account; to benefit from it.

The major idea is evident in many precepts in Scripture. "I desire then that in every place the men should pray, lifting holy hands without anger or quarreling" (1 Tim. 2:8). "Pray without ceasing, give thanks in all circumstances; for this is the will of God in Christ Jesus for you" (1 Thess. 5:17–18). "Continue steadfastly in prayer, being watchful in it with thanksgiving" (Col. 4:2). "Let the word of Christ dwell in you richly, teaching and admonishing one another in all wisdom, singing psalms and hymns and spiritual songs, with thankfulness in your hearts to God. And whatever you do, in word or deed, do everything in the name of the Lord Jesus, giving thanks to God the Father through him" (Col. 3:16–17). "Be constant in prayer" (Rom. 12:12), "praying at all times in the Spirit, with all prayer and supplication. To that end keep alert with all perseverance, making supplication for all the saints, and also for me, that words may be given to me" (Eph. 6:18–19). Many similar texts might be named, every one of which affords an argument for family praises.

First, if men must pray everywhere (that is convenient), then for certain in their families; therefore, second, if men must pray without ceasing, then for certain in their families. Third, if men must in everything give thanks, then surely in family mercies and then, according to the nature of them, together. Fourth, if men must continue in prayer and watch in it (for fit advantages and against impediments) and in thanksgiving, then doubtless they must not omit the singular advantages that are administered in families. Fifth, if we must continue instant in prayer and supplication and so on, then doubtless in family prayer, in our families, unless that is no place and no prayer. *Objection:* But this binds us no more to prayer in our families than anywhere else. *Answer:* Yea, it binds us to take all fit opportunities; and we have more fit opportunities in our own families than in other men's or in occasional meetings or in any ordinary societies, except the church.

And here let me tell you that it is ignorance to call for particular Scriptures to require praying in families, as if we thought the general commands did not comprehend this particular and were not sufficient. God does, in much wisdom, leave out of his written law the determination of some of those circumstances or the application of general precepts to some of those subjects to which common reason and the light of nature suffices to determine and apply them. The Scripture gives us the general, "praying at all times" (Eph. 6:18); that is, do not omit fit advantages and opportunities for prayer. What if God had said no more than this about prayer in Scripture? It seems some men would have said, "God has not required us to pray at all [when he requires us to pray always] because he tells us not when and where and how often and with whom and in what words and so on." So they would have concluded that God nowhere bids us pray in secret, nor pray in families, nor pray in assemblies, nor pray with the godly, nor pray with the wicked, nor pray every day, nor once a week, nor with a book, nor without a book, and therefore not at all. As if the general "praying at all times" was nothing.

But these men must know that nature and reason are God's light, and providence often determines such subjects and adjuncts; and the general law and these together do put all out of doubt. What if God tells you, "If anyone does not provide for his relatives, and especially for members of his household, he has denied the faith and is worse than an unbeliever," but does not tell you who are your families and who not or what provision you shall make for them, what food, what clothes, or how often they must feed and so on. Will you say God has not bid you to feed or clothe your child? It is enough that God charges you in the Scripture to provide for your families and that in nature he tells you who are your families and what provision to make for them and how often and in what quantity and so on. So if God bids you to pray in all places and at all times, on all occasions (that are fit for prayer), and experience and common reason tell you that families afford the most fit times, places, and occasions for prayer, is it not enough that there are such seasons, opportunities, and occasions for family prayer? I refer you to the particular discoveries of them in the beginning, where I proved the obligation[17] of worship in general. I refer you also to common reason itself, not fearing the contradiction of any man whose impiety has made him unreasonable and prevailed against the common light of nature. This first general argument is enough, if men were not so averse to their duty that they cannot know because they will not; but let us add some more.

Argument 2: If there are many blessings that the family needs

---

[17]*Dueness.*

and that they actually receive from God, then it is the will of God that the family prays for these blessings when they need them and give thanks for them when they have received them. But there are many blessings that the family, together,[18] needs and receives from God. Therefore the whole[19] family, and not only particular members secretly, should pray and give thanks for them.

The antecedent is past question: first, the continuance of the family as such in being, second, in well-being, third, for the preservation and direction of the essential members, and, fourth, the prospering of all family affairs are evident instances (to delve to particulars would be needless and tedious). The consequence is proved from many Scriptures that require those who want mercies to ask for them, and those who have received them to be thankful for them. *Objection:* So they may do singly. *Answer:* It is not only as single persons but as a society that they receive the mercy; therefore, not only as single persons but as a society should they pray and give thanks; therefore, they should do it in that manner as may be most fit for a society to do it, and that is, united[20] together, that it may be indeed a family sacrifice and that each part may see that the rest join with them. And especially that the ruler may be satisfied in this, to whom the oversight of the rest is committed, to see that they all join in prayer, which in secret he cannot see, it being not fit that secret prayer should have spectators or witness, that is, should not be secret. But this I intended to make another argument by itself, which, because we are fallen on it, I will add next.

Argument 3: If God has given charge to the ruler of the family to see that the rest worship him in that family, then ought the ruler to cause them solemnly or openly to join in that worship. And God has given charge to the ruler of the family to see that the rest worship God in that family.

The reason of the consequences is because otherwise he can with no convenience see that they do it. For, first, it is not fit that he should stand by while they pray secretly. Second, nor are they able vocally to do it in most families but have need of a leader, it not being expected of every woman and child that they should be able to pray

---

[18]*Conjunct.*
[19]*Conjunct.*
[20]*Conjunctly.*

without a guide, so as is fit for others to hear. Third, it would take almost all the time for the ruler of many families to go to them one after another and stand by them while they pray until all are done. What man in his wits can think this to be as fit a course as for the family to join together, the ruler being the mouth?

The antecedent I prove thus: first, the fourth commandment requires the ruler of the family not only to see that he himself sanctifies the Sabbath Day but also that his son, daughter, man-servant, maid-servant, and cattle (that is, so far as they are capable), yea, and the stranger who is within his gates should do it. Second, it was committed to Abraham's charge to see that all in his family were circumcised: so was it afterward to every ruler of a family, insomuch as the angel threatened Moses when his son was uncircumcised. Third, the ruler of the family was to see that the Passover was kept by everyone in his family (Ex. 12:2–3), and so the Feast of Weeks (Deut. 26:11–12). All that is said before tends to prove this, and much more might be said if I thought it would be denied.

Argument 4: If God prefers, and would have us prefer, the prayers and praises of many together[21] before the prayers and praises of those persons individually, then it is his will that the particular persons of Christian families should prefer joint[22] prayer and praises before individual.[23] The antecedent is true; therefore, so is the consequent. Or thus take it for the same argument or another. If it is the duty of neighbors, when they have occasion and opportunity, rather to join together in common concerns than to do it individually, then much more is this the duty of families. It is the duty of neighbors; therefore, etc.

In the former argument, the reason of the consequence is because that way is to be taken with which God is best pleased. The reason of the consequence in the latter is because family members are more nearly related than neighbors and have much more advantage and opportunity for union[24] and more ordinary reasons to urge them to it, from the similarity[25] of their interest and affairs.

Nothing needs proof but the antecedent, which I shall put past

---

[21]*Conjunct.*
[22]*Conjunct.*
[23]*Disjunct.*
[24]*Conjunction.*
[25]*Conjunction.*

all doubt by these arguments: First, "teaching and admonishing one another in all wisdom, singing psalms and hymns and spiritual songs, with thankfulness in your hearts to God" (Col. 3:16). Here is one duty of praise required to be done together and not apart only. I shall make further use of this text later. Second, "many were gathered together and were praying" (Acts 12:12). This was not an assembly of the whole church but a small part; they judged it better to pray together than alone. Third, Paul prayed together with all the elders of the church of Ephesus when he had them with him. He did not choose to let them pray alone (Acts 20:36). Fourth, James commands the sick to "call for the elders of the church, and let them pray over him, anointing him with oil in the name of the Lord" (James 5:14). He does not bid them to "call for them to pray for you," but he would have them join together. Fifth, church prayers are preferred before private on this ground, and we are commanded not to forsake the assembling of ourselves together (Heb. 10:25). Sixth, striving together in prayer is desired (Rom. 15:30). Seventh, "For where two or three are gathered in my name, there am I among them" (Matt. 18:20).

Eighth, therefore Christ came among the disciples when they were gathered together, after his resurrection, and sent down the Holy Ghost when they were gathered together: "All these with one accord were devoting themselves to prayer" (Acts 1:14, 24; 2:42). "And when they had prayed, the place in which they were gathered together was shaken, and they were all filled with the Holy Spirit" (Acts 4:31). Ninth, is not this implied in Christ's directing his disciples to pray in the plural number, "*Our* Father," "Give *us* this day," and so on? Tenth, the necessity of the persons, plural, proves it, in that few societies are such but that most are unable to express their own wants so largely as to affect their hearts as much as when others do it who are better stored with affection and expression. This is one of God's ways for communion and communication of grace so that those who have much may help to warm and kindle those who have less. Experience tells us the benefit of this. As all the body is not an eye or hand, so also not a tongue, and therefore the tongue of the church and family must speak for the whole body (not that each should not pray in secret too). 1. In secret the heart without the tongue may better serve in turn. But 2. They ought to prefer joint[26] prayer. And 3. The communion of saints is an article of our creed, which binds us to acknowledge doing as much of God's work as we can in communion with the saints, not going beyond our callings, nor into confusion.

Argument 5: It is a duty to receive all the mercies that God offers us. For a family to have access to God in joint prayers and praises is a mercy that God offers them; therefore, it is their duty to accept it. The major thesis is clear in nature and Scripture. "I have called and you refused to listen" (Prov. 1:24a) is God's great aggravation at the sin of the rebellious. "How often would I have gathered your children together as a hen gathers her brood under her wings, and you would not! . . . I . . . have stretched out my hand and no one has heeded" (Matt. 23:37; Prov. 1:24b). To refuse an offered kindness is contempt and ingratitude. The minor idea is undeniable by any Christian who ever knew what family prayers and praises were. Who dare say that it is no mercy to have such a joint access to God? Who does not feel that solidarity[27] helps his own affections, and who makes conscience of watching his heart?

Argument 6: Part of the duties of families is such that they apparently lose their chief life and excellency if they are not performed jointly; therefore, they are so to be performed. I mean, singing of psalms, which I before proved an ordinary duty of gathered[28] Christians, and so of families. The melody and harmony are lost by our separation, and consequently the alacrity and quickening that our affections should get by it. If part of God's praises must be performed together, it is easy to see that the rest must be so too (not to speak of teaching, which cannot be done alone).

Argument 7: Family prayer and praises are a duty owned by the teaching and sanctifying work of the Spirit; therefore, they are of God. I would not argue backwards from the Spirit's teaching to the Word's commanding but on these two suppositions: First, the experience is very general and undeniable. Second, many texts of Scripture have been brought already for family prayer, and this argument but seconds them and proves them truly interpreted. The Spirit and the

---

[26]*Conjunct.*
[27]*Conjunction.*
[28]*Conjunct.*

Word do always agree. If, therefore, I can prove that the Spirit of God commonly works in men's hearts to impress a love and savor of these duties, doubtless they are of God. Sanctification is a transcript of the precepts of the Word on the heart, written out by the Spirit of God; so much for the consequence.

The antecedent consists of two parts. First, the sanctified have in them inclinations to these duties. Second, these inclinations are from the Spirit of God. The first needs no proof, being a matter of experience. I appeal to the heart of every sound and stable Christian whether he does not feel a conviction of this duty and an inclination to the performance of it. I never met with anyone, to my knowledge, who was otherwise minded. *Objection:* Many in our times, who are good Christians, are quite against family prayer. *Answer:* I know none of them. I confess I once knew some very good Christians who were against these duties, but now they appear otherwise, not only in this but in other things. I know none who cast off these duties but they took up vile sins in their stead and cast off other duties as well as these. Let others observe and judge as they find. Second, the power of delusion may for a time make a Christian consider that unlawful to which his new nature is inclined. Some think it unlawful to pray in our assemblies, and some to join in sacraments; and yet they have a spirit within them that inclines their hearts to it still, and therefore they love it and wish it were lawful, even when they conceitedly consider that it is unlawful.

And so it is possible for a time some may do regarding family duties. But as I expect that these, before long, recover, so, for my part, I take all the rest to be graceless. Prejudice and error as temptations may prohibit the exercise of a duty, when yet the Spirit of God works in the heart an inclination to that duty in sanctifying it. Third, that these inclinations are indeed from the Spirit is evident, 1. In that they come in with all other grace. 2. And by the same means. 3. And are preserved by the same means, standing or falling, increasing or decreasing with the rest. 4. And are to the same end. 5. And are so generally in all the saints. 6. And so resisted by flesh and blood. 7. And so agreeable to the Word that a Christian sins against his new nature when he neglects family duties. God, by his Spirit, creates a desire after them and an estimation of them in every gracious soul.

Argument 8: Family prayer and praises are duties ordinarily crowned with admirable, divine, and special blessings; therefore, they are of God. The consequence is evident. Though common, outward prosperity may be given to the wicked, who have their portion in this life, prosperity of soul is not.

For the antecedent, I appeal to the experience of all the holy families in the world. Who ever used these duties seriously and found not the benefits? What families are they in which grace and heavenly mindedness prosper but those that use these duties? Compare in all your towns, cities, and villages the families that read Scriptures, pray, and praise God with those who do not and see the difference. Which of them abound more with impiety, oaths, cursings, railings, drunkenness, whoredoms, and worldliness? Which abound most with faith, patience, temperance, charity, repentance, and hope? The controversy is not hard to decide. Look to the nobility and gentry of England. Do you not see any difference between those who have been raised in praying families and the rest? I mean, taking them, as we say, proportionally. Look to the ministers of England. Is it praying families or prayerless families that have done most to furnish the universities?

Argument 9: All churches ought solemnly to pray to God and praise him—a Christian family is a church; therefore, etc. The major idea is past doubt; the minor I prove from the nature of a church in general, which is a society of Christians gathered for the worshipping and serving of God. I do not say that a family, as a family, is a church, but every family of Christians should, by such a combination, be a church. Yea, as Christians they are so combined, seeing Christianity ties them to serve God together in their relations. Scripture expresses it: "Aquila and Prisca, together with the church in their house, send you hearty greetings in the Lord" (1 Cor. 16:19). He does not say, "which *meets* in their house," but "in their house." So, "and the church in your house" (Philem. 2); "Greet also the church in their house" (Rom. 16:5); "Give my greetings to the brothers at Laodicea, and to Nympha and the church in her house" (Col. 4:15). Though some learned men take these to mean part of the churches assembling in these houses, yet Beza,[29] Grotius,[30] and many others acknowledge it to mean a family or domestic church, according to the sense of Tertullian,[31] *ubi tres licet laici ibi ecclesia* ("whereby it is permitted that three laymen [form] a church"). Yet I say not that such a family church is of the same species with an organized church of many families. But it could not (so much as analogically) be called a church if they might not and must not pray and praise God together.

Argument 10: If rulers must teach their families the Word of God, then they must pray with them, they must teach them; therefore, etc. The antecedent is fully proved by Scripture already; see also Psalm 128:4–6. Ministers must teach from house to house; therefore, rulers themselves must do it (Acts 5:42; 20:20).

The consequence is proved good: first, the apostles prayed when they preached or instructed Christians in private assemblies (Acts 20:36 and other places). Second, we have special need of God's assistance in reading the Scriptures, to know his mind in them and to make them profitable to us; therefore we must seek it. Third, the reverence due to so holy a business requires it. Fourth, we are commanded, "in everything by prayer and supplication with thanksgiving let your requests be made known to God" (Phil. 4:6), and therefore especially on such occasions as reading the Scriptures and instructing others. I think that few men who are convinced of the duty of reading Scripture and solemnly instructing their families will question the duty of praying for God's blessing on it when they set upon the work. Yea, a Christian's own conscience will provoke him, reverently, to begin all with God in imploring his acceptance, aid, and blessing.

Argument 11: If rulers of families are bound to teach their families to pray, then they are bound to pray with them. They are bound to teach them to pray; therefore, etc.

In the foregoing argument I speak of teaching in general; here I

---

[29]Theodore Beza (1519–1605) was an author, translator, educator, and leader of the Genevan Reformation after the death of John Calvin (1509–1564). Beza's critical edition of the Greek New Testament, the so-called *Codex Bezae*, was a popular and widely used anthology of Greek and Latin texts dating to the fifth century.

[30]Hugo Grotius (1583–1645) was a Dutch jurist and scholar whose fame largely rests on his contributions to international law. Grotius did write, however, several theological works, including biblical commentaries.

[31]Tertullian (c. 155–220) was an important early Christian polemicist and writer. He was largely responsible for introducing Latin into the vocabulary of Western Christianity.

speak of teaching to pray. The antecedent of the major I prove thus: first, they are bound to "bring them up in the discipline and instruction of the Lord" (Eph. 6:4) and therefore to teach them to pray and praise God, for "the discipline and instruction of the Lord" contains that. Second, they are bound to "teach [them] the fear of the LORD" (Ps. 34:11) and to "train up a child in the way he should go" (Prov. 22:6), and that is doubtless the way of prayer and praising God.

The consequence appears here to be sound, in that men cannot be well and effectually taught to pray without praying with them or in their hearing; therefore, they who must teach them to pray must pray with them. It is like music, which you cannot teach any man without playing or singing to him (seeing teaching must be by practicing).

If anyone questions this, I appeal to experience. I never knew anyone who was taught to pray without it being practiced before them. Those who know of someone may have more grounds to object, but I did not; still, such examples are so rare that it would not be the ordinary means of our endeavors any more than we should forbear teaching the most useful skills by visual demonstration[32] because some have learned by few words or of their own skill.[33] Those who do not teach their children by practice and example are cruel to their children.

Argument 12: "For everything created by God is good, and nothing is to be rejected if it is received with thanksgiving, for it is made holy by the word of God and prayer" (1 Tim. 4:4–5).

Here mark, first, that all our food is to be received with thanksgiving and not only with a disposition of thankfulness; second, that this is twice repeated here (verses 3–5), yea, three times in sense; third, that God created it so to be received; fourth, that this is made a condition of the goodness, that is, the blessing of the creature to our use; fifth, that the creature is said to be sanctified by God's Word and prayer, and so it is unsanctified before; sixth, that the same thing that is called thanksgiving in the two former verses is called prayer in the last; otherwise the consequence of the apostle could not hold when he thus argues, "for it is made holy by the word of God and prayer."

---

[32]*Curious artifices by ocular.*
[33]*Invention.*

Hence I will draw these two arguments: 1. If families must, with thanksgiving, receive their food as from God, then the thanksgiving of families is a duty of God's appointment. The former is true; therefore so is the latter. The antecedent is plain: all must receive their meat with thanksgiving; therefore families must. They eat together; therefore they must give thanks together. That prayer is included in thanksgiving in this text, I discussed before.

2. It is the duty of families to use the means so that all God's creatures may be sanctified to them. Prayer is the means to be used so that all God's creatures may be sanctified to them; therefore, it is the duty of families to use prayer.

Argument 13: "Likewise, husbands, live with your wives in an understanding way, showing honor to the woman as the weaker vessel, since they are heirs with you of the grace of life, so that your prayers may not be hindered" (1 Pet. 3:7). The prayers that are hindered by ignorant and unkind conversation are here meant. It is joint[34] prayer that is especially so hindered; therefore, etc. I know that secret, personal prayer is also hindered by the same causes, but not so directly and notably as joint[35] prayer is. With what hearts can husband and wife join together as one soul in prayer to God when they abuse and exasperate each other and come hot from chidings and dissensions? This seems the true meaning of the text. And so the joint[36] prayer of husband and wife being proved a duty (who sometimes constitute a family), the same reasons will include the rest of the family also.

Argument 14: From Colossians 3:16–18, "Let the word of Christ dwell in you richly, teaching and admonishing one another in all wisdom, singing psalms and hymns and spiritual songs, with thankfulness in your hearts to God. And whatever you do, in word or deed, do everything in the name of the Lord Jesus, giving thanks to God the Father through him. Wives, submit to your husbands, as is fitting in the Lord."

I may here fetch many arguments for family prayers. First, it appears to be family prayers chiefly that the apostle speaks of, for it is families that he speaks to (for in verses 16–17 he speaks

---

[34]*Conjunct.*
[35]*Conjunct.*
[36]*Conjunct.*

of prayer and thanksgiving; and in the next words he speaks to each family relation—wives, husbands, children, parents; and in the next words, continuing his speech to the same persons, he bids them, "Continue steadfastly in prayer, being watchful" [4:2]). If neighbors are bound to speak together in psalms, hymns, and spiritual songs, with grace in their hearts to the Lord, and to continue in prayer and thanksgiving, then families much more so, who are more closely related and have more necessities and opportunities. Third, if whatever we do in word or deed we must do all in the name of the Lord Jesus, giving thanks, then families must join in giving thanks, for they have much daily business, in word and deed, to be done together and apart.

Argument 15: "When Daniel knew that the document had been signed, he went to his house where he had windows in his upper chamber open toward Jerusalem. He got down on his knees three times a day and prayed and gave thanks before his God" (Dan. 6:10). Here note, first, the nature of the duty; second, the necessity of it. First, if it had not been open, family prayer that Daniel here performed, how could they have known what he said? It is not probable that he would speak so loudly in secret, nor is it likely they would have found him at it; so great a prince would have had servants in his outward rooms to keep out strangers before they could come so near. Second, the necessity of this prayer is such that Daniel would not be without it for a few days, even to save his life.

Argument 16: "But as for me and my house, we will serve the LORD" (Josh. 24:15). Here note, first, that it is a household that is here engaged; for if any would prove that it extends further, to all Joshua's tribe or kindred, yet his household would be included. Second, it is the same thing that Joshua promises for his house that he would have all Israel do for theirs. He makes himself an example to move them to it.

If households must serve the Lord, then households must pray to him and praise him; households must serve him; therefore, etc. The consequence is proved, in that prayer and praise are so necessary parts of God's service that no family or person can be said in general to be devoted to serve God that are not devoted to them. Calling upon God is often put in Scripture for all of God's worship, as being a most eminent part; and atheists are described to be fools who say, "There is no God" (Ps. 14:1).

Argument 17: The story of Cornelius in Acts 10 proves that he performed family worship. Observe, first, he is said to be "a devout man who feared God with all his household, gave alms generously to the people, and prayed continually to God" (verse 2); and he says, "I was praying in my house at the ninth hour" (verse 30); and he "called together his relatives and close friends" (verse 24). Fearing God includes prayer and is usually put for all of God's worship. Therefore, when he is said to fear God with all his house, it is also meant that he worshipped God with his house; and that he used to do it together[37] with them is implied in his gathering together his kindred and friends when Peter came, not mentioning the calling together of his household as being usual and supposed. When it is said that he prayed ἐν το οικο αυτου ("in my house"), it may signify his household, as in Scripture the word is often taken. However, the circumstances show that he did it.

Argument 18: "He must manage his own household well, with all dignity keeping his children submissive, for if someone does not know how to manage his own household, how will he care for God's church? . . . Let deacons each be the husband of one wife, managing their children and their own households well" (1 Tim. 3:4–5, 12). Here mark that it is the same ruling of their houses as of the church, *mutatis mutandis* ("with the respective differences having been considered"), that is, training them up in the worship of God and guiding them therein; for the apostle makes the defect of the one to be a sure discovery of their unfitness for the other. Now, to rule the church is to teach and guide it as their mouth in prayer and praises unto God as well as to oversee their lives. Therefore, it is such a ruling of their houses that is a prerequisite to prove them fit.

Those who must rule over their own houses (as may partly prove them fit to rule the church) must rule by holy instructions and guiding their family as their mouth in the worship of God. Those mentioned (1 Tim. 3) must so rule their houses; therefore, etc.

The pastors' ruling of the church consists most in going before them and guiding them in God's worship; therefore, so does the

---

[37]*Conjunctly.*

ruling of their own houses, which is made a qualification for their fitness. Though it does not reach so high or for many things, the conclusion is not affirmative, "He that rules his own house well is fit to rule the church of God," but rather negative: "If someone does not know how to manage his own household, how will he care for God's church?" It is so because, first, this is a lower degree of ruling, which will not prove him fit for a higher. Second, it is but one qualification of many that are required. It is apparent, however, that some degree of aptitude is here proved, and that from a similitude of the things. When Paul compares ruling the house to ruling the church, he cannot be understood to equate them as the same thing.[38] He would never have said, "He that cannot rule an army or regiment or a city, how shall he rule the church of God?" I conclude, therefore, that this text shows it is the duty of masters of families to rule well, instructing their families in the right worshipping of God, *mutatis mutandis*, as ministers must rule the church.

Argument 19: If families have a special necessity of praying together,[39] which cannot be supplied otherwise, then it is God's will that family prayer should be in use. Families have such necessities; therefore, etc. The consequent needs no proof; the antecedent is proved by instance. Families have family necessities that are larger than can be confined to a closet and yet more private than to be brought into the assemblies of the church. First, there are many worldly occasions about their callings and relations that are fit for them to mention among themselves but unfit to mention before the entire congregation. Second, there are many distempers in the hearts and lives of the members of the families, and many miscarriages and disagreements, that must be taken up at home and that prayer must do much to cure, and yet are not fit to be brought to the ears of the church assemblies. Third, if it were fit to mention them all in public, yet the number of such cases would be so great, it would overwhelm the minister and confound public worship; nay, one half of them in most churches could not be mentioned. Fourth, such cases are of ordinary occurrence and would therefore have all these inconveniencies.

There are many such cases that are not fit to be confined to our

---

[38]*Heterogeneous.*
[39]*Conjunctly.*

secret prayers, each one by himself, because 1. They often so sin together as makes it fit that they confess and lament together. 2. Some mercies they receive together, so it is fit that they seek and give thanks together. 3. Many works they do together, so it is fit that they seek a blessing together. 4. The presence of one another in confession, petition, and thanksgiving tends to the increase of their fervor and warming of their hearts and engaging them the more to duty and against sin; this is needful on the grounds laid down before. Nay, it is a kind of family schism in such cases to separate from one another and to pray in secret only, just as it is church schism to separate from the church assemblies and to pray in families only. Nature and grace delight in unity and abhor division. The light of nature and grace engages us to do as much of the work of God in unity, concord, and communion as we can.

Argument 20: If before the giving of the Law to Moses, God was worshipped in families by his own appointment and this appointment has not yet been reversed, then God is to be worshipped in families. The antecedent is certain; therefore, so is the consequent.

I think no man denies the first part of the antecedent, that before the flood in the families of the righteous and after, until the establishment of a priesthood, God was worshipped in families or households. It is a greater doubt whether he had any other public worship. When there were few or no church assemblies that were larger than families, no doubt God was worshipped in families. Every ruler of a family was as a priest to his own family. Cain and Abel offered their own sacrifices; so did Noah, Abraham, and Jacob.

If it is objected that this ceased when the office of the priest was instituted, thus denying the latter part of my antecedent, I reply, first, though some make a doubt of it, as to whether the office of the priesthood was instituted before Aaron's time, I think there is no great doubt to be made, seeing we find a priesthood then among other nations, who had it either by the light of nature or by tradition from the church; and Melchizedek's priesthood, which was a type of Christ,[40] is mentioned. Though family worship was the most usual, there was more public worship. Second, after the institution of Aaron's priesthood, family worship continued, as I have proved

---

[40]That is, Melchizedek's priesthood foreshadowed and anticipated the priesthood of Jesus Christ.

before; yea, the two sacraments of circumcision and the Passover were celebrated in families by the master of the house. Therefore, prayer was certainly continued in families. Third, if that part of worship that was afterward performed in synagogues and public assemblies was appropriated to them, that does not prove that the part assigned to families, as such, was transferred to those assemblies. Nay, it is a certain proof that part was left to families because we find that the public assemblies never undertook it. We find among them no prayer but church prayer, and not that which was fitted to families at all. Nor is there a word of Scripture that speaks of God reversing his command or order for family prayer or other family worship. Therefore, it is still obligatory.

Had I not been too long already, I should have urged to this end the example of Job in sacrificing daily for his sons (Job 1:2–5) and of Esther's keeping a fast with her maids (Est. 4:16). And Jeremiah 10:25, "Pour out your wrath on the nations that know you not, and on the peoples [KJV, "families"] that call not on your name." It is true that by "families" is meant "tribes of people," and by "call . . . on your name" is meant their worshipping the true God. But this is spoken of all tribes without exception, great and small, and tribes in the beginning (Abraham's, Isaac's, Jacob's, and so on) were confined to families. The argument holds from likeness[41] to a proper family. That calling on God's name is here put for worship is confirmed because it proves it to be the most eminent part of worship, or else the whole would be not signified by it. At least no reason can imagine it to be excluded; so much for the proof of the fourth proposition.

Objections Answered

Objection 1: Had it been a duty under the gospel to pray in families, we should certainly have found it more frequently required in the Scripture.

Answer: First, I have already shown you that it is plainly required in the Scripture. Men must not teach God how to speak or oblige him to make everything plain to blind, perverted minds. Second, those things that were plainly revealed in the Old Testament, and the church then held without any contradiction, even from the persecu-

---

[41]*Parity of reason.*

tors of Christ themselves, might well be passed over in the gospel and taken as supposed, acknowledged things. Third, the general precepts—that is, to pray always, with all prayer, in all places—being expressed in the gospel, and the light of nature making particular application to families, what need is there of more? Fourth, this reason makes apparent why Scripture does not speak of it more often: Before Christ's time, the worship of God was less spiritual and more ceremonial than afterward. Therefore, you find more mention of circumcision and sacrificing than of prayer. Yet prayer was still supposed to occur. After Christ's time on earth, most Christian families were disturbed by persecution, and Christians sold everything and lived in communities. Further, Scripture history was to describe to us the state of the churches rather than of particular families.

Objection 2: Christ himself did not often pray with his family, as appears by the disciples asking him to teach them to pray and by the silence of the Scripture on this point. Therefore, it is not our duty.

Answer: First, Scripture's silence is no proof that Christ did not use it. All things are not written that he did. Second, his teaching them the Lord's Prayer, and their desire of a common rule of prayer, might consist with his usual praying with them; at least with his using to pray with them after that, though at first he did not use it. Third, it is the consequence that I principally deny. 1. Because Christ did afterward call his servants to many duties that he did not put on them at first, as sacraments, discipline, preaching, more frequent praying, and so on, especially after the coming down of the Holy Spirit. As they understood not many articles of the faith until then, no wonder if they understood not many duties until then; for Christ would have them suddenly instructed and more fully sanctified by a miracle, that their ministry might be more credible, their mission being evidently divine, and they being past the suspicion of forgery and deceit. 2. It is evident that Christ did often bless the meal and sing hymns to God with his disciples (see Luke 22:17–18; Mark 14:22–23, 26; Matt. 26:27–28, 30), and it is very probable that he prayed with them often, as in John 17. Yet it could not be expected that he should ordinarily be their mouth in such prayers, as they daily needed.

His case and ours are exceedingly different. His disciples must daily confess their sins and be humbled for them and ask forgiveness; but Christ had to do none of this. They must pray for mortifying grace and help against sin; but he had no sin to mortify or pray against. They must pray for the Spirit and the increase of their imperfect graces; but Christ had fullness and perfection. They must pray for many means to these ends and for help in using them and a blessing on them, for which he had no use. They must give thanks for pardon and conversion and so on, for which Christ had no occasion to give thanks. So having a high priest so much separate from sinners, they had one who prayed for them but not one fit to join with them as their mouth to God in ordinary family prayers, such as they needed, as masters must do with their families.

Objection 3: God does not require either vain or abominable prayers. Family prayers are often vain and abominable; therefore, etc. The minor is proved thus: the prayers of the wicked are abominable; most families are wicked or have wicked persons; therefore, etc.

Answer: First, this is nothing against the prayers of godly families. Second, the prayers of a godly father[42] are neither abominable nor vain because of the presence of others who are ungodly. Otherwise Christ's prayers and blessings should have been vain or abominable because Judas was there, who was a thief and hypocrite. Further, the prayers of the apostles and ministers of those churches in Corinth, Galatia, and Ephesus would have been wicked if that were the case. Third, I refer you to my "Method for Peace of Conscience" as to how far the prayers of the wicked are or are not abominable. The prayers of the wicked as wicked are abominable, but not as they express their return to God and repenting of their wickedness. It is not the abominable prayer that God commands, but the faithful, penitent prayer. You mistake it, as if the wicked man were not the person commanded to pray; whereas you should rather say, "It is not the abominable prayer that is commanded him." He is commanded to pray such prayers as are not abominable, even as Simon Magus was commanded to repent and pray and "seek the LORD while he may be found; call upon him while he is near" (Acts 8:9–25; Isa. 55:6). So let the wicked pray, and his prayer will not be abominable. The command to pray implies the command to repent

---

[42]*Master.*

and depart from wickedness. For what is it to pray for grace but to express to God desires for grace? (It is not to tell God a lie by saying they desire what they hate.) Therefore, when we exhort them to pray, we exhort them to such desires.

Objection 4: Many masters of families cannot pray in their families without a book, and that is unlawful.

Answer: If their disability is natural, as a senseless person,[43] they are not fit to rule families. If it is moral and culpable, they are bound to use the means to overcome it (in the meantime they are to use a prayer book or form rather than not to pray in their families).

Frequency and Seasons of Family Worship

The last part of this work will speak of fit times for family worship, whether it should be every day, twice a day, or morning and evening. First, ordinarily it should be every day and twice a day; the morning and evening are usually the fittest seasons. Second, some greater duty may at times intervene, which, for that time, disobliges us. The occasions of some families may make some hours fit for one that are unfit for another.

Argument 1: We are bound to take all fit occasions and opportunities to worship God. Families have daily (morning and evening) occasions and opportunities; therefore, they are bound to take them.

Both major and minor ideas were proved before. Experience proves that family sins are committed daily and family mercies received daily; further, family necessities occur daily. Thus reason tells us, first, that it is seasonable every morning to give God thanks for the rest of the night past; second, to beg direction, protection, provisions, and blessing for the following day; third, then our minds are freed from weariness and worldly care. So reason tells us that the evening is a fit season to give God thanks for the mercies of the day, to confess the sins of the day, to ask forgiveness, and to pray for rest and protection in the night. Nature and reason tell us how often a man should eat and drink, how long he should sleep, and what clothing he should wear. Scripture does not need to tell us the particulars. So if Scripture commands your prayer in general, God may, by providence, tell you when and how often you must pray.

---
[43]*Idiot.*

Argument 2: The Lord's Prayer directs us daily to put up such prayers as belong to families. "Give us this day our daily bread." It is said in the plural, and the reason will oblige families as well as individual persons.

Argument 3: "Pray without ceasing, give thanks in all circumstances" (1 Thess. 5:17–18). "Masters, treat your slaves justly and fairly, knowing that you also have a Master in heaven. Continue steadfastly in prayer, being watchful in it with thanksgiving" (Col. 4:1–2). "And whatever you do, in word or deed, do everything in the name of the Lord Jesus, giving thanks to God the Father through him" (Col. 3:17). "Do not be anxious about anything, but in everything by prayer and supplication with thanksgiving let your requests be made known to God" (Phil. 4:6). It is easy to see that less than twice a day does not fulfill the command to pray "without ceasing . . . steadfastly . . . in everything"; the phrases seem to go much higher.

Argument 4: Daniel prayed in his house three times a day; therefore, less than twice a day under the gospel seems unreasonable.

Argument 5: "She who is truly a widow, left all alone, has set her hope on God and continues in supplications and prayers night and day" (1 Tim. 5:5). "Night and day" can be no less than morning and evening. If you say, "This is not family prayer," I answer that it is all kinds of prayer belonging to her, and if it commends the less, so much more the greater.

Argument 6: From Luke 6:12; 2:37; 18:7; Acts 26:7; 1 Thessalonians 3:10; 2 Timothy 1:3; Revelation 7:15; Nehemiah 1:6; Psalm 88:1; Joshua 1:8; Psalm 1:2, which show that Christ prayed night and day and that his servants prayed, meditated, and read the Scripture.

Argument 7: In Deuteronomy 6:7; 11:19, it is commanded that parents teach their children the Word of God when they "lie down, and when [they] rise"; and the likeness[44] and joining[45] of Word and prayer will prove that they should also pray with them lying down and rising up.

Argument 8: In Psalm 119:164, David praised God seven times a day; and 146:2, "I will praise the LORD as long as I live"; 5:3, "O LORD, in the morning you hear my voice; in the morning I prepare a

---

[44]*Parity of reason.*
[45]*Conjunction.*

sacrifice for you and watch"; 59:16, "But I will sing of your strength; I will sing aloud of your steadfast love in the morning"; 88:13, "in the morning my prayer comes before you"; 92:12, "The righteous flourish like the palm tree and grow like a cedar in Lebanon"; 119:147–148, "I rise before dawn and cry for help; I hope in your words. My eyes are awake before the watches of the night, that I may meditate on your promise"; 130:6, "my soul waits for the Lord more than watchmen for the morning." The priests were to offer sacrifices and thanks to God every morning (1 Chron. 23:30; Ex. 30:7; 36:3; Lev. 6:12; 2 Chron. 13:11; Ezek. 46:13–14; Amos 4:4). Christians are a "holy priesthood, to offer spiritual sacrifices acceptable to God through Jesus Christ" (1 Pet. 2:5, 9). David says, "Evening and morning and at noon I utter my complaint and moan, and he hears my voice" (Ps. 55:17). Thus, morning and evening sacrifices and burnt offerings were offered to the Lord; there is reason that gospel worship should be as frequent (1 Chron. 16:40; 2 Chron. 2:4; 13:11; 31:3; Ezra 3:3; 2 Kings 16:15; 1 Kings 18:29, 36; Ezra 9:5). There is no doubt that they prayed with their sacrifices, which David suggests in comparing them, "Let my prayer be counted as incense before you, and the lifting up of my hands as the evening sacrifice!" (Ps. 141:2). God calls for prayer and praise as better than sacrifice (1 Sam. 15:22).

All these show how frequently God's servants have been accustomed[46] to worship him and how often God expects it. It is reasonable that in gospel times of greater light and holiness, we should not come behind those who lived in times of the Law, especially when Christ prayed all night. You may observe that these Scriptures speak of prayer in general and do not limit it to private practice; therefore, these texts extend to all prayer, according to opportunity. No reason can limit these examples to the most secret and least noble sort of prayer. If two or three are gathered together in Christ's name, he is among them.

If you say that by this rule we must as frequently pray in the church assemblies, I answer, the church cannot so often assemble; but when it can be without great inconvenience, I doubt not but it would be a good work for many to meet the minister daily for prayer, as in some rich and populous cities they may do.

---

[46]*Wont.*

I have been more tedious on this subject than a holy, hungry Christian possibly may think necessary who needs not so many arguments to persuade him to feast his soul with God and to delight himself in the frequent exercises of faith and love. If I have said less than the other sort of readers think necessary, let them know that if they desire to open their eyes and recover their appetites and feel their sins and observe their daily wants and dangers and get a heart that loves God, these reasons will seem sufficient to convince them of so sweet, profitable, and necessary a work. If they observe the difference between praying and prayerless families and care for their souls and communion with God, much fewer words than these may convince them. It is a dead, graceless, carnal heart that must be cured before these men will be satisfied; a better appetite would help their reason. If God should say in general to all, "You shall eat as often as will do you good," the sick stomach would say, "Once a day, and that but a little, is enough, and as much as God requires"; another would say, "Three times a day is little enough." A good and healthy heart is a great help in the expounding of God's Word, especially of his general commandments. That which men love not but are weary of, they will not easily believe to be their duty. The new nature, holy love, desires, and experience of a sound believer make all these reasons needless to him. I confess I have written them, principally, to convince the carnal hypocrite and to stop the mouths of enemies.

Chapter Three

Directions for the
Holy Government of Families

The principal thing required for the right governing of families is the fitness of the governors and those governed, which was spoken of before in the directions for the constitution of the family. If persons, unfit for their relations, have joined themselves together in a family, their first duty is to repent of their former sin and rashness, to turn to God and seek after that fitness necessary for the right practice of their duties. In the governors of families, these three things are of greatest necessity: authority, skill, and holiness and readiness of will.

First, a *general direction*. Let governors maintain their authority in their families. For if that is lost, and you are despised by those you should rule, your word will be nothing to them; you do but ride without a bridle; your power of governing is gone when your authority is lost. You must first understand the nature, use, and extent of your authority; for as your relations are different to your wife and to your children, so also is your authority. Your authority over your wife is such as is necessary to the order of your family, the safe and prudent management of your affairs, and your comfortable cohabitation. The power of love and complicated interest must be more than magisterial commands. Your authority over your children is great, yet only such as, joined[1] with love, is needful for their good education and happiness.[2]

---

[1] *Conjunct.*
[2] *Felicity.*

Direction 1: Let your family understand that your authority is from God, who is the God of order, and that in obedience to him they are obliged to obey you. There is no power but from God; and there is none that the intelligent creature can so much reverence as that which is from God. All bonds are easily broken and cast away (by the soul at least, if not the body), which are not perceived to be divine. An enlightened conscience will say to ambitious usurpers, "I know God and his Son Jesus, but who are you?"

Direction 2: The more God appears to be with you, in your knowledge, holiness, and blameless life, the greater will your authority be in the eyes of your inferiors[3] who fear God. Sin will make you contemptible and vile; and holiness, being the image of God, will make you honorable. In the eyes of the faithful, "a vile person is despised, but [the faithful man] honors those who fear the LORD" Ps. 15:4). "Righteousness exalts a nation, but sin is a reproach to any people" (Prov. 14:34). "Those who honor me I will honor, and those who despise me shall be lightly esteemed" (1 Sam. 2:30). Those who give themselves to "dishonorable passions" and relations[4] (Rom. 1:26) will seem vile when they have made themselves so. Eli's sons were "blaspheming God" and made themselves vile by their sin (1 Sam. 3:13). I know men should discern and honor a person placed in authority by God, though they are morally and naturally vile; but this is so hard that it is seldom well done. God is so severe against proud offenders that he usually punishes them by making them vile in the eyes of others; at least, when they are dead, and men dare freely speak of them, their names will rot (Prov. 10:7). The instances of the greatest emperors in the world, both Persian, Roman, and Turkish, do tell us that if (by whoredom, drunkenness, gluttony, pride, and especially persecution) they will make themselves vile, God will permit them, by uncovering their nakedness, to become the shame and scorn of men. Shall a wicked master of a family think to maintain his authority over others while he rebels against the authority of God?

Direction 3: Do not show your natural weakness by passions or imprudent words or deeds. For if they show contempt to your

---

[3]Not inferior in value or importance, but subordinate to another's authority.
[4]*Conversations.*

family,[5] a little thing will draw them further, to despise your words. There is naturally in man so high an esteem of reason that men are hardly persuaded that they should rebel against reason to be governed, for order's sake, by folly. They are likely to think that reason should bear rule; therefore, any silly or weak expressions or inordinate passions or imprudent actions are likely to make you contemptible in the eyes of inferiors.

Direction 4: Do not lose your authority by not using it. If you suffer children a little while to be in control[6] and to have and say and do what they will, your government will be but a name or image. A moderate course between a lordly rigor and a soft subjection or neglect of exercising the power of your place will best preserve you from your inferiors' contempt.

Direction 5: Do not lose your authority by too much familiarity. If you make your children playfellows or equals and talk to them and allow them to talk to you as your companions, they will quickly grow upon you and hold their custom. Though another may govern them, they will scarce endure to be governed by you but will scorn to be subject where they have once been equal.

Second, a *general direction*: Labor for prudence and skillfulness in governing. Whoever undertakes to be the master of a family undertakes to be their governor; and it is no small sin or folly to undertake such a place as you are utterly unfit for when it is a matter of so great importance. You could discern this in a case that is not your own, as if a man undertakes to be a schoolmaster who cannot read or write or to be a physician who knows neither diseases nor their remedies or to be a ship's pilot who cannot tell how to do a pilot's work. Why cannot you much more discern it in your own case?

Direction 1: To get the skill of holy governing, it is needful that you be studied in the Word of God. Therefore, God commands the king that "he shall read in it all the days of his life" (Deut. 17:18–19), and it must "not depart from your mouth, but you shall meditate on it day and night" (Josh. 1:8). All parents must be able to "teach them diligently to your children, and shall talk of them when you sit in your house, and when you walk by the way, and when you lie down, and when you rise" (Deut. 6:6–7; 11:18–19). All government of men

---

[5]*Persons.*
[6]*To have the head.*

is subservient to the government of God and is to promote obedience to his laws. It is necessary that we understand the laws to which all laws and precepts must give place and serve.

Direction 2: Understand the different tempers of your inferiors, and deal with them as they are and as they can bear, and not with all alike. Some are more intelligent and some less so. Some are tender, and some have more hardened, impudent dispositions. Some will be best wrought upon by love and gentleness; and some have need of sharpness and severity. Prudence must fit your dealings to their dispositions.

Direction 3: You must recognize difference between their different faults, and accordingly suit your reprehensions. They must be most severely rebuked who have most willfulness and those who are faulty in matters of greatest weight. Some faults are so much through mere disability and unavoidable frailty of the flesh that there is but little of the will appearing in them. These must be more gently handled, as deserving more compassion than reproof. Some are habitual vices, and the whole nature is more depraved than in others. These must have more than a particular correction. They must be held to such a course of life as may be most effectual to destroy and change those habits. Some are upright at heart in the main and most momentous things but are guilty of some actual faults, and of these, some more seldom and some more frequent. If you do not prudently diversify your rebukes according to their faults, you will harden them and miss your ends; for there is a family justice that must not be overthrown unless you will overthrow your families, just as there is a more public justice necessary to the public good.

Direction 4: Be a good husband to your wife and a good father to your children, and let love have dominion in your governing, that your inferiors may easily find that it is in their interest to obey you. For interest and self-love are the natural rulers of the world. The most effectual way to procure obedience or any good is to make men perceive that it is for their own good and to engage in self-love, that they may see that the benefit is likely to be their own. If you do them no good but are sour and discourteous and closehanded to them, few will be ruled.

Direction 5: If you would be skillful in governing others, learn first to command yourselves. Can you ever expect to have others more at your will and government than yourselves? Is he fit to rule his family in the fear of God and a holy life who is unholy and fears not God himself? Or is he fit to keep them from passion, drunkenness, gluttony, lust, or any way of sensuality who cannot keep himself from it? Will not inferiors despise such reproofs, which are contradicted in your own lives? You know this is true of wicked preachers; is it not as true of other governors?

Third, a *general direction*: You must be holy persons if you would be holy governors of your families. Men's actions follow the bent of their dispositions. They will do as they are. An enemy of God will not govern a family for God; nor will an enemy of holiness (nor a stranger to it) set up a holy order in his house and in a holy manner manage his affairs. I know it is cheaper and easier to the flesh to call others to mortification and holiness of life than to bring ourselves to it; but yet when it is not a bare command or wish that is necessary but a course of holy and industrious government, unholy persons (though some of them may go far) have not the ends and principles that such a work requires.

Direction 1: To this end, be sure that your own souls are entirely subjected unto God and that you more accurately obey his laws than you expect any inferior should obey your commands. If you dare disobey God, why should they fear disobeying you? Can you more severely revenge disobedience, or more bountifully reward obedience, than God can? Are you greater and better than God is?

Direction 2: Be sure that you lay up your treasure in heaven, and make the enjoyment of God in glory to be the ultimate commanding end, both of the affairs and government of your family and of all things else with which you are entrusted. Devote yourselves and all to God, and do all for him; do all as passengers to another world whose business on earth is to provide for heaven and promote their everlasting interest. If thus you are separated unto God, you are sanctified; and then you will separate all that you have to his use and service, and this, with his acceptance, will sanctify all.

Direction 3: Maintain God's authority in your family more carefully than your own. Your own is but for his. More sharply rebuke

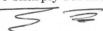

or correct those who wrong and dishonor God than those who wrong and dishonor you. Remember Eli's sad example. Do not make a small matter of any sins, especially great sins, of your children. It is an odious thing to slight God's cause when you are fiercely passionate for the loss of some small commodity of your own. God's honor must be greatest in your family. His service must have the preeminence of yours. Sin against him must be the most intolerable offense.

Direction 4: Let spiritual love to your family be predominant, and let your care be greatest for the saving of their souls, and your compassion greatest in their spiritual miseries. Be careful to provide them a portion in heaven and to save them from whatsoever would deprive them of it. Never prefer transitory riches[7] before their everlasting riches. Never be so cumbered about many things as to forget that one thing is necessary. Choose for yourselves and your children the better part (Luke 10:42).

Direction 5: Let your family neither be kept in idleness and flesh-pleasing, nor yet overwhelmed with such multitude of business as shall take up and distract their minds, diverting them from and unfitting them for holy things. Where God lays on you a necessity of excessive labors, it must patiently and cheerfully be undergone; but when you draw them unnecessarily on yourselves for the love of riches, you do but become the tempters and tormentors of yourselves and others, forgetting the terrible examples of those who have fallen from Christ and are pierced with many sorrows (1 Tim. 6:10).

Direction 6: As much as possible, settle a constant order for all your businesses, that every work may know its time, and confusion may not shut out godliness. It is a great assistance in every calling to do all in a set and constant order; it makes it easy, removes impediments, and promotes success. Distraction in your business causes a distraction in your minds in holy duty. Some callings can hardly be cast into any order or method, but others may, if prudence and diligence are used. God's service will be better done, and your work will be better done, to the quiet of your own minds. Foresight and skillfulness will save you an abundance of labor and vexation.

---

[7]*Pelf of earth.*

Chapter Four

Motives to Persuade Men to the Holy Government of Families

I f it were understood what benefits come by the holy governing of families, and what mischiefs come by its neglect, there would be few walking the streets among us who appear as odious as those careless, ungodly governors who do not know or mind their weighty duty. While we all suffer from the calamitous fruits of this neglect, I think it is worthwhile if, with some, the cause may be removed by awakening sluggish souls to do their designated work.

Motive 1: Consider that the holy government of families is a considerable part of God's own government of the world, and the contrary is a great part of the Devil's government. It has pleased God to settle a natural and so a political order in the world and to honor his creatures to be the instruments of his own operations. Though he could have produced all effects without any inferior causes and could have governed the world by himself alone without any instruments (he being not, as kings, constrained to make use of deputies and officers because of their own natural confinement and insufficiency), yet he is pleased to make inferior causes partakers in such excellent effects and takes delight in the frame and order of causes by which his will among his creatures is accomplished. As several justices in the countries govern as officers of the king, so every magistrate and master of a family governs as an officer of God. If his government by his officers is put down or neglected, it is contempt of God or rebellion against him. What is all the practical atheism,[1] rebellion, and ungodliness in the world but the rejecting of the government of God?

It is not with consideration against the being of God in itself that his enemies rise up with malignant, rebellious opposition; but it is against God as the holy and righteous Governor of the world, and especially of them. As in an army, if the corporals, sergeants, and lieutenants neglect their offices, the government of the general or colonels is defeated and of little force, so if the rulers of families and other officers of God corrupt or neglect their part of government, they do their worst to corrupt or cast out God's government from the earth. If God does not govern your families, who shall? The Devil is always the governor where God's government is refused. The world and the flesh are the instruments of his government; worldliness and living in the flesh are his service, and undoubtedly he is the ruler of the family where these prevail and where faith and godliness do not take place. What can you expect from such a master?

Motive 2: Consider also that an ungoverned, ungodly family is a powerful means to the damnation of all the members of it; it is the common boat or ship that hurries souls to hell and is bound for the devouring gulf. Whoever is the Devil's coach or boat is likely to go with the rest, as the driver or the boatman pleases. But a well-governed family is an excellent help to the saving of all the souls who are in it. As in an ungodly family there are continual temptations to ungodliness, swearing, lying, railing, wantonness, and contempt of God, so in a godly family there are continual provocations to a holy life, faith, love, obedience, and heavenly-mindedness. Temptations to sin are fewer there than in the Devil's shops and workhouses of sin; the authority of the governors, the behavior[2] of the rest, the examples of all are great inducements to a holy life.

As in a well-ordered army of valiant men, every coward is so linked in by order that he cannot choose but to fight and stand with the rest, and in a confused rout the most valiant man is cast[3] down by the disorder and must perish with the rest. Even so in a well-ordered, holy family, a wicked man can scarce tell how to live wickedly but seems almost to be a saint while he is among saints and

[1]That is, believing in God's existence but living as though he does not exist.
[2]*Conversation.*
[3]*Borne.*

hears no words that are profane or filthy and is kept in the constant exercises of religion by the authority and company of those with whom he lives. Oh, how easy and clean is the way to heaven in such a gracious, well-ordered family, in comparison of what it is to them who dwell in the distracted families of profane and worldly people![4] As there is greater probability of the salvation of souls in England, where the gospel is preached and professed, than in heathen or Islamic[5] countries, so there is a greater probability of their salvation who live in the houses and company of the godly than of the ungodly. In one the advantages of instruction, command, example, and credit are all on God's side; and in the other they are on the Devil's side.

Motive 3: A holy, well-governed family tends not only to the safety of the members but also to the ease and pleasure of their lives. To live where God's law is the principal rule and where you may be daily taught the mysteries of his kingdom and have the Scriptures opened to you and be led, as by the hand, in the paths of life, where the praises of God are daily celebrated and his name is called upon and where all speak the heavenly language and where God, Christ, and heaven are their daily work and recreation, where it is the greatest honor to be most holy and heavenly, and the greatest contention is who shall be most humble and godly and obedient to God and their superiors and where there is no reviling scorn at godliness, nor any profane and coarse language[6]—what a sweet and happy life is this! It is the closest thing to heaven on earth.

But to live where worldliness, profaneness, wantonness, and sensuality bear all the sway and where God is unknown and holiness and all religious exercises are matters of contempt and scorn and where he who will not swear and live profanely makes himself the hatred and derision of the rest and where men are known by their shape and speaking faculty to be men—nay, where men take not themselves for men but for animals[7] and live as if they had no rational souls or any expectations of another life or any higher employments or delights than the transitory concernments of the flesh—what a sordid, loathsome, filthy, miserable life is this! To live where there is no communion with God, where the marks of death

---

[4]*Sensual worldlings.*
[5]*Mahometan.*
[6]*Scurrilous talk.*
[7]*Brutes.*

and damnation are written, as it were, upon the doors, in the face of their impious, worldly lives, and where no man understands the holy language and where there is not the least foretaste of the heavenly, everlasting joys—what is this but to live as the serpent's seed, to feed on dust, and to be excommunicated from the face and favor of God and to be chained up in the prison of sexual desire[8] and malignity among his enemies until the judgment that is making haste comes and will render to all according to their works.

Motive 4: A holy and well-governed family tends to make a holy posterity and to propagate the fear of God from generation to generation. It is more comfortable to have no children than to beget and breed children for the Devil. Their natural corruption is advantage enough to Satan, to engage them to himself and use them for his service. This happens when parents shall also take the Devil's part and teach their children, by precepts or example, how to serve him and shall estrange them from God and a holy life and fill their minds with false conceits and prejudice against the means of their salvation, as if they had sold their children to the Devil. No wonder, then, if they have a black posterity that is trained to be heirs of hell.

Whoever trains up children for God must begin early, before things take deep possession of their hearts and custom increases the depravity[9] of their nature. Original sin is similar to the arched Indian fig tree, whose branches, turning downward and taking root, become as trees themselves. The acts that proceed from this habitual viciousness turn again into vicious habits. Thus sinful nature, by its fruits, increases itself. Other things consume themselves by breeding, and all that sin breeds is added to itself, and its breeding is its feeding, and every act confirms the habit. Therefore, no means in all the world more effectually tends to the happiness of souls than wise and holy education. This deals with sin before it has taken the deepest root and subdues[10] nature while it is but a twig. It prevents the increase of natural depravity[11] and keeps out those deceits, corrupt opinions, and carnal fantasies and lusts that otherwise would be serviceable to sin and Satan. It delivers the heart to Christ early or at least brings a disciple to his school to learn the way to eternal life

---

[8]*Concupiscence.*
[9]*Pravity.*
[10]*Bows.*
[11]*Pravity.*

and to spend those years acquainting himself with the ways of God that others spend growing worse and learning that which must be again unlearned and fortifying Satan's garrison in their hearts and defending it against Christ and his saving grace.

Motive 5: A holy, well-governed family prepares for a holy and well-governed church. If masters did their parts and sent such polished materials to the churches as they ought to do, the work and life of the pastors of the church would be more easy and delightful. It would do one good to preach to such an audience and to catechize and instruct them and examine them and watch over those who are prepared by a wise and holy education and understand and love the doctrine that they hear. To lay such polished stones in the building is an easy and delightful work; how teachable and tractable will such be! How prosperously will the labors of their pastors be laid out upon them! How comely and beautiful will the churches be that are composed of such persons! How pure and comfortable will their communion be! If the churches are sties of unclean beasts, and if they are made up of ignorant and ungodly persons who savor nothing but the things of the flesh and worship what they do not know, we may thank ill-governed families for this. It is difficult for ministers to preach to those who cannot understand them, for they must always be feeding them with milk and teaching them basic principles and catechizing them in the church when they should have been so taught at home. Yea, it is hard for them that there are so many wolves and swine among the sheep of Christ and that holy things are administered to the enemies of holiness and that the godly live in communion with the haters of God and godliness. They are troubled that the Christian religion is dishonored before the heathen world by the worse than heathenish lives of Christian professors.[12]

The pollutions of the churches hinder the conversion of the unbelieving world. Those who judge our religion only by those who profess it judge it by the lives of those who are, in their heart, its enemies. When the haters of Christianity and godliness are the Christians by whose lives[13] the infidel world judges Christianity, you may easily conjecture what judgment they are likely to make. Thus pastors are discouraged, churches defiled, religion disgraced, and infidels hard-

---

[12]That is, professing believers.
[13]*Conversations.*

ened through the impious disorder and negligence of families! What
universities would we have if all the grammar schools neglect their
duties and graduate their students as untaught as they received
them! If all tutors must teach their pupils first to spell and read! Such
churches we are likely to have when every pastor must first do the
work that their masters of families should have done and the part
of many score or hundreds or thousands must be performed by one.

Motive 6: Well-governed families tend to make a happy state and
commonwealth. A good education is the first and greatest work to
make good magistrates and subjects because it tends to make good
men. Though a good man may be a bad magistrate, yet a bad man
cannot be a very good magistrate. The ignorance or worldliness or
sensuality or enmity to godliness that grew up with such persons in
their youth will show itself in all the places and relations that ever
they come into. When an ungodly family has once confirmed them
in wickedness, they will do wickedly in every state of life. When a
deceitful[14] parent betrays his children into the power and service of
the Devil, they will serve him in all relations and conditions. This
is the school from which come all the injustice, cruelties, and perse-
cutions, the impieties of magistrates, and all the murmurings and
rebellions of subjects. This is the soil and seminary where the seed
of the Devil is first sown and where he nurses the plants of covetousness, pride, ambition, revenge, malignity, and sensuality until he
transplants them for his service into several offices in church and
state and into all places of inferiority, where they may disperse their
venom and resist all that is good and contend for the interest of the
flesh and hell, against the interest of the Spirit and of Christ. But
oh, what a blessing to the world would they be who come prepared
by a holy education to places of government and subjection! How
happy is that land that is ruled by such superiors and consists of
such prepared subjects as have first learned to be subject to God and
to their parents!

Motive 7: If governors of families faithfully performed their
duties, that would be a great supply as to any defects on the pastor's part and a means to propagate and preserve religion in times
of public negligence or persecution. Therefore, Christian families

---

[14]*Perfidious.*

are called "churches" because they consist of holy persons who worship God and learn, love, and obey his Word. If you lived among the enemies of religion who forbade Christ's ministers to preach his gospel and forbade God's servants to meet in church assemblies for his worship, the support of religion and the comfort and edification of believers would then rest almost wholly upon the right performance of family duties. There masters might teach the same truths to their households that ministers are forbidden to preach in the assemblies. There you might pray together as fervently and spiritually as you can. There you may keep as holy converse and communion and as strict a discipline as you please. There you may celebrate the praises of your blessed Creator, Redeemer, and Sanctifier and observe the Lord's Day in as exact and spiritual a manner as you are able. You may there provoke one another to love and good works, rebuke every sin, mind each other to prepare for death, and live together as passengers to eternal life. Thus, holy families may keep up religion and the life and comfort of believers and supply the absence[15] of public preaching in those countries where persecutors prohibit and restrain it or where unable or unfaithful pastors neglect it.

Motive 8: The duties of your families are such as you may perform with greatest peace and least exception or opposition from others. When you go further and would be instructing others, they will think you go beyond your call, and many will be suspicious that you take too much upon you; and if you do but gently admonish such as the Sodomites, perhaps they will say, "This fellow came to sojourn, and he has become the judge!" (Gen. 19:9). But your own house is your castle; your family is your charge. You may teach them as often and as diligently as you will. If the ungodly scorn you for it, yet no sober person will condemn you or trouble you for it, if you teach them no evil. All men must confess that nature and Scripture oblige you to it as your unquestionable work. Therefore, you may do it, among sober people, with approbation and quietness.

Motive 9: Well-governed families are honorable and exemplary to others. Even the worldly and ungodly bear a certain reverence to them; for holiness and order have some witness that commends them in the consciences of many who never practiced them. A worldly,

---

[15]*Want.*

ungodly, disordered family is a den of snakes, a place of hissing, railing, folly, and confusion; it is like a wilderness overgrown with briars and weeds. But a holy family is a garden of God; it is beautified with his graces and ordered by his government and fruitful by the showers of his heavenly blessing. The sluggard, who will not suffer the cost and pains to make a garden of his thorny wilderness, may yet confess that a garden is more beautiful and fruitful and delightful; and if wishing would do it, his wilderness should be such. Even so, the ungodly, who will not suffer the cost and pains to order their souls and families in holiness, may yet see a beauty in those that are so ordered and wish for the happiness of such if they could have it without the labor and cost of self-denial. And no doubt the beauty of such holy and well-governed families has convinced many and has drawn them to a great approbation of religion and occasioned them at last to imitate them.

Motive 10: Lastly, consider that holy, well-governed families are blessed with the presence and favor of God. They are his churches where he is worshipped, his houses where he dwells. He is engaged, by love and promise, to bless, protect, and prosper them (Ps. 1:3; 128). It is safe to sail in the ship that is bound for heaven, for Christ is the pilot. But when you reject his government, you refuse his company, condemn his favor, and forfeit his blessing by despising his presence, interest, and commands.

It is an evident truth that most of the mischiefs that now infest or seize upon mankind throughout the earth are caused by ill-governed families. These are the schools and shops of Satan, from which proceeds ignorance, lust, sensuality, devilish pride, malignity, and cruelty against the holy ways of God, which have so unmanned the progeny of Adam. These are the nests in which the serpent hatches the eggs of covetousness, envy, strife, revenge, tyranny, disobedience, wars, and bloodshed and all the leprosy of sin that has so odiously contaminated human nature and all the miseries by which they make the world calamitous. Do you wonder that there can be persons and nations so blind and barbarous as we read of the Turks, Mongols,[16] Indians, and most of the inhabitants of the earth? A wicked education is the cause of all, which, finding nature depraved,

---

[16]*Tartarians.*

increases the venom that should, through education, have been cured. From the wickedness of families national wickedness arises.

Do you wonder why so much ignorance, deceit, and stubbornness in errors, contrary to common sense, can be found among professed Christians, great and small, high and low, throughout all the papal kingdoms? Though the pride, covetousness, and wickedness of a worldly clergy is a great cause, the sinful negligence of parents is as great a cause, if not the greatest. Do you wonder how, even in Reformed churches, there can be so many unreformed sinners who hate the serious practice of religion? It is poor education in ungodly families that is the cause of this. Oh, therefore, how great and necessary a work it is to cast salt into these corrupt fountains! Cleanse and cure these corrupt[17] families, and you may cure almost all the calamities of the earth. To tell what the emperors and princes of the earth might do, if they were wise and good, to remedy this common misery is the idle talk of those negligent persons who condemn themselves in condemning others. Even those rulers and princes who are the pillars and patrons of heathenism, Islam,[18] popery, and ungodliness in the world did themselves receive that venom from their parents, in their birth and education, which inclines them to all this mischief. Family reformation is the easiest and most likely way to a common reformation, or at least to send many souls to heaven and train up multitudes for God if it reaches not to national reformation.

---

[17]*Vitiated.*
[18]*Mahometanism.*

Chapter Five

Motives for a Holy and Careful Education of Children

B ecause the chief part of family care and government consists in the right education of children, I shall provide motives to quicken considerate parents to this duty. Most that I have to say for it is already said in my *Saints' Everlasting Rest*[1] and shall, therefore, here be largely omitted. I shall say something, however, unless the absence of instruction for parents should seem too great.

Motive 1: Consider how deeply nature itself engages you to the greatest care and diligence for the holy education of your children. They are, as it were, parts of yourselves and those whom nature teaches you to love and provide for and take most care for, next to yourselves; and will you be regardless of their chief concerns and the neglect of their souls? Will you in no other way show your love to your children than every beast or bird will to their young, to cherish them until they can go abroad and shift for themselves for bodily[2] sustenance? You do not bring dogs or beasts into the world but children who have immortal souls. Therefore, it is a care and education suitable to their natures that you owe them, even such as conduces most effectually to the happiness of their souls. Nature teaches them some natural things without you, as it does the bird to fly, but it has

---

[1]See *The Saints' Everlasting Rest*, Part 3, Chapter 14, Section 11. *The Saints' Everlasting Rest; or, A Treatise of the Blessed State of Saints in Their Enjoyment of God in Glory* was published throughout the seventeenth, eighteenth, and nineteenth centuries. It was first abridged by John Wesley in 1754 and has been translated into Welsh, Gaelic, German, and French. Several editions, both abridged and unabridged, of the work are still in print.

[2]*Corporeal.*

committed it to your trust and care to teach them the greatest and most necessary things. If you should think that you have nothing to do but to feed them and leave all the rest to nature, then they would not learn to speak. If nature itself would condemn you if you do not teach them to speak, it will much more condemn you if do not teach them to understand both what they should speak and do.

They have an everlasting inheritance of happiness to attain, and it is that for which you must bring them up. They have an endless misery to escape, and it is that which you must diligently teach them. If you do not teach them to escape the flames of hell, what thanks do they owe you for teaching them to speak and do? If you do not teach them the way to heaven and how they may make sure of their salvation, what thanks do they owe you for teaching them how to get their living a little while in a miserable world? If you do not teach them to know God and how to serve him and be saved, you teach them nothing, or worse than nothing.

It is in your hands to do them the greatest kindness or cruelty in all the world. Therefore, help them to know God and to be saved, and you do more for them than if you helped them to be lords or princes. If you neglect their souls and breed them in ignorance, worldliness, ungodliness, and sin, you betray them to the Devil, the enemy of souls, even as truly as if you sold them to him. You thus sell them to be slaves to Satan; you betray them to him who will deceive them and abuse them in this life and will torment them in the next. If you saw but a burning furnace, much more the flames of hell, would you not think that man or woman more fit to be called a devil than a parent who could find it in his or her heart to cast the child into it or to put him into the hands of one who would do it? What monsters, then, are you who read in Scripture the way to hell and who they are whom God will deliver to Satan to be tormented by him and yet will bring up your children in that way and will not take pains to save them from it! What a stir do you make to provide them food and clothing[3] and a competent maintenance in the world when you are dead! How little pains do you take to prepare their souls for the heavenly inheritance! If you seriously believe there are such joys or torments for your children (and for you) as soon as death removes

---

[3]*Raiment.*

you, is it possible that you should take this for the least of their concerns and make it the least and last of your cares to assure them of an endless happiness? If you love them, show it in those things on which their everlasting welfare depends. Do not say you love them and then lead them to hell. If you do not love them, do not be so unmerciful as to damn them. Your saying, "God forbid" and "We hope better" will not make it better or be any excuse for you. What can you do more to damn them if you studied to do it as maliciously as the Devil himself? You cannot possibly do worse than to bring them up in ignorance, carelessness, worldliness, sensuality, and ungodliness. The Devil can do nothing else to damn either them or you but by tempting you to sin and drawing you from godliness. There is no other way to hell. No man is damned for anything but this. And yet, will you bring them up in such a life and say, "God forbid, we do not desire to damn them"?

It is no wonder when you do for your children as you do for yourselves. Who can expect a man to be reasonable for his child who is so unreasonable for himself? Or that those parents should have any mercy on their children's souls who have no mercy on their own. You do not desire to damn yourselves, but yet you do it if you live ungodly lives; and so you will do to your children if you train them up in ignorance of God and in the services of the flesh and the world. You act like one who would set fire on his house and say, "God forbid, I did not intend it to burn" or like one who casts his child into the sea and says, "I did not intend him to drown" or trains him in robbing and thievery and says, "I did not intend him to be hanged." But you intend to make a thief, and so it is all one effect, as if you intended his hanging. For the law determines, and the judge will intend it. So, if you intend to train your children in ungodliness, as if they had no God or souls to mind, you may as well say that you intend to have them damned. And is not an enemy, yea, even the Devil, more excusable for dealing thus cruelly with your children than you who are their parents, bound by nature to love them and prevent their misery? It is odious in ministers who take charge of souls to betray them by being negligent and so be guilty of their everlasting misery; but in parents it is more unnatural and therefore more inexcusable.

Motive 2: Consider that God is the Lord and Owner of your children, both by title of creation and redemption. Therefore, in justice you must resign them to him and educate them for him. Otherwise you rob God of his own creatures and rob Christ of those for whom he died, and this is to give them to the Devil, the enemy of God and them. It was not the world, the flesh, or the Devil that created them or redeemed them but God. It is not possible for any right to be built upon a fuller title than to make them of nothing and redeem them from a state far worse than nothing. After all this, shall the parents of such children steal them from their absolute Lord and Father and sell them to slavery and torment?

Motive 3: Remember that in their baptism you dedicated them to God; you entered them into a solemn vow and covenant, to be wholly his and to live to him. Therein they renounced the flesh, the world, and the Devil; therein you promised to bring them up virtuously, to lead a godly and Christian life, that they might keep God's will and commandments and walk in the same all the days of their lives. After all this, will you break so solemn a promise and cause them to break such a vow and covenant by bringing them up in ignorance and ungodliness? Did you understand and consider what you then did? How solemnly you yourselves engaged them, in a vow to God, to live a mortified and a holy life! Will you so solemnly do in an hour what all their life you will endeavor to destroy?

Motive 4: Consider how great a power the education of children has upon all of their lives. Other than nature and grace, there is nothing that usually prevails so much with them. Indeed, natural viciousness often frustrates a good education. If any means are likely to do them good, it is this; but ill education is more successful in making them evil. This cherishes those seeds of wickedness that spring up when they come of age; this makes so many proud, idle, flesh-pleasing, licentious, lustful, and covetous, and all that is nothing. Whoever tries to root out these vices, which ungodly education has deeply rooted,[4] has a hard task. Ungodly parents serve the Devil so effectually in the first impressions on their children's minds that it is more than magistrates and ministers and all reforming means can afterward do to recover them from that sin to God. Whereas, if you would first engage their hearts to God by a religious education, piety

---

[4]*Radicated.*

would then have all those advantages that sin has now. "Train up a child in the way he should go; even when he is old he will not depart from it" (Prov. 22:6). The language you teach them to speak when they are children, they will use all their life after, if they live with those who use it. And so the opinions that they first receive and the customs that they are used to at first are hardly changed afterward.

I do not doubt that a godly education is God's first and appointed means for causing[5] actual faith and other graces in the children of believers. Many may have beginning[6] grace before, but they cannot sooner have actual faith, repentance, love, or any grace than they have reason in act and exercise. The preaching of the Word by public ministers is not the first ordinary means of grace to any but those who were graceless until they come to hear such preaching; that is, to those on whom the first appointed means has been neglected or proved in vain. It is the second means to do that which was not done by the first. The proof is undeniable: God appoints parents to teach their children the doctrine of his Holy Word before they come to the public ministry. Thus, parents' teaching is the first teaching; and parents' teaching is for this end, as well as public teaching, even to cause[7] faith, love, and holiness. God appoints no means to be used by us on which we may not expect his blessing. Therefore, it is apparent that the appointed means for the first actual grace is parents' godly instruction and education of their children. Public preaching is appointed for the conversion of those who have missed the blessing of the first appointed means. Therefore, if you deny your children religious education, you deny them the first appointed means of their actual faith and sanctification, and then the second comes to disadvantage.

Motive 5: Consider also how many and great are your advantages above all others for your children's good. First, nothing takes so much with anyone as that which is known to come from love. The greater love is discerned in your instruction, the greater success may you expect. Now your children are more confident of their parents' love than of any others. Whether ministers and strangers speak to them in love, they cannot tell; but of their parents' love they make

---

[5]*Begetting.*
[6]*Seminal.*
[7]*Beget.*

no doubt. Second, their love to you is as great a preparative to your success. We all hearken to them whom we dearly love with greater attention and willingness than to others. They do not love the minister as they do their parents. Third, you have them in your care before they receive any false opinions or bad impressions, before they have any sin but that which was born with them. You are to make the first impressions upon them; you have them while they are most teachable, flexible, and tender and make least resistance against instruction. They will not rise up, at first, against your teaching with self-conceit and proud objections. When they come to the minister, however, they are as paper that is written on or printed before, unable to receive another impression. They have much to be untaught before they can be taught. They come with proud and stiff resistance to strive against instruction rather than to readily receive it. Fourth, your children wholly depend on you for their provision,[8] and much for their future livelihood and portions; therefore, they know that it is in their interest to obey and please you. As interest is the common bias of the world, so with your children; they are easier to rule when you have this handle to hold them than any other have who do not have this advantage. They know they do not serve you for nothing.

Fifth, your authority over your children is unquestionable. They will dispute the authority of ministers, yea, and of magistrates, and ask them who gave them the power to teach them and to command them, but parents' authority is beyond all dispute. They will not call you tyrants or usurpers or bid you prove the validity of your ordination or the continuance[9] of your succession. Therefore, father and mother, as the first natural power, are mentioned rather than kings or queens in the fifth commandment. Sixth, you have the power of the rod to force them. "Folly is bound up in the heart of a child, but the rod of discipline drives it far from him" (Prov. 22:15). Your correction will be better understood to come from love than that of the magistrate or any other. Seventh, you have the best opportunity to know both the diseases and temperature of your children, which is a great advantage for choosing and applying the best remedy. Eighth, you have opportunity of watching over them and discerning all their

---

[8]*Maintenance.*
[9]*Uninterruptedness.*

faults in time, but if a minister speaks to them he can know no more what fault to reprehend than others tell him. You may also discern what success your former exhortations had and whether your children amend or still go on in sin and whether you should proceed to more severe remedies.

Ninth, you have opportunity to speak to them in the most familiar manner, which is better understood than the set speech of a minister in the pulpit, which few of them mark or understand. You can quicken their attention by questions that put them upon answering you and so awaken them to a serious regard of what you say. Tenth, you are so frequently with them that you can repeat your instructions and drive them home, and what is not done at one time may be done at another; whereas other men can seldom speak to them, and what is so seldom spoken is easily neglected or forgotten. Eleventh, you have power to place them under the best means and to remove many impediments out of their way, which usually frustrate other men's endeavors. Twelfth, your example is near them and continually in their sight, which is a continual and powerful sermon. By all these advantages God has enabled you, above all others, to be instruments of your children's good and the first and greatest promoters of their salvation.

Motive 6: Consider how great a comfort it would be to you to have your children such as you may hope are the children of God, being brought to know, love, and serve him through your own endeavors in their pious education. First, you may love your children upon a higher account than as they are yours, as they are God's, adorned with his image and quickened with a divine celestial life; and this is to love them with a higher kind of love than mere natural affection. You would rejoice to see your children advanced to be lords or princes; but, oh, how much greater cause for joy to see them made members of Christ and quickened by his Spirit and sealed for eternal life! Second, when your children are made the children of God by the regeneration of the Spirit, you may be freer from care and trouble for them than before. Now you may boldly trust them to the care of their heavenly Father, who is able to do more for them than you are able to desire. He loves them better than you can love them; he is bound by promise to protect them and provide for them and to see that all things work together for their good. He who clothes the lilies of the fields and does not suffer the young lions or ravens to hunger[10] will provide food for his own children (though he will have you also do your duty for them, as they are your children). While they are the children of Satan and the servants of sin, you have cause to fear, not only lest they be exposed to miseries in this world, but much more lest they be snatched away in their sin to hell. Your children, while they are ungodly, are worse than among wolves and tigers. But when they are renewed by the Spirit of Christ, they are the charge of all the blessed Trinity and under God the charge of angels. Living or dying they are safe, for the eternal God is their portion and defense. Third, it may be a continual comfort to you to think what a deal of drudgery and calamity your child is freed from; to think how many oaths he would have sworn, and how many lies and curses he would have uttered, and how beastly and fleshly a life he would have lived, how much wrong he would have done to God and men, and how much he would have pleased the Devil, and what torments in hell he must have endured as the reward of all. And then to think how mercifully God has prevented all this, and what service your child may do God in the world and finally live with Christ in glory—what a joy is this to a considering, believing parent who takes the mercies of his children to be his own!

Fourth, religion will teach your children to be more dutiful to yourselves than nature can teach them. It will teach them to love you even when you have no more to give them, as well as if you had the wealth of all the world. It will teach them to honor you though you are poor and contemptible in the eyes of others. It will teach them to obey you, and if you fall into want, to relieve you according to their power. It will fit them to comfort you in the time of your sickness and distress, when ungodly children will be as thorns in your feet or eyes and cut your hearts and prove a greater grief than any enemies to you. A gracious child will bear with your weaknesses, when a Ham will not cover his father's nakedness. A gracious child can pray for you and pray with you and be a blessing to your house, when an ungodly child is fitter to curse and prove a curse to those with whom he lives. Fifth, is it not an exceeding joy to think of the

---

[10]*Be unprovided for.*

everlasting happiness of your child? That you may live together in heaven forever? The foreseen misery of a graceless child will grieve you whenever you look him in the face. Sixth, it will be a great addition to your joy to think that God blessed your instructions and made you an instrument of all that good that is done to your children and all the good that is done by them and of the happiness they have forever. To think this was conveyed to them by your means will give you a larger share in the delights of it.

Motive 7: Remember that your children's original sin and misery is by you; therefore, in justice, you who have undone them are bound to do your best to save them. If you had but conveyed leprosy or some hereditary disease to their bodies, would you have not done your best to cure them? Oh, that you could do them but as much good as you do them hurt! It is more than Adam's sin that runs down into the natures of your children, yea, and that brings judgments on them; and even Adam's sin does not come to them but by you.

Motive 8: Lastly, consider what great need they have of the most help you can afford them. It is not a bodily[11] disease, an easy enemy, a tolerable misery that we call to you for their help; it is against sin, Satan, and hellfire. It is against a body of sin; not one, but many; not small, but pernicious, having seized on the heart; deep-rooted sins that are not easily plucked up. All the teaching, diligence, and watchfulness that you can use are little enough, and may prove too little. They are obstinate vices that have possessed them; they are not quickly nor easily cast out, and the remnants and roots are apt to be still springing up again when you thought they had been quite destroyed. Oh, then, what wisdom and diligence is requisite to so great and necessary a work!

Now let me speak to the hearts of those careless and ungodly parents who neglect the holy education of their children; yea, and to those professors of godliness who slobber over so great a work with few formal duties and words that are next to a total omission of it. Oh, do not be so unmerciful to the souls that you have helped bring into the world! Do not think so basely of them, as if they were not worth your labor. Do not treat your children like your animals,[12] to make no provision for them but for their flesh. Remember that they

---

[11]*Corporal.*
[12]*Beasts.*

are not animals[13] but men whom you have brought into the world; educate them, then, and treat them as men, for the love and obedience of their Maker. Oh, pity and help the souls of those you have defiled and undone! Have mercy on the souls that must perish in hell if they are not saved in this day of salvation! Oh, help them who have so many enemies to assault them! Help them who have so many temptations to pass through, so many difficulties to overcome, and so severe a judgment to undergo! Help them who are so weak and so easily deceived and overthrown! Help them while your advantages continue, before sin hardens them and grace forsakes them, before Satan places a stronger garrison in their hearts. Help them while they are teachable,[14] before they are grown up and despise your help; before you and they are separated asunder, and your opportunities are at an end. You do not think it difficult from year to year to make provision for their bodies; oh, do not be cruel to their souls! Do not sell them to Satan, and for nothing! Do not betray them by your ungodly negligence to hell. Or if any of them perishes, do not let it be by you who are so much bound to do them good. The undoing of your children's souls is a work better suited for Satan than for their parents.

Remember how comfortable a thing it is to work with Christ for the saving of souls. You think the calling of ministers is honorable and happy; and so it is, because they serve Christ in so high a work. But if you will not neglect it, you may do for your children more than any minister can do. This is your preaching place; here God calls you to exercise your parts, even in the holy instruction of your families. Your charge is small in comparison to the minister's; he has many hundreds of souls to watch over, scattered throughout the parish. Will you think it much to instruct and watch over those few of your own who are under your roof? You can speak odiously of unfaithful, soul-betraying ministers; and do you not consider how odious a soul-betraying parent is? If God entrusts you with earthly talents, take heed how you use them, for you must be accountable for your trust; and when he has entrusted you with souls, even your children's souls, will you betray them? If any rulers forbid you the instructing and well-governing of your families and restrain you by law (as they would have restrained Daniel from praying in his house, Daniel 6),

---

[13]*Beasts.*
[14]*Tractable.*

then you would think them monsters of impiety and inhumanity; you would cry out about a satanic persecution that would make men traitors to their children's souls and drive away all religion from the earth. Yet, how easily can you neglect such duties when none forbid them and never accuse you of any such horrid impiety or inhumanity! What hypocrisy and blind partiality is this! Like a lazy minister who would cry out about persecution if he were silenced by others and yet will not be provoked to be laborious but by his slothfulness silences himself and makes no matter of it. Would it be so heinous a sin in another to restrain you? Is it not as heinous for you, who are so much obliged to it, voluntarily to restrain yourselves? Oh, then, deny not this necessary diligence to your children, as you love their souls, as you love the happiness of the church or commonwealth, as you love the honor and interest of Christ, and as you love your present and everlasting peace.

Do not see your children the slaves of Satan here and the firebrands of hell forever if any diligence of yours may contribute to prevent it. Do not give conscience such matter of accusation against you as to say, "All this is your fault! If you would have instructed them diligently and watched over them and corrected them and done your part, they would have never come to this." You till your fields, and you weed your gardens. What pains you take for your grounds and cattle! Will you not take more pains for your children's souls? Alas, what creatures will they be if you leave them to themselves? Will they not become ignorant, careless, rude, and beastly? Oh, what a lamentable case have ungodly parents brought the world into! Ignorance and selfishness, sensuality and devilish malignity have covered the face of the earth as a deluge and have driven away wisdom, self-denial, piety, charity, justice, and temperance out of the world, thus confining them to the breasts of a few obscure, humble souls who love virtue for virtue's sake and look for their reward from God alone and expect that by abstaining from iniquity they make themselves a prey to wolves (Isa. 59:15). Wicked education has undone[15] the world, subdued it to Satan, and made it like a hell. Oh, do not join with the sons of Belial in this unnatural, horrid wickedness!

---

[15]*Unmanned.*

Chapter Six

Mutual Duties of Husbands and Wives Toward Each Other

I t is the subversion of all societies, and so of the world, that selfish, ungodly persons enter into all relations with a desire to serve themselves and fish out all that gratifies their flesh without any sense of the duty of their relation. They consider[1] what honor, profit, or pleasure their relation will afford them, but not what God and man require or expect from them (Gen. 2:18; Prov. 18:22). All their thought is what they shall have, but not what they shall be and do. They are very sensible what others should be and do to them but not what they should be and do to others. Thus it is with magistrates and with people, with too many pastors and their flocks, with husbands and wives, with parents and children, and all other relations. Our first care should be to know and perform the duties of our relations and please God in them and then to look for his blessing by way of encouraging reward. Study and do your parts, and God will certainly do his.

Direction 1: The first duty of husbands is to love their wives (and wives their husbands) with a true, entire, married[2] love. "Husbands, love your wives, as Christ loved the church and gave himself up for her. . . . In the same way husbands should love their wives as their own bodies. He who loves his wife loves himself. For no one ever hated his own flesh, but nourishes and cherishes it, just as Christ does the church. . . . However, let each one of you love his

---

[1]*Bethink.*
[2]*Conjugal.*

wife as himself, and let the wife see that she respects her husband"
(Eph. 5:25, 28–29, 33). See Genesis 2:24. It is a relation of love that
you have entered. God has made it your duty for your mutual help
and comfort, that you may be as willing and ready to comfort[3] one
another as the hand is to help the eye or other members and that
your converse may be sweet and your burdens easy and your lives
comfortable. If love is removed but for an hour between husband and
wife, they are as a bone out of joint; there is no ease, no order, no
work well done till they are restored and set in joint again. Therefore,
be sure that married[4] love be constantly maintained.

The directions for maintaining married[5] love are such as these:

First, choose one at first who is truly amiable, especially in
the virtues of the mind. Second, do not marry until you are sure
that you can love entirely. Do not be drawn for sordid ends to join
with one for whom you have but ordinary affections. Third, do not
be too hasty, but know beforehand all the imperfections that may
tempt you afterward to loathing. If these duties have been sinfully
neglected, yet, fourth, remember that justice commands you to love
one who has, as it were, forsaken the world for you and is content to
be the companion of your labors and sufferings and an equal sharer
in all conditions with you and your companion until death. It is
worse than barbarous inhumanity to entice such a one into a bond
of love and fellowship[6] with you and then to say that you cannot
love her. This was, by deviousness,[7] to draw her into a snare to her
undoing. What comfort can she have in her converse with you and
care and labor and necessary sufferings if you deny her married[8]
love? Especially if she does not deny love to you, the inhumanity is
the greater. Fifth, remember that women are ordinarily affectionate,
passionate creatures, and as they love themselves, so they expect
much love from you. When you joined yourself to such a nature,
you obliged yourself to answerable duty. If love does not love, it is
an ungrateful and unjust contempt. Sixth, remember that you are
under God's command. To deny married[9] love to your wives is to

---

[3]*Succor.*
[4]*Conjugal.*
[5]*Conjugal.*
[6]*Society.*
[7]*Perfidiousness.*
[8]*Conjugal.*
[9]*Conjugal.*

deny a duty that God has urgently imposed on you. Obedience, therefore, should command your love.

Seventh, remember that you are relatively, as it were, one flesh. You have drawn her to forsake father and mother, to cleave to you; you are joined for procreation of children as must bear the image and nature of you both; your possessions and interests are in a manner the same. Therefore, such nearness should command affection; they who are as you should be most easily loved as yourselves. Eighth, take more notice of the good that is in your wives than of the evil. Do not let the observation of their faults make you forget or overlook their virtues. Love is kindled by the sight of love or goodness. Ninth, do not make infirmities to seem odious faults but excuse them as far as lawfully you may, by considering the frailty of the sex, their tempers, and considering also your own infirmities and how much your wives must bear with you. Tenth, stir up in them most what is best, and do not stir up that which is evil; then the good will most appear, and the evil will be as buried, and you will more easily maintain your love. There is some uncleanness in the best on earth; yet if you will be daily stirring in the filth, no wonder if you have the annoyance; and for that you may thank yourselves. Draw out the fragrance of that which is good and delectable in them, and do not, by your own imprudence or peevishness, stir up the worst, and then you shall find that even your faulty wives will appear more amiable to you.

Eleventh, overcome them with love. Then whatever they are in themselves, they will be loving you, and consequently lovely. Love will cause love, as fire kindles fire. A good husband is the best means to make a good and loving wife. Do not make them detestable[10] by your bad[11] behavior and then say, "I cannot love them." Twelfth, give them examples of amiableness in yourselves; set them the pattern of a prudent, lowly, loving, meek, self-denying, patient, harmless, holy, heavenly life. Try this a while, and see whether it will not shame them from their faults and make them walk more amiably themselves.

Direction 2: Another duty of husbands and wives is to live together[12] and, where age does not prohibit, a sober and modest join-

---

[10]*Froward.*
[11]*Froward.*
[12]*Cohabitation.*

ing[13] for procreation, which avoids lasciviousness, unseasonableness, and whatever tends to corrupt the mind, make it vain and filthy, and hinder from holy employment. Therefore, lust must not be cherished in the married, but the mind must be brought to a moderate, chaste, and sober frame. The remedy must not be turned into an increase of the disease but used to extinguish it. For if the mind is left to the power of lust, and only marriage trusted to for the cure, with many it will be found an insufficient cure. Lust will rage as it did before, and you will be so much the more desperate and your case the more miserable as your sin prevails against the remedy. Yet marriage being appointed for a remedy against lust, for avoiding all unlawful congress, the apostle has plainly described your duty: "'It is good for a man not to have sexual relations with a woman.' But because of the temptation to sexual immorality, each man should have his own wife and each woman her own husband. The husband should give to his wife her conjugal rights, and likewise the wife to her husband. For the wife does not have authority over her own body, but the husband does. Likewise the husband does not have authority over his own body, but the wife does. Do not deprive one another, except perhaps by agreement for a limited time, that you may devote yourselves to prayer; but then come together again, so that Satan may not tempt you because of your lack of self-control" (1 Cor. 7:1–5).

Therefore, those persons live contrary to the nature of their relation who live a great part of their lives apart,[14] as many do for worldly respects, when they have several houses, possessions, or trades and the husband must live at one and the wife at another for their commodity's sake and only come together once in a week or in many weeks. When this is done without great necessity, it is a constant violation of their duties. And so it is for men who go trade or live beyond the sea or in another land and leave their wives behind them; yea, though they have their wives' consent, it is an unlawful course except in a case of mere necessity or public service or when they are able on good grounds to say that the benefits are greater to soul and body than the loss and that they are confirmed against the danger of incontinence. The offices that husband and wife are bound to perform for one another are such as, for the most part, suppose

---

[13]*Conjunction.*
[14]*Asunder.*

their cohabitation, like the offices of the members of the body for each other, which they cannot perform if they are dismembered and divided.

Direction 3: Do not only abhor adultery but all that tends to impurity[15] and the violation of your marriage covenant (for adultery, see Gen. 6:2–3; 34:27; Lev. 21:9; Num. 25:1–9; Deut. 23:2; Judg. 20:10; 2 Sam. 12:10; 13:22; Prov. 2:17; 6:32, 35; 22:14; Jer. 5:7–9; 23:14; Hos. 4:2–3; Mal. 2:15; Matt. 5:31–32; 19:9; John 8:4–5; 1 Cor. 6:15, 19). Adultery is so contrary to the married[16] bond and state of life that though *de facto* ("as a matter of fact") it does not actually dissolve the bond and nullify the marriage, yet it so far disobliges the wronged and innocent party that *de jure* ("as of right") it is to such a sufficient ground to warrant a divorce. God required that it be punished by death (Lev. 20:10). When lust is the chief cause of marriage, and when married persons do not live in the fear of God but pamper the flesh and live licentiously, no wonder if marriage proves to be an insufficient remedy against such cherished lust. Such carnal, beastly persons are still casting fuel on the fire; by wanton, unbridled thoughts and speeches, by gluttony, drinking, sports, and idleness, by vain, enticing company, and not avoiding occasions, opportunities, and temptations, they burn as much when they are married as they did before. The Devil, who blows up this fire in their flesh, conducts and accommodates them in the satisfying of their lusts, so that their brutish lust[17] is like a fire burning in the sea; water itself will not quench it. One woman will not satisfy their bestiality; and perhaps they loathe their own wives and run after others though their own, in the eye of any impartial man, be the more comely and amiable, and their whores be never so deformed or impudent, filthy lumps of dirt that one would think that they had no other reason to love and follow such unlovely things but only because God forbids it. It is as if the Devil did it to show his power over them, that he can make them do that, as in despite of God, which else they would abhor themselves.

When once their sensuality and their forsaking of God has provoked God to forsake them and give them up to the rage of that sensuality, an unclean spirit sometimes takes possession of them and

---

[15]*Unchasteness.*
[16]*Conjugal.*
[17]*Concupiscence.*

wholly inclines them to wallow in uncleanness. They can scarcely look a comely person in the face, that is, of the other sex, but unclean thoughts are rising in their hearts. They think of filthiness when they are alone; they dream of filthiness in the night; they talk of filthiness with others. The tongues of the dogs that licked Lazarus's sores were not used in such a filthy employment as theirs are. "They were well-fed, lusty stallions, each neighing for his neighbor's wife" (Jer. 5:8); "They proclaim their sin like Sodom; they do not hide it" (Isa. 3:9). Usually when they are given over to this filthy sin, it utterly debauches their consciences and makes them like blocks or beasts, insensible of their misery and the wrath of God and given over to other villainies, and even to hate and persecute godliness, if not civility itself (Prov. 5:20; 2 Pet. 2:10, 12, 14; Rev. 21:8).

I have known some adulterers who sin so much against their consciences that they live in continual despair, tormented in the sense of their own unhappiness and sinning still, as if the Devil would make them a derision; and yet these are the better sort, as there is some sense[18] of a better life remaining in their minds. Others, having become callous, "have given themselves up to sensuality, greedy to practice every kind of impurity" (Eph. 4:19), "especially those who indulge in the lust of defiling passion and despise authority . . . these, like irrational animals, creatures of instinct, born to be caught and destroyed, blaspheming about matters of which they are ignorant, will also be destroyed in their destruction" (2 Pet. 2:10–12). Take heed, therefore, of the causes of this odious sin and of all appearance of it; do not suffer your eye or thought to go after a stranger or to begin a breach in your covenant and fidelity.

Direction 4: Husband and wife must take delight in the love, company, and converse of each other. There is nothing that man's heart is so inordinately set upon as delight; and yet the lawful delight allowed them by God, they can turn into loathing and disdain. The delight that would entangle you in sin and turn you from your duty and from God is that which is forbidden you; but this is a delight that is helpful to you in your duty and would keep you from sin. When husband and wife take pleasure in each other, it unites them in duty; it helps them with ease to do their work and bear their burdens. This

---

[18]*Testimony.*

is not the least part of the comfort of the married state. "Rejoice in the wife of your youth, a lovely deer, a graceful doe. Let her breasts fill you at all times with delight; be intoxicated always in her love" (Prov. 5:18–19). Therefore, a wife is called "the delight of your eyes" (Ezek. 24:16). Avoid all things that may represent you as unpleasant or unlovely to each other, and use all lawful means to cherish complacency and delight—not by foolish, ridiculous, or proud attire or immodest actions but by cleanness, decency, and gentle conduct.[19] Nastiness, uncleanness, unseemly carriage, foolish speech, and whatever is loathsome in body or mind must be shunned as temptations that would hinder you from that love, pleasure, and contentment that husband and wife should have in one another.

Yet, it is a foolish, fleshly person who will continue love no longer than it is cherished with all this care. If there is any deformity of the body or anything unseemly in behavior, or if God should visit them with any loathsome sores or sickness, they must for all that love each other, yea, and take pleasure in their converse. It is not a true friend who leaves you in adversity; nor is it true, married[20] affection that is blasted by a loathsome sickness. The love of mothers to their children will make them take pleasure in them, notwithstanding their sickness or uncleanness; and so should their love be between a husband and his wife. He who considers that his own flesh is liable to the same diseases and, before long, will be as loathsome will do as he would be done by and not turn away in the time of her affliction, from her who has become his flesh. Much less excusable is the crime of them who when they have nothing extraordinary to distaste or disaffect them are weary of each other's company and would rather be in their neighbor's houses than in their own and find more pleasure in the company of a stranger than in one another.

Direction 5: It is a great duty of husbands and wives to live in quietness and peace and avoid all occasions of wrath and discord. Because this is a duty of so great importance, I shall, first, open to you the great necessity of it and then give you more particular directions to perform it.

1. It is a duty that your union or near relation especially requires. Will you fall out with yourselves? Cannot you agree with your own

---

[19]*Kind deportment.*
[20]*Conjugal.*

flesh? 2. Your discord will be your pain and the vexation of your lives, like a bile, wound, or fracture in your own bodies that will pain you until it is cured. You will hardly keep peace in your minds when peace is broken so near you in your family. As you would take heed of hurting yourselves, and as you would hasten the cure when you are hurt, so should you take heed of any breach of peace and quickly seek to heal it when it is broken. 3. Dissension tends to cool your love; often falling out tends to leave a habit of distaste and averseness on the mind. Wounding is separating; to be tied together by any outward bonds, when your hearts are separated, is but to be tormented and to have the insides of adversaries while you appear to be married.[21] As the difference between my house and my prison is that I willingly and with delight dwell in the one but am unwillingly confined to the other, such will be the difference between a quiet and an unquiet life in your married state. It turns your dwelling and delight into a prison, where you are chained to those calamities that, in a free condition, you might overrun.

4. Dissension between the husband and the wife disorders their family affairs; they are like oxen unequally yoked that can do no work for striving with one another. Nothing is well done because of the variance of those who should do it or oversee it. 5. It unfits you for the worship of God; you are not fit to pray together or to confer together of heavenly things or to be helpers to each other's souls. I do not need to tell you this because you feel it by experience. Wrath and bitterness will not allow you so much exercise of love and holy composedness of mind as every one of those duties requires. 6. Dissension disables you to govern your families aright. Your children will follow your example or think they are at liberty to do what they will[22] when they find you taken up with such work between yourselves. They will think that you are unfit to reprove them for their faults when they see you guilty of such faults and folly of your own; nay, you will become the shame and secret derision of your family and bring yourselves into contempt. 7. Your dissensions will expose you to the malice of Satan and give him advantage for diverse[23] temptations. A house divided cannot stand; an army divided is easily

---

[21]*Have conjugal outsides.*
[22]*List.*
[23]*Manifold.*

conquered and made a prey to the enemy. You cannot foresee what abundance of sin you put yourselves in danger of. By all this you may see what dissensions between husband and wife tend to and how they should be avoided.

Second, for avoiding them, observe these directions:

1. Keep up your love[24] in a constant heat and vigor. Love will suppress wrath; you cannot have a bitter mind upon small provocations against those whom you dearly love; much less can you proceed to reviling words or to averseness and being estranged[25] or any abuse of one another. Or if a breach and wound is unhappily made, the calming[26] quality of love will heal it. But when love cools, small matters exasperate and breed distaste.

2. Both husband and wife must mortify their pride and passion, which are the causes of impatience. They must pray and labor for a humble, meek, and quiet spirit. For it is the diseased temper of the heart that causes dissension more than the occasions or matters of offense do. A proud heart is troubled and provoked by every word or behavior[27] that seems to tend to its undervaluing. A perverse and naughty[28] mind is like sore and ulcerated members that will be hurt if they are touched. He who must live near such a sore, diseased, impatient mind must live even as the nurse does with a child, making it her business to rock, lull, and sing the child quiet when he cries, for to be angry with the child will do no good. If you have married one with a sick or childish temper, you must resolve to bear and use it accordingly. But no Christian should bear with such a vexatious malady in themselves or be patient with such impatience of mind. Once get the victory over yourselves, and get the cure of your own impatience, and you will easily keep peace with one another.

3. Remember that you are both diseased persons, full of infirmities; therefore, expect the fruit of those infirmities in each other. Do not make a strange matter of it, as if you had never known it before. If you had married one who is lame, would you be angry with her for limping?[29] Or if you had married someone with an ulcer, would

---

[24]*Conjugal love.*
[25]*Estrangedness.*
[26]*Balsamic.*
[27]*Carriage.*
[28]*Peevish and froward.*
[29]*Halting.*

you fall out with her because it smells? Did you not know beforehand that you married a person of such weaknesses as would yield you some matter of daily trial and offense? If you could not bear this, you should not have married her; if you resolved that you could bear it then, you are still obliged to bear it now. Resolve, therefore, to bear with one another, remembering that you took one another as sinful, frail, imperfect persons and not as angels or as blameless and perfect.

4. Remember that you are one flesh; therefore, be no more offended with the words or failings of each other than you would be if they were your own. Do not fall out with your wife for her faults more than you would for your own faults if her faults had been your own. This will allow you such anger and displeasure against a fault as tends to heal it but not such as tends to fester and vex the diseased part. This will turn anger into compassion and speedy, tender diligence for the cure.

5. Agree together beforehand that when one is in a diseased, angry fit, the other shall silently and gently bear it until it is past and you are come to yourselves again. Do not be angry both at once. When the fire is kindled, quench it with gentle words and conduct,[30] and do not fuel the fire[31] by answering with sharp and provocative words or by multiplying words and answering wrath with wrath. Remember, the work you are called to is to mollify and not to exasperate, to help and not to hurt, to cure one another rather than to right yourself. If another fall and hurt himself, your business is to help him up and not to tread upon him.

6. Look before you, and remember that you must live together until death and must be the companions of each other's fortunes and the comforts of each other's lives, and then you will see how absurd it is for you to disagree and vex each other. Anger is the principle of revenge, and falling out tends toward separation. Therefore, those who must not revenge should not give way to anger; and those who know they must not part should not fall out.

7. As far as you are able, avoid all occasions of wrath and falling out about the matters of your families. Some by their slothfulness bring themselves into want; and then being unable to bear it, they

---

[30]*Carriage.*
[31]*Cast on oil or fuel.*

contract a discontented, perverse[32] habit, and in their impatience they wrangle and disquiet one another. Some plunge themselves into a multitude of business and have to do with so many things and persons that one or the other is still offending them, and then they are impatient with one another. Some have neither skill nor diligence to manage their business aright; and so things become cross and go out of order, and then their impatience turns itself against each other. Avoid these occasions if you would avoid sin, and see that you are not without[33] patience to bear that which cannot be avoided.

8. If you cannot quickly quench your passion, yet at least refrain your tongues; do not speak reproachful or provoking words. Talking it out hotly blows the fire and increases the flame. Be silent, and you will sooner return to your serenity and peace. Foul words tend to more displeasure. Socrates said when his wife first railed at him and next threw a vessel of foul water upon him, "I thought when I heard the thunder, there would come rain"; so you may foresee[34] worse following when foul, unseemly words begin. If you cannot easily allay your wrath, you may hold your tongues, if you are truly willing.

9. Let the sober party condescend to speak with fairness and to entreat the other (unless it is with a person so insolent as will be the worse). Usually a few sober, grave admonitions will prove as water to the boiling pot. Say to your angry wife or husband, "You know this should not be between us. Love must allay it, and it must be repented of. God does not approve it, and we shall not approve it when the heat is over. This frame of mind is contrary to a praying frame, and this language is contrary to a praying language; we must pray together instantly.[35] Let us do nothing contrary to prayer now; sweet water and bitter do not come from the same spring." Some calm and condescending words of reason may stop the torrent and revive reason, which passion had overcome.

10. Confess your faults to one another when passion has prevailed against you. Ask forgiveness of each other, and join in prayer to God for pardon; this will lay a greater engagement on you to forbear the next time. You will surely be ashamed to do that which you have confessed and asked forgiveness for, of God and man. If you will

---

[32]*Peevish.*
[33]*Unfurnished of.*
[34]*Portend.*
[35]*Anon.*

practice these ten directions, your marital[36] and family peace may
be preserved.

Direction 6: A principal duty between husband and wife is, with
special care, skill, and diligence, to help each other in the knowledge,
worship, and obedience of God, in order to their salvation. Because
this is a duty in which you are the greatest helps and blessings to
each other if you perform it, I shall, first, endeavor to quicken you to
make conscience of it and then, second, direct you how to do it.

First, consider how little it can stand with rational love to neglect
the souls of one another. I suppose you believe that you have immortal souls and an endless life of joy or misery to live; then you cannot
help[37] but know that your great concernment and business is to
make sure provision for those souls and for endless life. Therefore,
if your love does not help one another in this which is your main
concernment, it is of little worth and little use. Everything in this
world is as valuable as it is useful. A useless or unprofitable love is a
worthless love. It is a trifling or a childish or a beastly love that helps
you only in trifling, childish, or beastly things. Do you love your wife
and yet will leave her in the power of Satan or will not help to save
her soul? What! Love her and yet let her go to hell? And rather let her
be damned than you will be at the pains to endeavor her salvation?
If she were in bodily pain or misery, and you refused to do your part
to succor her, she would take it for cold, unprofitable love, though
you were never so kind to her in compliments and trifles. The Devil
makes show of such a love as that; he can bestow[38] men pleasures,
wealth, and honor, so that he may see the perdition of their souls.

If your love to your wife or husband tends to no greater matters
than the pleasures of this life while the soul is left to perish in sin,
seriously consider[39] how little more kindness you show them than
the Devil. Oh, can you see the danger of one whom you love so dearly
and do no more to save him or her from it? Can you think of the damnation of so dear a friend and not do all that you are able to do to prevent it? Would you be separated from them in the world to which you
are going? Would you not live with them in heaven forever? Never
say you love them if you will not labor for their salvation. If ever they

---

[36]*Conjugal.*
[37]*Choose.*
[38]*Vouchsafe.*
[39]*Bethink yourselves.*

come to hell, or if ever you see them there, both they and you will then confess that you did not behave as such as loved them. It does not deserve the name of love if it can leave a soul to endless misery.

What then shall we say of those who do not only deny their help but are hinderers to the holiness and salvation of each other, as Eve was Adam's tempter (1 Kings 11:4; Job 2:9; Acts 5:2)! And yet (the Lord have mercy on the poor miserable world!) how common a thing is this among us! If the wife is ignorant and ungodly, she will do her worst to make or keep her husband such as herself. If God puts any holy inclinations into his heart, she will be to it as water to the fire, to quench or keep it under; and if he will not be as sinful and miserable as herself, he shall have little quietness or rest. If God opens the eyes of the wife of a bad man and shows her the amiableness and necessity of a holy life, and she resolves to obey the Lord and save her soul, what an enemy and tyrant will her husband prove to her (if God does not restrain him). The Devil himself scarcely does more against the saving of souls than ungodly husbands and wives do against each other.

Second, consider also that you live not up to the ends of marriage, or of humanity, if you are not helpers to each other's souls. To help each other only for your bellies is to live together like beasts. You are appointed to live together as "heirs . . . of the grace of life" (1 Pet. 3:7). "Husbands, love your wives, as Christ loved the church and gave himself up for her . . . so that he might present the church to himself in splendor, without spot or wrinkle or any such thing, that she might be holy and without blemish" (Eph. 5:25–27). That which is the purpose[40] of your life and being must be the purpose[41] of your relations and daily converse.

Consider also, if you neglect each other's souls, what enemies you are to one another and how you prepare for your everlasting sorrows. When you should be preparing for your joyful meeting in heaven, you are laying up for yourselves everlasting horror. What a dreadful meeting and greeting will you have at the bar of Christ, or in the flames of hell, when you shall find how perversely you have done (Gen. 35:2, 4; Lev. 19:18; 1 Cor. 7:5; Heb. 12:15; Eph. 4:16; 1 Thess. 5:11)! It will be better to be praising God together in glory than to be

---

[40]*End.*
[41]*End.*

raging against each other in the horror of your consciences and flying in each other's faces with such accusations as these: "Oh, cruel husband! Oh, merciless, deceitful wife! It was after a while that I came to this miserable and woeful end! I might have lived with Christ and his saints in joy, but now I am tormented in these flames in desperation! You were commanded by God to warn me and tell me of my sin and misery and to never let me rest in it but to instruct and entreat me until I had come home by Christ, that I might have escaped this place of torment. But you never spoke to me of God and my salvation unless you did it in jest! If the house had been on fire, you would have been more earnest to have quenched it than you were to save my soul from hell! You never told me, seriously, of the misery of a natural and unrenewed state! Nor did you tell me the great necessity of regeneration and a holy life; nor did you ever talk to me of heaven and hell, as matters of such consequence should have been mentioned. Rather, morning and night your talk was nothing but of the world and the things in the world [Num. 16:27, 32]. Your idle talk, jesting, naughty,[42] carnal, and unprofitable discourse filled all the time; we did not have one sober word of salvation. You never told me of this day or prayed with me or read the Scripture and good books to me. You never took pains to instruct me or humble my hardened heart or to save me from it or to draw me to the love of God and holiness by faith in Christ. You did not go before me with a good example of a holy and heavenly conduct.[43] Rather, you led by an evil example, an ungodly, fleshly, worldly life. You neither cared for your own soul, nor for mine; nor I for yours or my own; and now we are justly condemned together because we would not live in holiness together!" Oh, foolish, miserable souls who, by your ungodliness and negligence in this life, will prepare each other for a life of endless woe and horror! Resolve, therefore, without delay to live as heirs of heaven and to be helpers to each other's souls! To this end I will give you these directions that, if practiced, will make you to be blessings to one another:

Direction 1: If you would help save each other's souls, you must be sure that you have a care of your own and retain a deep and lively apprehension of those great and everlasting matters of which you are to speak to others (Gen. 2:18). It cannot be reasonably expected

---

[42]*Froward.*
[43]*Conversation.*

that he should have a due compassion to another's soul who has none to his own, that he should be at the pains that are needful to help another to salvation who sets so little by his own as to sell it for the base and momentary ease and pleasure of the flesh. Nor is it to be expected that a man should speak with any suitable weight and seriousness about those matters whose weight his heart did never feel and about which he was never serious himself. First see that you feel thoroughly that which you would speak profitably and that you are what you persuade another to be and that all your counsel may be perceived to arise from the bottom of your heart and that you speak of things that you are well acquainted with by experience.

Direction 2: Take those opportunities that your nearness and familiarity afford you to be speaking seriously to each other about the matters of God and your salvation. When you lie down and rise together, do not let your worldly business have all your talk, but let God and your souls have the first and the last and the freest and sweetest of your speech, if not the most. When you have said so much of your common business as its nature and dispatch requires, lay it by, and talk together of the state and duty of your souls toward God and of your hopes of heaven as those who take these for their greatest business. Do not speak lightly or irreverently or in a rude and bickering[44] manner but with gravity and sobriety, as those who are advising together about the greatest matter that they ever had to do in the world.

Direction 3: When either husband or wife is speaking seriously about holy things, let the other be careful to cherish and not to extinguish and put an end to the discourse. There are two ways to cherish such discourse. The first is by taking your turn and bearing a due proportion in the discourse with wisdom and gravity. All cannot do this. Some are learners, and those must take the second way, which is to ask for resolution in matters of which they doubt or are uninstructed and to draw on more by pertinent questions. The two ways by which such discourse is silenced are these: first, by the constant silence of the hearer, as when a man talks to a post that gives no answer or does not put forth any pertinent questions; he will be wearied at last and will give up. The second is by a cross, when

---

[44]*Wrangling.*

one contradicts, cavils, and bickers[45] against what is spoken or by interruptions and diversions. When you come in presently with some worldly or impertinent talk and wind about from sober conference to something that is unedifying and talk that will not seem merely profane but vain and worldly, that will destroy all holy, fruitful conference, even by a kind of religious talk, carrying you away from heart-searching and heavenly discourse to some doctrinal, formal, or historical controversy that is sufficiently distant from the heart and heaven. Take heed of these courses if you would help each other.

Direction 4: Watch over the hearts and lives of one another, and labor to discern the state of one another's souls and the strength or weakness of each other's sins and graces and the failings of each other's lives, so that you may be able to apply to one another the most suitable help. What you are unacquainted with, you cannot be very helpful in (Matt. 27:19). You cannot cure unknown diseases; you cannot give wise and safe advice about the state of one another's souls if you are mistaken in them. God has placed you nearest to each other, that you might have so much interest in each other as to quicken you to a loving care and so much acquaintance with each other as to keep you from misunderstanding and so from neglecting or deceiving one another. You should be always provided with those fit remedies that are most needful and suitable to each other's case. If that preacher is dull and unsuccessful who is all about mere doctrine and offers little or nothing in close and lively application, you may conceive that it will be so also with those with whom you are in closest relationship.[46]

Direction 5: See that you neither flatter one another through fond and foolish love, nor exasperate one another by a passionate or contemptuous kind of reprehension. Some persons are so blinded with fond affection that they can scarcely see in husband, wife, or children any aggravated sin or misery. They think all is well that they do or not so ill as they would perceive in another; but this is the same course that self-loving sinners take with their own souls, to their delusion and perdition. This flattering of yourselves or others is the Devil's charm to keep you from effectual repentance and salvation. The ease of anodynes and narcotics endures but a little while.

---

[45]*Wrangles.*
[46]*Familiar conference.*

On the other side, some cannot speak to one another of their faults without such bitterness of passion or contempt as tends to make the stomach of the receiver to loathe the medicine and so to refuse it or to case it up. If common reproofs to strangers must all be offered in love, much more between the nearest relations.

Direction 6: Be sure that you keep up true, married[47] love to one another and that you do not grow to despise[48] each other. For if you do, you will despise each other's counsels and reproofs. Those who slight, loathe, or are weary of each other will disdain reproofs and will scorn advice from one another when entire affection greatly disposes to the right entertainment of instruction.

Direction 7: Do not discourage each other from instruction or reproof by taking it the wrong way[49] or by rude[50] reflections and being stubborn.[51] When you will not learn or will not amend, you discourage your instructor and reprover. Men will be apt to give up when they are requited with ingratitude and snappish retorts or when they perceive that their labor is in vain. As it is the heaviest judgment of God that befalls any upon earth when he withdraws his advice and help and leaves sinners wholly to themselves, so it is the saddest condition in your relations when the ignorant and sinning party is forsaken by the other and left to his or her own opinions and ways. Indeed, this should not be so because while there is life there is hope.

Direction 8: So far as you are able to instruct or quicken one another, call in for better helps. Engage each other in the reading of the most convincing, quickening books and in attendance on the most powerful ministry and in profitable conversation with the most holy persons. Do not do this to neglect your duty to one another, but that all helps concurring may be more effectual. When the other finds that you speak to him or her the same things that ministers and other Christians do, it will be the more easily received.

Direction 9: Do not conceal the state of your souls or hide your faults from one another. You are as one flesh and should have one heart. As it is dangerous for a man not to know his own needs, so it

---

[47]*Conjugal.*
[48]*Disaffect.*
[49]*Ill.*
[50]*Churlish.*
[51]*Obstinate unreformedness.*

is hurtful for a husband or wife not to know the other's needs. It is foolish tenderness when you conceal your disease from your physician or your helpful friend. Who should be so tender and helpful to you as you should be to one another? Indeed, in some few cases where the opening of a fault or secret tends to quench affection and does not get assistance from another, it is wisdom to conceal it. But that is not the ordinary case. Opening your hearts to each other is necessary to your mutual help.

Direction 10: Avoid as much contrariety of opinions in religion as possible. For if you hold different judgments in matters that you take to be of great concernment, you will be tempted to disaffect, condemn, or undervalue one another and so despise the help that you might receive. If you fall into several sects and follow several teachers, you will hardly avoid that strife[52] and confusion that prove a great advantage to the Devil and an impediment to your spiritual good.

Direction 11: If differences in judgment arise between you, be sure that it is managed with holiness, humility, love, and peace and not with carnality, pride, stinginess, or strife.[53] First, to manage your differences holily is to take God for the Judge and to refer the matter to his Word and to aim at his glory and the pleasing of his will and to use his means for the harmony of your opinions.[54] This is to search the Scripture and consult with the faithful, able pastors of the church and soberly and patiently to debate the case and pray together for the illumination of the Spirit. On the contrary, your differences are carnally managed when carnal reasons breed or feed them—when you run after this or that sect or party, through admiration of the persons, and do not value persons for the sake of truth but measure truth by the opinion and estimate of the persons or when you end your differences by selfish, carnal principles and respects. Hence, it comes to pass that if the husband is a papist or otherwise in error,[55] it is two to one that the wife will soon share his erroneous religion, not because of any cogent evidence but because he is the stronger person and has constant opportunity to persuade and because love prepares and inclines her to share his opinion. Thus man, instead of God, is the master of the faith of many.

---

[52]*Contention.*
[53]*Uncharitableness or contention.*
[54]*Concord of your judgments.*
[55]*Erroneous.*

Second, your differences are managed in humility when you have a just and modest suspicion of your own understanding and debate and practice your differences with meekness and submission. Do not proudly overvalue your own apprehensions and despise another's reasons, as if they were not worthy of your consideration. Third, your differences must be managed in love, not that mere love should make you turn to another's opinion, be it true or false, but that you must be desirous to be of the same mind, and if you cannot, must take it for a sore affliction and bear with the tolerable mistakes of one another as you bear your own infirmities, that they do not cool love or alienate your hearts from one another but provoke you to tender, healing, compassionate care and endeavor to do each other good. Fourth, you must manage your differences in quietness, without any passionate quarrel[56] and dissensions, that no bitter fruits may be bred by it in your families among yourselves. Thus, all true Christians must manage their differences in matters of religion, but married persons above all.

Direction 12: Do not be either blindly indulgent to each other's faults or too censorious of each other's state, lest Satan get an advantage to alienate your affections from one another. To make nothing of the faults of those whom you love is to love them foolishly, to their hurt, and to show that it is not for their virtues that you love them. To make too great a matter of one another's faults is to help the tempter to quench your love and turn your hearts from one another. Thus, many good women who have husbands who are guilty of too much coldness in religion or worldly mindedness or falling into ill company and misspending their time are the first to overlook the possibility of any seed of grace in them; then, looking on them as ungodly persons, they abate too much their love and duty to them. There is great wisdom and watchfulness requisite in this case, to keep you from being carried into either extreme.

Direction 13: If you are married to one who is indeed an infidel or an ungodly person, you must still keep up the love[57] that is due for the relation's sake. Though you cannot love them as true Christians, you can love them as husband or wife. Even heathens are bound to love those who are thus related to them. The apostle has determined

---

[56]*Wranglings.*
[57]*Conjugal love.*

that Christians must perform their duties to husbands or wives who are unbelievers (1 Cor. 7). The faults of another do not discharge you from your duty. As Satan has deceived some by separating principles about church communion, to deny almost all God's ordinances to many to whom they are due, so he deceives some persons in family relations and draws them from the duties they owe for one another's good.

Direction 14: Join together in frequent and fervent prayer. Prayer forces the mind into some composedness and sobriety and affects the heart with the presence and majesty of God. Pray also for each other when you are in secret, that God may do that work that you desire most upon each other's hearts.

Direction 15: Lastly, help each other by living an exemplary life. Be the way that you desire your husband or wife to be; excel in meekness, humility, charity, dutifulness, diligence, self-denial, and patience as far as you excel in the profession of religion. Saint Peter says that even those who will not be won by the Word may be won without it, by the conduct[58] of their wives (1 Pet. 3:1). That is, the excellency of religion may appear to them by its fruits in their wives, inclining them to think well and honorably of it and so to inquire into the nature and reason of it and to hearken to their wives. This can all be done without public ministry. A life of genuine[59] holiness, heavenliness, self-denial, meekness, love, and mortification is a powerful sermon that, if you are constantly preaching before those who are near you, will hardly miss having a good effect. Works are more clearly[60] significant and persuasive than words alone.

Direction 16: Another great marital[61] duty is to be helpful to each other for the health and comfort of your bodies (see Gen. 2:18; Rom. 13:13–14; Eph. 5:29, 31); that is, not to pamper each other's flesh or cherish the vices of pride, sloth, gluttony, or sexual addiction[62] but to further the health and cheerfulness of the body and to fit it for the service of the soul and God. Such cherishing or pleasing of the flesh, which is unlawful in each person, is also unlawful, ordinarily, to use to another. But such as you may use for yourself, you may use also for your wife or husband. Not to live above your estates

---

[58]*Conversation.*
[59]*Undissembled.*
[60]*Palpably.*
[61]*Conjugal.*
[62]*Voluptuousness.*

or as servants to your guts, to serve the appetites of one another by delicious fare, but to be careful of that health without which your lives will be made unserviceable or uncomfortable. This must proceed from such a love to one another as you have for yourself in time of health and sickness.

First, in health you must be careful to provide for each other not so much pleasing as wholesome food and to keep each other from what is hurtful to your health, dissuading the other from gluttony and idleness, which are the two great murderers of mankind. If the bodies of the poor in hunger, cold, and nakedness must be relieved, much more those who are your own flesh.

Second, also in sickness you are to be tenderly regardful of each other. You are not to spare any costs or pains by which the health of the other may be restored (or your souls confirmed) and your comforts cherished (Gen. 27:14). You must neither loathe the bodies of each other in the most loathsome sickness, nor shun them through loathing, no more than you would your own (Job 2:9; 19:17; Eph. 5:29, 31). "A friend loves at all times, and a brother is born for adversity" (Prov. 17:17); much more those who are so nearly bound in sickness and health till death shall separate them. It is an odious sin to be weary of a sick or suffering friend and desirous that God would take them merely so that you may be eased of the trouble. Usually such persons meet with such measure as they measure to others; those to whom they look for help and comfort will perhaps be as weary of them and as glad to be rid of them.

Direction 17: Another duty of husbands and wives is to be helpful to each other in their worldly business and estates (see Gen. 31:40; Prov. 31; 1 Tim. 5:14; 5:8; Titus 2:5), not for worldly ends or with a worldly mind but in obedience to God, who will have them labor, as well as pray, for their daily bread and has determined that in the sweat of their brows they shall eat their bread and that six days they shall labor and do all that they have to do and that he who will not work must not eat. The care of their affairs lies upon them both, and neither of them must cast it off and live in idleness (unless one of them is deficient in reasoning[63] or so witless as to be unfit for care or so sick or lame as to be unfit for labor).

---

[63]*An idiot.*

Direction 18: Also, you must be careful for the lawful honor and good names of one another (Gen. 9:22, 25; 1 Sam. 25:25; 2 Sam. 6:20; Prov. 31:28; Eccles. 7:1; Matt. 1:19; 18:16). You must not divulge but conceal the dishonorable failings of each other, as did Abigail, unless compassion or justice requires you to open to another for a cure or to clear the truth. The reputation of each other must be as dear to you as your own. It is a sinful and unfaithful practice of many, both husbands and wives, who, among their companions, open the faults and infirmities of each other that they are bound, in tenderness, to cover. As if they did not perceive that in dishonoring the other, they dishonor themselves. Love will cover a multitude of faults (1 Pet. 4:8). Nay, many disaffected, perverse[64] persons will aggravate the faults of the other, behind their backs, to strangers and sometimes slander them and speak more than is true. Many a man has had to clear his name from the slanders of a jealous or passionate wife. An open enemy is not capable of doing so much wrong as she who is in his bosom, for she will be easily believed, supposedly knowing him better than anyone else.

Direction 19: It is also a great part of the duty of husbands and wives to be helpful to one another in the education of their children and in the government of the family (Gen. 18:19; 35:2; Josh. 24:15; Ps. 101; 1 Tim. 2:4, 12). Some men cast all the care of their young children upon their wives; and many women, by their passion and indiscretion, make themselves unfit to help their husbands in the government of their children. Still, this is one of the greatest parts of their employment. As to the man's part, to govern his house well, the duty is unquestionable. Further, this duty is not to be denied to the wife: "I would have younger widows marry, bear children, manage their households" (1 Tim. 5:14). Bathsheba taught Solomon (Lemuel; Prov. 31:1). Abigail took better care of Nabal's house than he did himself. They who have a joint interest and are one flesh must have a joint part in government, though their power is not equal, and one may better oversee some business, and the other another business. Yet, in their places they must divide the care and help each other. They are not to be as it is with many wicked persons who are the most unruly part of the family and the chief cause of its being ungov-

---

[64]*Peevish.*

erned and ungodly, where one party hinders the other from keeping order or doing good.

Direction 20: Another part of their duty is to help each other in works of charity and hospitality (Gen. 18:6; Job 29:13; 31:20; Prov. 11:20, 28; 19:17; Neh. 8:10; Luke 16:9; Acts 20:35; Rom. 12:13; 2 Cor. 9:6; Heb. 13:2; 1 Tim. 3:2; 5:10). While they have opportunity, they must do good to all, especially to those of the household of faith. They must sow to the Spirit, that from the Spirit they may reap everlasting life; yea, they must sow plentifully, that they may reap plentifully (Galatians 6). If their houses are able, they must afford relief and sustenance[65] for the needy, especially for Christ's servants for their Master's sake, who promised, "The one who receives a prophet because he is a prophet will receive a prophet's reward, and the one who receives a righteous person because he is a righteous person will receive a righteous person's reward. And whoever gives one of these little ones even a cup of cold water because he is a disciple, truly, I say to you, he will by no means lose his reward" (Matt. 10:41–42). The woman of Shunem lost nothing by sustaining[66] Elisha, saying to her husband, "Behold now, I know that this is a holy man of God who is continually passing our way. Let us make a small room on the roof with walls and put there for him a bed, a table, a chair, and a lamp, so that whenever he comes to us, he can go in there" (2 Kings 4:9–10). But now how common is it for people to think too little of this, and if one is addicted to works of charity, the other is covetous and always hindering the first.

Direction 21: Lastly, it is a great part of the duty of husbands and wives to be helpers and comforters of each other in order to have a safe and happy death. First, in the time of health, you must often and seriously remind[67] each other of the time when death will make the separation. You must live together, in your daily converse, as those who are expecting the parting hour. Help to awaken each other's souls, to make ready all those graces that will then prove necessary. Live in a constant preparation for your change. Reprove all in one another that will be unsavory and ungrateful to your review at death. If you see each other dull and slow in your preparations or

---

[65]*Entertainment.*
[66]*Entertaining.*
[67]*Remember.*

live in vanity, worldliness, or sloth, as if you had forgotten that you must shortly die, stir up one another to do all without delay that the approach of such a day requires. Second, when death is at hand, oh, then what abundance of tenderness, seriousness, skill, and diligence is needful for one who has the last office of love to perform to the departing soul of so near a friend! Oh, then what need will there be of your most wise, faithful, and diligent help! What skill and holy seriousness will be necessary when nature fails and the pains of flesh divert the mind, when temptations are strongest, when the body is weakest, when a languishing body and a doubting, fearful, troubled mind calls for your compassion and help!

Oh, what a calamity it is to have a carnal, unsanctified husband or wife who will neither help you to prepare for death, nor speak a serious word of counsel or comfort to you at your dying hour—one who can do nothing but stand by and weep over you but has no sensible word to say about the life you are going to or the duty of a departing soul or against the temptations and fears that overwhelm you. Those who are utterly unprepared and unfit to die themselves can do little to prepare or help another. Those who live together as heirs of heaven and converse on earth as fellow travelers to the land of promise, however, may help and encourage each other's soul and joyfully part at death, expecting quickly to meet again in life eternal.

If it is not over-tedious, I shall next speak of the manner how husbands and wives must perform their duties to each other. First, it should be done in such an entire love as makes the case of the other as your own. Second, all must be done in patience and mutual forbearance. Third, it must be done in familiarity and not with strangeness, distance, sourness, or affected compliment. Fourth, it must be done in secrecy, and I shall show you in what cases secrecy may be broken and in what not. Fifth, it must be done in confidence of each other's fidelity and not in suspicion, jealousy, and distrust. Sixth, and in prudence, to manage things aright and to foresee and avoid impediments and inconveniencies. Seventh, in holiness, that God may be the first and last and all in all. And lastly, in constancy, that you cease not your duties for one another until death.

Chapter Seven

Duties of Husbands to Their Wives

He who will expect duty or comfort from his wife must be faithful in doing the duty of a husband. Your failing in this duty may cause the failing of another to you or at least will in some other way afflict you and will be more bitter to you in the end than if a hundred failed in their duty to you. A good husband will either make a wife good or will easily and profitably endure a bad one. I shall, therefore, give you directions for your own part of duty as that with which your happiness is most concerned.

Direction 1: The husband must undertake the principal part of the government of the whole family, even of the wife herself. He must labor to be fit and able for that government that he undertakes. This ability consists, first, in holiness and spiritual wisdom, that he may be acquainted with the end to which he is to conduct them, the rule by which he is to guide them, and the principal works that they are to do. An ungodly, irreligious man is both a stranger and an enemy to the chief part of family government. Second, his ability consists in an acquaintance with the works of his calling and the labors in which his servants are to be employed. For he that is utterly unacquainted with their business will be very unfit to govern them in it, unless he commits that part of government to his wife. Third, he must be acquainted with the common temper and infirmities of mankind, that he may know how much is to be borne and the particular temper, faults, and virtues of those whom he is to govern. Fourth, he must have prudence to direct himself in his carriage to them and justice to deal with everyone as they deserve and love to do them all the good he can, for soul and body. Being thus able, he must make it his daily work and be sure that he governs himself well, that his example may be part of his government of others.

Direction 2: The husband must so unite authority and love that neither of them may be omitted or concealed, but both will be exercised and maintained. Love must not be exercised so imprudently as to destroy the exercise of authority; and authority must not be exercised over a wife so magisterially and imperiously as to destroy the exercise of love. As your love must be a governing love, so your commands must be loving commands. Do not lose your authority, for that will disable you from doing the office of a husband to your wife. It must be maintained by no means inconsistent with married[1] love and therefore not by fierceness or cruelty, by threatening or stripes (unless by distraction or loss of reason the husband ceases to be capable of behavior[2] otherwise due to a wife). There are many cases of equality in which authority is not to be exercised, but there is no case of inequality or unworthiness so great in which married[3] love is not to be exercised, and therefore nothing must exclude it.

Direction 3: It is the duty of husbands to preserve the authority of their wives over their children. They are joint governors with them over their children.[4] The infirmities of women are apt many times to expose them to contempt, so that children will be likely to slight and disobey them if the husband does not interpose to preserve their honor and authority. Yet this must be done with such cautions as these: First, do not justify any error, vice, or weakness in your wives. They may be concealed and excused as far as may be, but never owned or defended. Second, do not urge obedience to any unlawful command of theirs. No one has authority to contradict the law of God or disoblige any from his government. You will diminish your own authority with persons of any understanding if you justify anything that is against God's authority. If the thing commanded is lawful, though it may have some inconveniences, you must rebuke

---

[1]*Conjugal.*
[2]*Carriage.*
[3]*Conjugal.*
[4]*All the inferiors.*

the disobedience of children[5] and not suffer them to slight the commands of your wives, nor to set their own reason and wills against them and say, "We will not do it." How can they help you in ruling your home[6] if you allow[7] them to be disobeyed?

Direction 4: You must preserve the honor as well as the authority of your wives. If they have any dishonorable infirmities, they are not to be mentioned by your children. As in the natural body we cover most carefully the most dishonorable parts, for our attractive[8] parts have no need (1 Cor. 12:23–24), so must it be here. Children must not be allowed[9] to carry themselves contemptuously or rudely toward them, nor to despise them or speak unmannerly, proud, or disdainful words to them. The husband must vindicate them from all such injury and contempt.

Direction 5: The husband is to exceed the wife in knowledge and be her teacher in the matters that belong to her salvation. He must instruct her in the Word of God, direct her in particular duties, help her to subdue her own corruptions, and labor to fortify[10] her against temptations. If she doubts anything that he can strengthen[11] her in, she is to ask for his help,[12] and he is to open to her at home the things she did not understand in the congregation (1 Cor. 14:35). But if the husband is ignorant[13] or is unable to instruct his wife, she is not bound to ask him in vain to teach her what he does not understand. Those husbands who despise the Word of God and live in willful ignorance do not only despise their own souls but their families also, and making themselves unable for their duties, they are usually despised by many;[14] for God has said in his message to Eli, "Those who honor me I will honor, and those who despise me shall be lightly esteemed" (1 Sam. 2:30).

Direction 6: The husband must be the principal teacher of the family. He must instruct, examine, and rule them about the matters of God as well as his own service and see that the Lord's Day and worship be observed by all who are within his gates. Therefore, he

---

[5]*Inferiors.*
[6]*Government.*
[7]*Suffer.*
[8]*Comely.*
[9]*Suffered.*
[10]*Confirm.*
[11]*Resolve.*
[12]*Resolution.*
[13]*Be indeed an ignorant sot.*
[14]*Their inferiors.*

must labor for such understanding and ability as is necessary. If he is unable or negligent, it is his sin and will be his shame. If the wife is wiser and abler, and it is cast upon her, it is to his dishonor. If neither of them do it, the sin, shame, and suffering will be common to both.

Direction 7: The husband is to be the mouth of the family in their daily family[15] prayers unto God. Therefore, he must be able to pray and also have a praying heart. He must be the priest of the household and, therefore, should be the most holy, that he may be fit to stand between them and God and to offer up their prayers to him. If this is cast on the wife, it will be to his dishonor.

Direction 8: The husband is to be the chief provider for the family. It is supposed that he is most able in mind and body and is the chief disposer of the estate. Therefore, he must be careful that his wife and children lack nothing that is fit for them, so far as he can procure it.

Direction 9: The husband must be strongest in family patience, bearing with the weakness and passions of the wife, not to make light of any sin against God but so as not to make a great matter of any frailty as against him and so to preserve the love and peace that is the natural temper of their relation.

Direction 10: The manner of all these duties must also be carefully regarded: first, that they are done in prudence and not in folly, rashness, or inconsiderateness. Second, that all is done in married[16] love and tenderness, as over one who is tender and the weaker vessel, and that he does not teach, command, or reprove a wife in the same commanding tone[17] as a child. Third, that due familiarity is maintained and that he does not keep at a distance and strangeness from his wife. Fourth, that love is confident, without base suspicions and causeless jealousies. Fifth, that all is done in gentleness and not in passion, roughness, or sourness. Sixth, that there is no unjust and causeless concealment of secrets, which should be common to both. Seventh, that there is no foolish opening of secrets to her as may become her snare, as she is not able to bear or keep. Eighth, that none of their own matters, which should be kept secret, be made known to others. His teaching and reproving her should be for the most part secret. Ninth, that he is constant and not weary of his love or duty.

---

[15]*Conjunct.*
[16]*Conjugal.*
[17]*Imperious manner.*

Chapter Eight

Duties of Wives to Their Husbands

The wife who expects comfort in a husband must make conscience of her own duty to her husband. For though it is his duty to be kind and faithful to her though she proves unkind and hard to please,[1] yet men are frail and apt to fail in such difficulties as well as women. It is so ordered by God that comfort and duty shall go together, and you shall miss comfort if you cast off duty.

Direction 1: Be especially loving to your husbands. Your natures give you the advantage in this, and love feeds love. This is your special requital for all the troubles that your infirmities put them through.

Direction 2: Live in a voluntary subjection and obedience to them. If their softness or yieldingness causes them to relinquish their authority, and for peace they let you have your will, yet remember that it is God who has appointed them to be your heads and governors. If they are so silly as to be unable, you should not have chosen such to rule you as are unfit; but having chosen them, you must assist them with your better understanding in a submissive and not a ruling, masterly way. A servant who has a foolish master may help him without becoming master. Do not deceive yourselves by giving the bare titles of government to your husbands when you must have your will in all things, for this is but mockery and not obedience. To be subject and obedient is to take the understanding and will of another to govern you

---

[1]*Froward.*

before, though not without, your own and to make your understanding and will to follow the conduct of the one who governs you. Being self-willed[2] is contrary to subjection and obedience.

Direction 3: Learn from your husbands, as your appointed teachers, and do not be self-conceited and wise in your own eyes, but ask them such instructions as your case requires. "The women should keep silent in the churches. For they are not permitted to speak, but should be in submission, as the Law also says. If there is anything they desire to learn, let them ask their husbands at home. For it is shameful for a woman to speak in church" (1 Cor. 14:34–35)—unless, of course, the husband is so ignorant as to be unable, which is his sin and shame; it is vain to ask those who do not know.

Direction 4: Set yourselves to amend all those faults that they reprove in you. Do not take it wrongly[3] to be reproved; do not swell against it, as if they did you harm or wrong. It is not a good sign to "reject reproof" (Prov. 10:17; 15:10, 31–32; 17:10). What does their government of you signify if you will not amend the faults that are reproved in you but continue impenitent and begrudge the reproof? It is a miserable folly to desire to be flattered and soothed by any, but especially by one who is bound to be faithful to you and whose intimacy should make you as ready to hear of your faults from him as to be acquainted with them yourselves, and especially when it concerns the safety or benefit of your souls.

Direction 5: Honor your husbands according to their superiority. Do not behave toward them with irreverence and contempt in titles, speeches, or any behavior. If the worth of their persons does not desire honor, yet their place does. Do not speak of their infirmities to others, behind their backs, as some trifling[4] gossips do who do not know that their husbands' dishonor is their own and that to open it causelessly before others is to double their shame. Those who silently hear you will tell others behind your back how foolish and shamefully you spoke against your husbands. If God has made your nearest friend an affliction to you, why should you complain to one who is farther off (unless it is to some prudent friend, in cases of true necessity, for advice)?

---

[2]*Self-willedness.*
[3]*Ill.*
[4]*Twattling.*

Direction 6: Live in a cheerful contentedness with your condition, and take heed of an impatient, murmuring spirit. It is a continual burden to a man to have an impatient, discontented wife. Many a poor man can easily bear his own poverty but is not able to bear his wife's impatience under it. To hear her night and day complaining and speaking distrustfully and to see her live disquietedly is far heavier than his poverty. If his wife could bear it as patiently as he, it would be light to him. Yea, in cases of suffering for righteousness' sake, the impatience of a wife is a greater trial to a man than all the suffering itself; and many a man who could easily have suffered the loss of his estate, banishment, or imprisonment for Christ has betrayed his conscience and yielded to sin because his wife has grieved him with impatience and could not bear what he could bear. A contented, cheerful wife helps make a man cheerful and contented in every state.

Direction 7: In a special manner strive to subdue your passions and to speak and do all in meekness and sobriety. The weakness of your sex usually subjects you more to passions than men; and it is the common cause of the husband's disquietness and the calamity of your relation. It is the vexation and sickness of your own minds. You will not find yourselves at ease as long as you are passionate. Then comes the grief and disquietness of your husbands, and being provoked by you, they provoke you more; and so your disquietness increases, and your lives are made a burden to you. By all means, subdue passion and keep a composed, patient mind.

Direction 8: Take heed of a proud and contentious disposition, and maintain a humble, peaceable temper. Pride will make you turbulent and unquiet with your husbands and contentious with your neighbors. It will make you foolish and ridiculous in striving for honor and superiority[5] and in envying those who exceed or go before you. In a word, it is the Devil's sin and would make you a shame and trouble to the world. But humility is the health, peace, and ornament of the soul. "Let your adorning be the hidden person of the heart with the imperishable beauty of a gentle and quiet spirit, which in God's sight is very precious" (1 Pet. 3:4). Write those words in your bedroom,[6] on the walls, where they may be daily before your

---

[5]*Precedency.*
[6]*Bedchamber.*

eyes. "Put on then, as God's chosen ones, holy and beloved, compassionate hearts, kindness, humility, meekness, and patience, bearing with one another and, if one has a complaint against another, forgiving each other; as the Lord has forgiven you, so you also must forgive" (Col. 3:12–13). If this is the duty of all to one another, much more of wives to husbands. "Clothe yourselves, all of you, with humility toward one another, for 'God opposes the proud but gives grace to the humble'" (1 Pet. 5:5). Proud women often ruin their husbands' estates and quietness and their own souls.

Direction 9: Do not affect a childish gaudiness of apparel or a vain, costly, or troublesome curiosity in anything about you. Uncleanness and nastiness is a fault, but very small in comparison with this pride and curiosity. It dishonors your sex and yourselves to be so childish as to over-mind such trivial[7] things. If you have to be proud, be proud of something that is of worth and proper to a person. To be proud of reason, wisdom, learning, or goodness is bad enough. But to be proud of fashions and fine clothes, of blemishes[8] and nakedness, of sumptuous entertainments and neat rooms is to be proud of your shame and not your virtue; it is to be proud of things for which you are not commendable. The cost, time (oh, precious time!) that they must lay out upon their dressings, entertainments, and other curiosities will be the shame and sorrow of their souls, whenever God shall open their eyes and make them know what time was worth and what greater matters they had to mind. If vain and empty persons commend you for your bravery or curiosity, a judicious and sober person, whose commendation is worth much, will not.

Yet I must here with grief take notice that when some who in other matters seem wise and religious are themselves a little tainted with this childish curiosity and pride and speak words of disparagement against those whose dress, dwellings, and entertainments are not so curious as their own, that proves the greatest maintainer of this sin and the most notable service to the Devil. For then an abundance will plead for this sinful curiosity and pride and say, "Otherwise, I shall be accounted base or sordid; even such and such will speak against me." Take heed if you will be such that howl[9]

---

[7]*Toyish.*
[8]*Spots.*
[9]*Prate.*

against others who are not as vain and curious as you; for the nature of man is more prone to pride and vanity than to humility and the improvement of their time and cost in great matters. While you think you speak against indecency, you become the Devil's preachers and do him more service than you know. You may as wisely speak against people for eating or drinking too little when there is not one of a multitude who lives in excess; and so excess will get advantage by it.

Direction 10: Be careful in the government of your tongues. Let your words be few and well considered before you speak them. A double diligence is needful in this because it is the most common misconduct[10] of your sex. A loose,[11] running tongue is so great a dishonor to you that I never knew a woman full of words but she was the pity of her friends and the contempt of others. They will, behind her back, make a scorn of her and talk of her as some crack-brained or half-witted person. Yea, though your talk is good, it will be tedious and contemptible if it is poured out and too cheap. "When words are many, transgression is not lacking, but whoever restrains his lips is prudent" (Prov. 10:19). You must answer in judgment for "every careless word" (Matt. 12:36). You dislike to be accounted fools and made the derision of those who talk of you; judge by the Scripture what occasion you give them. "For a dream comes with much business, and a fool's voice with many words. . . . For when dreams increase and words grow many, there is vanity; but God is the one you must fear" (Eccles. 5:3, 7). "The words of a wise man's mouth win him favor, but the lips of a fool consume him. The beginning of the words of his mouth is foolishness, and the end of his talk is evil madness. A fool multiplies words" (Eccles. 10:12–14). But a woman who is cautious[12] and sparing of her words is commonly reverenced and considered[13] to be wise. If you have no higher design than merely to be thought well of and honored by men, you can scarcely take a surer way than to let your words be few and weighty. The avoiding of sin and disquietude[14] should prevail with you much more.

Direction 11: Be willing and diligent in your proper part of the care and labor of the family. As the primary provision of maintenance

---

[10]*Miscarriage.*
[11]*Laxative.*
[12]*Cautelous.*
[13]*Supposed.*
[14]*Unquietness.*

belongs most to the husband, so the secondary provision within doors belongs to the wife. Read over and over the thirty-first chapter of Proverbs, especially the care of nursing your own children, teaching and watching over them when they are young, and also watching over the family at home when your husband is abroad.

Direction 12: Do not dispose of your husband's estate without his knowledge and consent. You are not only to consider whether the work is good that you lay it upon but what power you have to do it.

Question: But may a woman give nothing or lay out nothing in the house without her husband's consent?

Answer: First, if she has his general or implicit consent, it may suffice; that is, if he allows her to follow her judgment or if he commits such a proportion to her power, to do what she will with it. Or if she knows that if he knew it, he would not be against it. Second, if the law, or his consent, gives her any propriety in any part of his estate or makes her a joint-proprietor, she may proportionally dispose of it in a necessary case (see Dr. Gouge on family relations, who says most against women's giving).[15] The husband is considerable either as a proprietor or as her governor. As a proprietor, he only may dispose of the estate when he is the sole proprietor; but where consent or the law of the land makes the woman joint-proprietor, she is not disabled from giving for want of propriety. But then no law exempts her from his government; and therefore she is not to give anything in a way of disobedience, though it is her own, except when he forbids what is her duty or what he has no power to forbid. In the case of joint-propriety, she may give without him, as long as she does not exceed her proportion. Also, if it is a case of duty, he may not hinder her, as to save the lives of the poor in extreme necessity, famine, imprisonment, or the like.

Third, if the thing is wholly her own, excepted from his propriety, and she is sole proprietor, then she does not need to ask for his consent any other way than as he is her guide, to direct her to the best way of disposing of it. If he forbids her instead of directing her, she is

---

[15]William Gouge's (1575–1653) *Of Domestical Duties* was published in 1622. Gouge, a clergyman in Blackfriars, preached his *magnum opus* on family life to his congregation, which, though popular in its time, incurred the wrath of wealthy city wives. See Anthony Fletcher, "The Protestant Idea of Marriage," in *Religion, Culture, and Society in Early Modern Britain: Essays in Honor of Patrick Collinson*, ed. Anthony Fletcher and Peter Roberts (Cambridge: Cambridge University Press, 2006), 167.

not excusable before God for abusing her trust and talents. Fourth, I conceive that *ad aliquid*, as to certain absolutely necessary uses, the relation makes the woman a joint-proprietor (2 Kings 4:9, 22; 1 Sam. 25:18, 29–30; Prov. 31:11–13, 20), as if her husband will not allow her such food and clothing[16] as is necessary to preserve the lives and health of herself and all her children. She is bound to do it without or against his will (if she can and if it is not to a greater hurt and the estate is his own) rather than let her children contract such diseases as will follow to the hazard of their lives, yea, and to save the life of another who in famine is ready to perish, for she is not as a stranger to his estate. But out of these cases if a wife shall secretly waste or give or lay it out on bravery or vanity or set her wit against her husband's and because she thinks him too strait or penurious therefore will dispose it without his consent, it is thievery, disobedience, and injustice.

Question 1: But as the case stands with us in England, does the wife have a joint-propriety or not?

Answer: Three ways, at least, she may have propriety. First, by a reserve of what was her own before, which, however some question it, may in some cases be done in their agreement at marriage. Second, by the law of the land. Third, by the husband's consent or donation. What the law of the land says in such a case, I leave to lawyers, but it seems to me that his words at marriage, "With all my worldly goods I you endow," signifies his consent to make her a joint-proprietor. His consent is sufficient to the collation of a title to that which was his own, unless any can prove that law or custom otherwise expounds the words as an empty formality and that at the contract this was or should be known to her to be the sense. The laws allowing the wife the third part upon death or separation implies a joint-propriety before.

Question 2: If the husband lives upon unlawful gain, as cheating, stealing, robbing on the highway, and so on, is not the wife guilty as a joint-proprietor in retaining such ill-gotten goods if she knows it? Is she bound to accuse her husband or to restore such goods?

Answer: Her duty is first to admonish her husband of his sin and danger and endeavor his repentance while disclaiming all consent

---

[16]*Raiment.*

and reception of the goods. If she cannot prevail for his repentance, restitution, and reformation, she has a double duty to perform. The one is to help them to their goods whom he has injured and robbed, by prudent and just means; the other involves his robbing of others in the time to come. But these must be done with great difficulty.

First, if she foresees that by her husband's displeasure or by the cruel revenge of the injured party, the hurt of revealing[17] the fraud or robbery will be greater than the good, then I think that she is not bound to disclose[18] it but by some secret, indirect way should help the owner regain his own, if it may be done without a greater hurt.

Second, to prevent his sin and other men's future suffering by him, she seems to me to be bound to reveal her husband's sinful purposes to the magistrate, if she cannot prevail with her husband to forbear. My reasons are, because the keeping of God's law and the law of the land and the public order and good and the preventing of our neighbors' hurt by robbery or fraud, and so the interest of honesty and right, are of greater importance than any duty to her husband or preservation of her own peace, which seems to be against it. But then I must suppose that she lives under a magistrate who will take a just revenge. For if she knows the laws and magistrate to be unjust, as to punish a fault with death that it does not deserve, she is not to tell the magistrate but is to preserve her neighbors' safety by some other way.

If anyone thinks that a wife may in no case accuse a husband to the hazard of his life or estate, let them remember what God obliged parents to do against the lives of incorrigible children (Deut. 21:18–21). Remember also that the honor of God and the lives of our neighbors should be preferred before the life of one offender, and their estates before his estate alone. The light of reason tells us that a wife is to reveal a treason against the king that is plotted by a husband and, therefore, also the robbing of the king's treasury or deceiving him in any matter of great concernment. Therefore, in due proportion the laws and common good and our neighbors' welfare are to be preserved by us, though against the nearest relation. Only all due tenderness of the life and reputation of the husband is to be

---

[17]*Discovering.*
[18]*Discover.*

preserved in the manner of proceedings as far as will stand with the interest of justice and the common good.

Question 3: May the wife go hear sermons when the husband forbids her?

Answer: There are some sermons that must not be heard; there are some sermons that may be heard and must when no greater matter diverts us; and there are some sermons that must be heard, whoever shall forbid it. Those that must not be heard are such as are heretical and such as are superfluous and at such times when greater duties call us another way. Those that may be heard are either occasional sermons or such lectures as are neither of necessity to ourselves, nor to the acknowledgment[19] of God and his public worship. One who lives where there are daily or hourly sermons may hear them as often as suits one's condition and one's other duties. But this case, the command of a husband with the inconveniences that will follow disobeying him may make it a duty to forbear. But that we do sometimes publicly own God's worship and church ordinances and receive ministerial teaching for our edification is of double necessity, so that we do not deny God or betray or desert our own souls. This is especially necessary on the Lord's Day, which is appointed for these uses. Here the husband has no power to forbid the wife, nor should she obey his prohibition. But as affirmatives do not bind *ad semper* ("in every circumstance"), and no duty is a duty at every season, so it is possible that on the Lord's Day it may extraordinarily become a duty to forbear from hearing sermons or attending sacraments or other forms of public worship when any greater duty calls us away, as to quench a fire, to save men's lives, to save our country from an enemy in time of war, to save our own lives (if we knew the assembly would be assaulted), or to preserve our liberty for greater service. Christ set us to learn the meaning of this lesson, "I will have mercy and not sacrifice." In such a case a mischief may be avoided, even from a husband, by the omission of a duty at that time (when it would be no duty), for this is but a transposition of it. But this is an act of prudent self-preservation and not an act of formal disobedience.

Question 4: If a woman has a husband so incorrigible in vice that by long trial she finds that speaking against it makes him worse and

---

[19]*Owning.*

causes him to abuse her, is she bound to continue her dissuasion or to forbear?

Answer: This is not a duty that is not a means to do some good; and this is no means that we know beforehand is likely, if not certainly, to do no good or to do more harm. We must not by weariness, laziness, or censoriousness take a case to be desperate that is not; nor must we so easily desist with so near a relation, as with a stranger or a neighbor. But Christ's indulgence of not exposing ourselves to be torn by dogs, and his Word trodden in the dirt by swine, extends to relations as well as others. But then you must observe that she who is justly discouraged from sharp reproofs may have hope that gentle and humble persuasions may succeed. She who is discouraged from open or frequent or plain reproofs may have hope that secret or more seldom or more distant and general admonitions may not be lost. She who is discouraged from one way of doing him good may have many other ways (as to set some minister whom he reverences to speak to him, to put some suitable book into his hand, etc.). She who is discouraged at the present ought not totally to despair but may make some more attempts thereafter, either in some sickness or time of mortality or danger or affliction or when possibly time and consideration may have better prepared him to hear. In the meantime, she is to continue all marital[20] affection and duty and a convincing, winning course of life, which may prove the most effectual reproof.

Question 5: What should a woman do in disputed[21] cases of religion, when her judgment and her husband's differ?

Answer: Some make a controversy of what with all good Christians or sober persons should be past controversy; and some controversies are indeed of real, not insuperable difficulty. Second, some controversies are about important, necessary things and some about things of lesser moment. Third, some are about mere opinion or other men's practice and some about our own practice.

1. In all differences of judgment, the wife must exercise self-suspicion, modesty, and submission, as may signify her due sense both of the weakness of her sex and her subjection to her husband. 2. In things indifferent, she must in practice obey her husband, unless superior powers forbid it and in cases where their authority

---
[20]*Conjugal.*
[21]*Controverted.*

is greater. 3. She may modestly give her reasons of dissent. 4. She must not turn it into a troublesome[22] quarrel or matter of disaffection or pretend any differences against her married[23] duties. 5. In dark and difficult cases she should not be peremptory and self-conceited or importunate; but if she has faith (that is, more knowledge than he) she is to have it to herself, in quietness and silence, and seek further information lest she err. 6. She must not speak untruth or commit any known sin, in obedience to her husband's judgment. 7. When she strongly suspects sin, she must not do it merely in obedience to him but seek for better satisfaction. For she is sure that he has no power to force her to sin and, therefore, has no more assurance of his power in that point than she has of the lawfulness of the thing. 8. If she proves to be in error, she will still sin on either side until she repents.[24] 9. If a husband is in dangerous error, she must wisely, without weariness, seek his reformation, by herself or through others.

Cases about Divorce and Separation

Question 1: Is it lawful for a husband and wife to be absent from each other for a while? How long, and in what cases?

Answer: It is lawful to be absent either in the case of prayer, which Paul mentions, or in case of the needful affairs of their estates, so long as there may be no danger to them as to mental or corporal incontinency[25] or any other hurt that would be greater than the benefits of their absence or cause them to be guilty of the neglect of any real duty. Therefore, the cases of several persons differ according to the different tempers of their minds, bodies, and affairs. He who has a wife with a chaste, contented, prudent temper may stay apart many months or years in some cases when, all things considered, it tends to more good than hurt. For example, lawyers, by their callings, are often necessitated to follow their callings at terms and assizes;[26] and merchants may be some years absent in some weighty cases. But if you ask whether getting money is a sufficient cause, I answer, it is sufficient to those whose families must be maintained

---

[22]*Unpeaceable.*
[23]*Conjugal.*
[24]*Recovers.*
[25]That is, a lack of sexual self-control.
[26]That is, a legislative sitting, such as a courtroom.

and their wives are easily self-restrained,[27] and so the good of their gain is greater than any loss or danger that comes by it. But when covetousness puts them upon it needlessly, and their wives cannot bear it, or in any case when the hurt that is to follow is greater than the good, it is unlawful.

Question 2: May husband and wife be separated by the command of princes if they make a law that in certain cases they shall part, as for, suppose, ministers, judges, or soldiers?

Answer: You must distinguish between the command or law and the reasons and ends of that command, and so between a lawful command and an unlawful. In some cases a prince may justly command a separation for a time or such as is likely to prove for perpetuity, and in some cases he may not. If a king commands a separation without sufficient cause, so that you have no motive but his authority, and the question is whether formally you are bound to obedience, I answer no because what God has joined, no man has power to put asunder. Nor can prince, pope, or prelate dispense with your marriage covenant. In such a case it is as a private act, because God has given them no authority for it; and therefore their commands or laws are nullities. If a prince says, "He who will be a judge or a justice shall part with his wife," it is lawful to leave the office and so obey the law. But if he says to all ministers of the gospel, "You shall forsake your wives or your ministry," they should do neither because they are divinely obliged to both, and he has no power to forbid them or to dispense with that obligation.

But it may fall out that the ends of the command are so great as to make it lawful, and then it must be obeyed both formally for the authority of the prince and finally for the reasons of the thing. As an example, if the safety of the commonwealth should require that married persons be soldiers and that they go far off, yea, though there is no likelihood of returning to their families, and they cannot take their wives with them without detriment or danger to their service, in this case men must obey the magistrate and are called by God to forsake their wives as if it were by death. Nor is it any violation of their marriage covenant because that was intended or meant to sup-

---

[27]*Continent.*

pose the exception of any such call of God, which cannot be resisted when it will make a separation.

Question 3: May ministers leave their wives to go abroad to preach the gospel?

Answer: If they can neither do God's work as well at home, nor take their wives with them, nor be excused from doing that part of service by other men doing it who have no such impediment, they may and must leave their wives behind. In this case the interest of the church and of the souls of many must overrule the interest of wife and family. Those pastors who have fixed stations must neither leave flock nor family without necessity or a clear call from God. But in several cases a preacher may be necessitated to go abroad, as in cases of persecution at home or of some necessity of foreign or remote parts that cannot be otherwise supplied or when some door is opened for the conversion of infidels, heretics, or idolaters, and no one else is fit to do the work. In any such case, when the cause of God in any part of the world, *consideratis considerandis*, requires his help, a minister must leave wife and family, yea, and a particular flock, to do it. For our obligations are greatest to the catholic[28] church and public good, and the greatest good must be preferred. If a king commands a subject to be an ambassador in the remotest part of the world, and the public good requires it, if wife and children cannot be taken with him, they must be left behind, and he must go. So must a consecrated minister of Christ for the service of the church refuse all entanglements that would more hinder this work than the contrary benefits would countervail. This exception was supposed in the marriage contract, that family interests and comforts must give way to the public interest and to God's disposals.

Therefore, ministers should not rashly venture upon marriage or any woman who is wise venture to marry a minister until she is well prepared for such accidents as may separate them for a shorter or a longer time.

Question 4: May one leave a wife to save his life, in case of personal persecution or danger?

Answer: Yes, if she cannot be taken with him; for the means that are for the helps of life do suppose the preservation of life itself. If he

---

[28]That is, universal.

lives, he may further serve God and possibly return to his wife and family; but if he dies, he is removed from them all.

Question 5: May husband and wife part by mutual consent if they find it is for the good of both?

Answer: If you do not speak of dissolving the bond of their relations but withdrawing as to cohabitation, I answer, it is not to be done upon passions and discontents, to feed and gratify each other's vicious distempers or interest; for then both the consent and the separation are their sins. But if such an incurable unsuitableness lies between them as their lives are miserable by their cohabitation, I do not know if they may live apart;[29] so be it that after all other means are used in vain, they do it by deliberate, free consent. If one of them should by craft or cruelty constrain the other to consent, it is unlawful to the constrainer. Nor must impatience make either of them despair of the cure of any unsuitableness that is really curable. Many sad instances might be given in which cohabitation may be a constant calamity to both, and distance may be their relief and further them both in God's service and in their bodily[30] concernments. Yet I do not say that this is no sin, for their unsuitableness is their sin, and God still obliges them to lay down the sin that makes them unsuitable and, therefore, does not allow them to live apart,[31] being still their duty to live together in love and peace. To say that they cannot does not free them from their duty; but moral impotency may make such a separation, as before said, to be a lesser sin than their painful[32] cohabitation.

Question 6: May not the relation itself be dissolved by mutual, free consent, so that they may marry others?

Answer: As to the relation, they will still be related as those who did covenant to live in a married state[33] and are still allowed it and obliged to it if the impediments were removed; it is but the exercise that is hindered. They may not consent to marry others, first, because the contracted relation was for life (Rom. 7:2), and God's law accordingly obliges them. Marriages *pro tempore* ("for the time being"), dissoluble by consent, are not God's institution but contrary

---

[29]*Asunder.*
[30]*Corporal.*
[31]*Asunder.*
[32]*Unpeaceable.*
[33]*Conjugal society.*

to it. Second, they do not know whether their impediments may be removed. Third, if he who marries an innocent, divorced woman commits adultery, it will likewise[34] be so here. If you say, "What if either of them cannot contain his or her desires?" I answer, he who will not take heed before must be patient afterward and not make advantage of his own folly, to the fulfilling of his lusts. If he will do what he ought to do in the use of all means, he may live chastely. And, fourth, the public interest must overrule the private, and that which would be unjust in private respects may for public good become a duty. It seems unjust, with us, that the innocent country should repay every man his money who between sun and sun is robbed on the road; yet, because it will engage the country to watchfulness, it is just, being for the common good. He who consents to be a member of a commonwealth consents to submit his own right to the common interest. So here, if all should have leave to marry others when they consent to part, it would bring utter confusion and would encourage wicked men to abuse their wives till they forced them to consent. Therefore, some must bear the trouble that their folly has brought on themselves rather than the common order being confounded.

Question 7: Does adultery dissolve the bond of marriage or not? Amesius says it does.[35] Mr. Whately, having said so, afterward recanted, being persuaded by other divines.[36]

Answer: The difference is only about the name, and not about the matter itself. The reason that moved Dr. Ames is because the injured person is free and so not bound; therefore, the bond is dissolved. The reason that Mr. Whately could not answer is, because it is not fornication, it is lawful if they continue their married[37] familiarity after adultery. Therefore, that bond is not dissolved. In all, it is easy to perceive that one man takes the word *vinculum* ("bond") in one

---

[34]*By parity of reason.*

[35]This is the Latin name for William Ames (1576–1633), an English theologian best known for his writings on ethics and Reformed theology. He served on the Synod of Dort and was a virulent opponent of Arminianism. He was professor of theology at Franeker in Friesland for a few years. Among his many works, two are considered representative, his *Medulla Theologiae* (1623), or "Marrow of Theology," and his *De Conscientia et Ejus Jure vel Casibus* (1632), a treatise on the cases of conscience. The latter text was for many years considered the standard work on Christian ethics by the Dutch Reformed Church. Both texts were issued in English editions, in 1642 and 1639 respectively.

[36]William Whately (1583–1639) was an early seventeenth-century theologian and scholar. His work on marriage, *A Bride-Bush; or, A General Direction for Married Persons,* was the most famous of the seventeenth-century conduct books. See Lloyd Davis, ed., *Sexuality and Gender in the English Renaissance: An Annotated Edition of Contemporary Documents* (New York: Routledge, 1998), 245.

[37]*Conjugal.*

sense, that is, "for their covenant obligation to continue their relation and mutual duties." The other takes it in another sense, that is,
"for the relation itself as by it they are allowed conjugal familiarity,
if the injured person will continue it." The first *vinculum*, or bond,
is dissolved; the second is not. In the matter we are agreed that the
injured man may put away an adulterous wife if he pleases, but also
that he may continue the relation if he pleases. So his continued
consent shall suffice to continue it a lawful relation and exercise;
and his will, on the contrary, shall suffice to dissolve the relation
and disoblige him.

Question 8: Is not the injured party obliged to separate, left free?

Answer: Considering the thing simply in itself, he is wholly free
to do as he pleases. But accidents or circumstances may make it one
man's duty to divorce and another's duty to continue the relation,
according as it is likely to do more good or hurt. Sometimes it may
be a duty to expose the sin to public shame for the prevention of it in
others, and also to deliver oneself from a calamity. Sometimes there
may be so great repentance and hope of better effects by forgiving
that it may be a duty to forgive. Prudence must lay one thing with
another, to discern on which side the duty lies.

Question 9: Is it only the privilege of the man, that he may put
away an adulterous wife? Or of the woman also, to depart from an
adulterous husband? The reason of the doubt is because Christ mentions the man's power only (Matthew 5 and 19).

Answer: The reason Christ speaks only of the man's case is
because he was occasioned only to restrain the vicious custom of
men's causelessly putting away their wives, having no occasion
to restrain women from leaving their husbands. Men, having the
rule, abused it to the woman's injury, which Christ forbids. As it
is an act of power, it concerns the man alone; but as it is an act
of liberty, it seems to me to be supposed that the woman has the
same freedom, seeing the covenant is violated to her wrong. The
apostle, in 1 Corinthians 7, makes the case of the man and woman
to be equal in the point of infidelity and desertion. I confess that it
is unsafe to extend the sense of Scripture beyond the importance of
the words, upon pretense of a likeness[38] (as many of the perjured do

---

[38]*Parity of reason.*

by Leviticus 27 in the case of vows), lest man's deceitful wit should make a law to itself as divine, upon pretense of interpreting God's laws. When the plain text speaks of one case, that is, of men's putting away their wives, he who will, from that, gather an exclusion of the woman's liberty seems, by addition, to be a corrupter of the Law. Where the context plainly shows a likeness,[39] and that reason is made the ground of the determination of the text, there it is safe to expound the Law extensively, as it suits. Surely the covenant of marriage has its conditions on both parts. Some of those conditions are necessary to the very being of the obligations, though others are needful to the well-being of the parties in that state. Therefore, though putting away is only the part of the husband as being the ruler and usually the owner of the habitation, yet departing may be the liberty of the wife. I know no reason to blame those countries whose laws allow the wife to sue for a divorce as well as the husband.

Question 10: May the husband put away his wife without the magistrate or the wife depart from her husband without a public legal divorce or license?

Answer: Where the laws of the land take care for the prevention of injuries and make any determination in the case not contrary to the law of God, it is a Christian's duty to obey those laws. Therefore, if you live under a law that forbids any putting away or departing without public sentence or allowance, you may not do it privately upon your own will. For the civil governors are to provide against the private injuries of any of the subjects. If persons might put away or depart at pleasure, it would introduce both injury and much weakness into the world. Where the laws of men leave persons to their liberty in this case, they need look no further than to the laws of God alone. But usually the sentence of the civil power is necessary only in case of appeal or complaint of the injured party. A separation may be made without such a public divorce, so that each party may make use of the magistrate to right themselves if wronged. If the adultery is not openly known, and the injuring party desires rather to be put away privately[40] than publicly (as Joseph purposed to do with Mary), I see not but it is lawful so to do in the case that the law or the necessity of making the offender an example does not require

---

[39]*Parity of reason.*
[40]*Privily.*

the contrary, or scandal or other accidents forbid it not. See Grotius's learned notes on Matthew 5:31–32, 19, and 1 Corinthians 7 about these questions.

Question 11: Is not the case of sodomy or buggery a ground for warrantable divorce as well as adultery?

Answer: Yes, and it seems to be included in the word itself (Matt. 5:31–32), which signifies "uncleanness," or at least is fully implied in the reason of it. See Grotius also on this, in the same place as before.

Question 12: What if both parties commit adultery? May either of them put away the other or depart, or must they forgive each other?

Answer: If they both do it at the same time, they both forfeit the liberty of seeking any compensation for the injury, the injury being equal (however, some would give the advantage to the man). However, if one person commits adultery and then the other, the last offender either knew of the first or not. If not, then it seems all one, as if it had been done at once. But if yea, then they did either act on a supposition of the dissolution of the matrimonial obligation, as being loosed from the first adulterer, or otherwise upon a purpose of continuing in the first relation. In the latter case, it is still all one, as if it had been done by them at once, and it is a forfeiture of any satisfaction. In the former case, though the last adulterer did sin, yet being before set at liberty, it does not renew the matrimonial obligation; yet, if the first offender desires the continuance of it and the return of the first injured party, shame and conscience of their own sin will rebuke them if they plead injury for continuance of the separation.

Question 13: What if one purposely commits adultery to be separated from the other?

Answer: It is in the other's power and choice whether to be divorced and depart or not, as he or she finds the good or evil consequents preponderant.

Question 14: Does not infidelity dissolve the relation or obligation, seeing there is no communion between light and darkness, between a believer and an infidel?

Answer: It makes it unlawful for a believer to marry an infidel except in cases of true necessity because they can have no communion in religion. But it does not nullify a marriage already made, nor does it make it lawful to depart or divorce because they may have married[41] communion still, as the apostle purposely determines the case (1 Corinthians 7).

Question 15: Does not the desertion of one party disoblige the other?

Answer: First, it must be considered what true desertion is. Second, whether it is a desertion of the relation itself and its continuance or only a temporary desertion of cohabitation or congress.[42] Third, what the temper and state of the deserted party is. It is sometimes easy and sometimes hard to discern who the departing party is. If the wife goes away from the husband without warrant, though she requires him to follow her and says that she does not desert him, yet it may be taken for a desertion because it is the man who is to rule and choose the habitation. But if the man goes away, and the woman refuses to follow, he is not therefore the deserter.

Question: But what if the man does not have sufficient cause to go away, and the woman has great and urgent reasons not to go? As an example, suppose that the man will go away in hatred of an able preacher and good company, and the woman if she follows him must leave all those helps and go among ignorant, profane, heretical persons or infidels. Which is the deserter then?

Answer: If she is one who is likely to do good to the infidels, heretics, or bad persons with whom they must converse, she may suppose that God calls her to receive good by doing good; or if she is a confirmed, well-settled Christian and not very likely, either by infection or by want of helps, to be unsettled and miscarry, it seems to me the safest way to follow her husband. She will lose God's public ordinances by following him, but it is not imputable to her, as being outside her choice. She must lose the benefits and neglect the duties of the married[43] ordinance if she does not follow him. But if she is a person under such weaknesses as makes her removal apparently dangerous as to her perseverance and salvation, and her husband will by no means be prevailed upon to change his mind, the case, then, is very difficult as to what is her duty and who is the deserter, unless he leads her into a country where her life is likely to be taken away, as under the Spanish Inquisition, unless her suffering is likely

---

[41]*Conjugal.*
[42]That is, sexual relations.
[43]*Conjugal.*

to be as serviceable to Christ as her life. Indeed, these cases are so difficult that I will not decide them. The inconveniencies, or mischiefs rather, are great whatever way she takes.

I most incline to judge as follows: It is considerable, first, what marriage obligates her to simply of its own nature and what it may do next by any superadded contract or by the law or custom of the land or any other accident. As to the first, it seems that everyone's obligation is first to God and then to their own souls and lives. Marriage, as such, which is for mutual help, as a means to higher ends, does not obligate her to forsake all the communion of saints and the place or country where God is lawfully worshipped, to lose all the helps of public worship, and to expose her soul both to spiritual famine and infection, to the apparent hazard of her salvation (and perhaps bring her children into the same misery); nor has God given her husband any power to do her so much wrong, nor is the marriage covenant to be interpreted to intend it. But what any human law or contract or other accident that is of greater public consequence may do more than marriage in itself is a distinct case that must have a particular discussion.

Question: But what if the husband would only have her follow him to the forsaking of her estate and undoing herself and their children in the world (as in the case of Galeacius Carracciolus),[44] yea, and if it were without just cause?

Answer: If it is for greater spiritual gain, as in his case, she is bound to follow him; but if it be apparently foolish, to the undoing of her and her children without any cause, I do not see that marriage obliges a woman to follow a fool in beggary or out of a calling to her ruin. But if it is at all a controvertible case, whether the cause is just or not, then the husband, being governor, must judge. The laws of the land are supposed to be just, which allow a woman by trustees to secure some part of her former estate from her husband's disposal. Much more may she beforehand secure herself and children from being ruined by his willful folly. She can by no contract except herself from his true government.

---

[44]Galeazzo Carraccioli di Vico (d. 1586), an Italian of distinguished ancestry and a nephew of Pope Paul IV, because of his Reformed faith (he was converted under the ministry of Peter Martyr) left Naples and his wife and family and settled in Geneva. His story was well known in the fifteenth and sixteenth centuries. John Calvin praised Carraccioli's self-sacrifice and devoted the second edition of his commentary on 1 Corinthians to him.

Yet, she must consider whether she can live continently in his absence; otherwise the greatest sufferings must be endured to avoid incontinency.

Moreover, in all these cases a temporary removal may be followed rather than a perpetual separation[45] because it has fewer evil consequents.

If either party renounces the relation itself, that is a fuller desertion and a clearer discharge of the other party than a mere removal is.

Question 16: What if a man or wife knows that the other, in hatred, intends by poison or other murder to take away his or her life? May he or she not depart?

Answer: They may not do it upon a groundless or rash surmise, nor upon a danger that by other lawful means may be avoided (as by vigilance or the magistrate or especially by love and duty). But in plain danger that is not otherwise to be avoided, I do not doubt that it may be done, and ought. For it is a duty to preserve our own lives as well as our neighbors'. And when marriage is contracted for mutual help, it is naturally implied that they shall have no power to deprive one another of life (however some barbarous nations have given men power over the lives of their wives). Killing is the grossest kind of desertion and a greater injury and violation of the marriage covenant than adultery and may be prevented by avoiding the murderer's presence if that way is necessary. None of the ends of marriage can be attained where the hatred is so great.

Question 17: If there is a fixed hatred of each other, is that inconsistent with the purposes[46] of marriage? Is parting lawful in such a case?

Answer: The injuring party is bound to love and not to separate and can have no liberty by his or her sin. And to say, "I cannot love" or "My wife or husband is not amiable" is no sufficient excuse; every person has something that is amiable, if it is but human nature; and that should have been foreseen before your choice. As it is not an excuse for a drunkard to say, "I cannot leave my drink," so it is not for an adulterer or hater of another to say, "I cannot love them," for that is to say, "I am so wicked that my heart or will is against my duty." But the innocent party's case is harder, though commonly both

---

[45]*Transmigration.*
[46]*Ends.*

parties are faulty, and therefore both are obliged to return to love and not to separate. If hatred does not proceed to adultery, murder, or intolerable injuries, you must remember that marriage is not a contract for years but for life and that it is possible that hatred may be cured, no matter how unlikely that may seem. Therefore, you must do your duty, wait, pray, and strive by love and goodness to recover love, and then stay to see what God will do, for mistakes in your choice will not warrant a separation.

Question 18: What if a woman has a husband who will not suffer her to read the Scriptures or go to God's worship, public or private, or who beats or abuses her (it cannot be expected that human nature should be, in such a case, kept fit for any holy action), or if a man has a wife who scolds at him when he is praying or instructing his family and makes it impossible for him to serve God with freedom or peace and comfort?

Answer: The woman must, at necessary seasons, though not when she would, both read the Scriptures and worship God and suffer patiently what is inflicted on her. Martyrdom may be as comfortably suffered from a husband as from a prince. But yet if neither her own love, duty, and patience, nor friends' persuasion, nor the magistrate's justice can free her from such inhumane cruelty as quite disables her for her duty to God and man, I do not see why she may not depart from such a tyrant. But the man has more means to restrain his wife from beating him or doing such intolerable things, either by the magistrate or by denying her what otherwise she might have or by his own violently restraining her, as belongs to a governor[47] and as circumstances shall direct a prudent man. In case that unsuitableness or sin is so great that after long trial there is no likelihood of any other cohabitation but what will tend to their spiritual hurt and calamity, it is their lesser sin to live apart[48] by mutual consent.

Question 19: May one part from a husband or wife who has leprosy or syphilis[49] because of his or her adulterous practices when the innocent person's life is endangered by it?

Answer: If it is an innocent person's disease, the other must cohabit and tenderly cherish and comfort the diseased, yea, so as somewhat to hazard their own lives, but not so as apparently to cast

---

[47]*Conjugal ruler.*
[48]*Asunder.*
[49]*The French pox.*

them away upon a danger that cannot be avoided unless the other's life or some greater good is to be seen by it. If it is the pox of an adulterer, the innocent party is at liberty by the other's adultery and the saving of their own lives. Without adultery, the disease alone will not excuse them from cohabitation, though it may from sexual union.[50]

Question 20: Who are they who may or may not marry again when they are parted?

Answer: They who are released by divorce upon the other's adultery, sodomy, etc., may marry again. The case of the rest is harder. They who part by consent, to avoid mutual hurt, may not marry again; nor the party who departs for self-preservation or for the preservation of estate, children, comforts, or liberty of worship, as before said, because it is an intermission of marital[51] fruition and not a total dissolution of the relation. The innocent party must wait to see whether there is any hope of return. Yea, Christ seems to answer this in Matthew 5:31–32, where an adulterer who marries an innocent party is put away; the other living in adultery, their first contracted relation seems to be still in being. But Grotius and some others think that Christ means this only of the man who over-hastily marries the innocent divorced woman before it is seen whether he will repent and reassume her. But how can that hold if the husband after adultery frees her? May it not be meant that the woman must stay unmarried in hope of his reconciliation, till such time as his adultery with his next married wife disobliges her? Then it must be taken as a law for Christians, for the Jew who might have many wives does not disoblige one by taking another.

A short desertion must be endured in hope; but in the case of a very long or total desertion or rejection, if the injured party should have an untamable lust, the case is difficult. I think there are some who by just means may abstain. If there are any who cannot, after all means, without such trouble as overthrows their peace and so plainly hazards their continence, I dare not say that marriage, in that case, is unlawful for the innocent party.

Question 21: Is it lawful to suffer or tolerate, yea, or contribute to the matter of known sin in a family, in wife or child or consequently in any other relations?

---

[50]*Congress.*
[51]*Conjugal.*

Answer: In this some lukewarm men are apt to run into the extreme of remissness and some inexperienced young men who never had families into the extreme of censorious rigor, not knowing what they talk of.

First, it is not lawful either in family, commonwealth, church, or anywhere to allow sin or to tolerate it or to leave it uncured when it is truly in our power to cure it. Second, as to the question, when is it and when is it not in our power? I shall answer by some instances.

It is not in our power to do that which we are naturally unable to do. No law of God binds us to impossibilities. And natural impotency is found in these several cases. *When we are overmatched in strength, and wife or child is too strong for the master of the house, so that he cannot correct them or remove them.* A king is not bound to punish rebellious or offending subjects when they are too strong for him and he is unable, either because of their numbers or other advantages. If a pastor censures an offender, and all the church is against the censure, he cannot see it executed but must acquiesce in having done his part and leave their guilt upon themselves.

When the thing to be done is impossible, at least morally, as to hinder all the persons of a family, church, or kingdom from ever sinning. It is not in their own power so far to reform themselves, much less in a ruler so far to reform them. Even as to ourselves, perfection is but desired in this life, not attained; much less for others.

When the principal causes do not cooperate with us, and we are but subservient moral causes. We can but [attempt to] persuade men to repent, believe, and love God and goodness. We cannot save men without and against themselves. Their hearts are out of our reach; therefore, in all these cases we are naturally unable to hinder sin.

It is not in our power to do anything that God forbids us. That which is sinful is to be accounted out of our power in this sense. To cure the sin of a wife by such cruelty or harshness as is contrary to our married[52] relation and to the office of necessary love is out of our power because forbidden, as contrary to our duty; and so of other actions.

Those actions are out of our power that are acts of higher authority than we have. A subject cannot reform by such actions as are proper to the sovereign or a layman by actions proper to the pastor, for want of authority. So a schoolmaster cannot do that which is

---

[52]*Conjugal.*

proper to a patient, nor the master of a family that which is proper to the magistrate, as to punish with death, etc.

We do not have power to do that which a superior power forbids us unless it is what God commands us. The wife may not correct a child or turn him away when the husband forbids it. The master of a family may not punish a sin in a way that the king or laws forbid.

We do not have the power to do that for the cure of sin that is likely to do more harm than good, yea, perhaps to prove a pernicious mischief. If my sharp reproof is likely to do more hurt, or less good, than milder dealings, if I have reason to believe that correction will make things worse, I am not to do it, because we have power to edification and not to destruction. God has not told us to speak such and such words or to use this or that correction but to use reproofs and corrections only in that time, measure, and manner as true reason tells us is most likely to attain their end. To do it, if it would do never so much hurt, with a *fiat justitia etsi pereat mundus* ("let righteousness be done even if purity is done away") is to be righteous overmuch.

Yea, great and heinous sins may be endured in families sometimes to avoid a greater hurt and because there is no other means to cure them. For instance, a wife may be guilty of notorious pride and of malignantly deriding the exercises of religion and of railing, lying, slandering, backbiting, covetousness, swearing, cursing, and the husband be necessitated to bear it, not so far as not to reprove it, but so far as not to correct her, much less cure her. Divines used to say that it is unlawful for a man to beat his wife; the reason is not that he lacks authority to do it but because he is by his relation obliged to a life of love with her and, therefore, must so rule as tends not to destroy love. Further, it may often do more hurt to her and the family than good. It may make her furious and desperate and make her contemptible in the family and diminish the reverence of children, both to wife and husband, for living so distasteful[53] a life.

Question: Is there any case in which a man may silently bear the sins of a wife or children without reproof or urging them to amend?

Answer: Yes, in case, first, that reproof has been tried to the utmost, and, second, it is most evident by full experience that it is likely to do more hurt than good.

---

[53] *Uncomely.*

The rule given by Christ extends to families, as to others, not to cast pearls before swine or to give that which is holy to dogs (Matt. 7:6); it is more to the discomposure of a man's own peace to have a wife turn again and rend him than a stranger. As the church may cease admonishing a sinner after a certain time of obstinacy, when experience has ended their present hopes of bringing the person to repentance, and thereupon may excommunicate him, so a husband may be brought to the same despair with a wife and may be dis-obliged from ordinary reproof, though the nearness of the relation forbids him to eject her. In such a case where the family and neigh-borhood know the intractableness and obstinacy of the wife, it is no scandal or sign of approbation or neglect of duty for a man to be silent at her sin (Ps. 81:11; Rev. 22:10–11; Prov. 1:24–25), because they look upon her as incorrigible by that means. It is the sharpest reproof to such a one to be obstinate[54] and to be let alone in her sin, just as it is God's greatest judgment on a sinner to leave him to himself and say, "Be filthy still."

There are some women whose fantasies and passions are natu-rally so strong that it seems to me that in many cases they have not so much as natural free will or power to restrain them. But if in all other cases they acted as in some, I should take them for mere animals[55] that had no true reason; they seem naturally neces-sitated to do as they do. I have known the long profession of piety that in other respects has seemed sincere to consist in a wife with such unbridled,[56] furious passion that she could not before strang-ers forbear throwing what was in her hand in her husband's face or thrusting the burning candle into his face and slandering him of the filthiest sins, and when the passion was over, to confess all to be false and her rage to be the reason of her speech and actions, and the man, though a minister of more than ordinary wit and strength, yet will-ing[57] to endure all without returns of violence till her death. Those who never knew such a case by trial can tell how all might be cured easily, but those who bear it are hard-pressed for the cure.

There are some other women of the same incurable strength of imagination and passion who in other respects are very pious and

---

[54]*Unreproved.*
[55]*Brutes.*
[56]*Unmastered.*
[57]*Fain.*

prudent too and too wise and conscionable to wrong their husbands with their hands or tongues, who yet are utterly unable to forbear any injury of the highest nature to themselves. They are so utterly impatient of being crossed of their wills that it would in all likelihood cast them into melancholy or madness or some mortal sickness; and no reason signifies anything to debate such passions. In case of pride or some sinful custom, they are not able to bear reproof and to be hindered in the sin without apparent danger of distraction or death. I suppose these cases are but few. What to do in such cases when they come is the present question.

Nay, the question is yet harder: whether to avoid such inconvenience one may contribute toward another's sin by affording him the means of committing it.

Answer: No man may contribute to sin as sin, formally considered. No man may contribute to another's sin for sinful ends, nor in a manner forbidden and sinful in himself. No man may contribute to another's sin when he is not naturally or morally necessitated to it but might forbear it.

But as it is consistent with the holiness of God to contribute those natural and providential mercies that he knows men will abuse in sin, so is it in some cases with us, his creatures, to one another. God gives all men their lives and time, their reason and free will, which he knows they will abuse in sin. He gives them the meat, drink, riches, health, and vigor of senses that are the usual means of the sin and the undoing of the world.

Objection: But God is not under any law or obligation as we are.

Answer: His own perfection is above all law and will not consist with a consent or acting of anything that is contrary to holiness and perfection. But this I confess, that many things are contrary to the order and duty of the creature that are not contrary to the place and perfection of the Creator.

First, when man generates man, he knowingly contributes to a sinful nature and life; for he knows that it is unavoidable, and that which is born of the flesh is flesh (John 3:6; Eph. 2:2–3). And yet he does not sin by so doing because he is not bound to prevent sin by forbearing procreation.

Second, when one advances another to the office of magistracy or ministry, knowing that he will sin in it, he contributes accidentally to his sin; but he is not culpable for so doing.

Third, a physician has to do with a difficult[58] and intemperate patient who will please his appetite or else if he be denied, his passion will increase his disease and kill him. In this case he may lawfully say, "Let him take a little rather than kill him," though by so doing he contributes to his sin; this is a not hindering that which he cannot hinder without greater evil. The sin is only his that chooses it.

It is specially to be noted that that which physically is a positive act and contributing to the matter of the sin yet morally is but a not hindering the sin by such a withholding of materials as we are not obliged to withhold (which is the case also of God's contributing to the matter of sin). If the physician in such a case or the parent of a sick and hard to please[59] child actually gives them what they sin in desiring, the giving is a furthering of the sin as cannot be lawfully forborne lest we do hurt and, therefore, is morally but a not hindering it when we cannot hinder it.

Fourth, if a man has a wife so proud that she will go mad or disturb him and his family by rage if her pride is not gratified by some sinful fashions, curiosities, or excesses, if he gives her money or materials to do it with, to prevent her distraction, it is like the foresaid case of the physician or parents of a sick child.

In these cases I will give you a rule to walk by and a caution on how to judge others.

First, be sure that you leave nothing undone that you can lawfully do for the cure and prevention of others' sins, and that it be not for want of zeal against sin, through indifference or slothfulness, that you forbear to hinder it but merely through disability. Second, see that in comparing the evil that is likely to follow the hindering,[60] you do not mistake, but be sure that it be indeed a greater evil that you avoid by not hindering that particular sin. Third, see that your own carnal interest does not weigh more with you than there is cause and that you do not account fleshly suffering a greater evil than sin. Fourth, that dishonor that may be cast upon religion and the good of souls, which may be hindered by a bodily suffering, may come into the comparison.

---

[58]*Froward.*
[59]*Froward.*
[60]*Impedition.*

Fifth, your own duties to men's bodies (as to save men's lives or health or peace) are to be numbered with spiritual things, and the materials of a sin may in some cases be administered for the discharge of such a duty. If you knew a man would die if you give him not hot water,[61] and he will be drunk if you do give it to him, in this case you do but your duty, and he commits the sin. You do that which is good and are not bound to forbear it because he will turn it to sin, unless you see that the hurt by that sin is likely to be so great, besides the sin itself, as to discharge you from the duty of doing good.

As to others, put them on to their duty, and do not spare. But do not censure them for the sins of their families till you are acquainted with the case. It is usual with rash and carnal censurers to cry out about some godly ministers or gentlemen that their wives are as proud and their children as bad as others. But are you sure that it is in their power to remedy it? Malice and rashness judge at a distance things that men do not understand and sin in speaking against sin.

Question 22: If a gentleman of modest wealth could spare half his yearly rents for his children and charitable uses, and his wife is so proud and prodigal that she will waste it all in keeping the house and excesses and will rage, be unquiet, or go mad if she is hindered, what is a man's duty in such a case?

Answer: This is an instance of the case mentioned before and must be answered. First, it is supposed that she is incurable by all wise and rational means of persuasion. Second, he is wise to compare the greatness of the evil that will come by crossing her with the good that may come by the improvement of his estate and the forbearance of those excesses. If her rage or distraction or disquietude[62] were likely, by any accident, to do more hurt than his estate may do good, he might consider himself disabled from hindering the sin; and though he gives her the money that she misspends, he is not sinning but only not hindering sin when he is unable. Third, ordinarily some small or tolerable degree of sinful waste and excess may be tolerated to avoid such mischiefs as else would follow, but not too much. Though no just measure can be assigned at what rate a man may lawfully purchase his own peace and consequently his liberty to serve God, or at what rate he may save his wife from madness

---

[61]Alcoholic beverage.
[62]*Unquietness.*

or some mortal mischiefs of her discontent, yet the case must be resolved by such considerations; and a prudent man who knows what is likely to be the consequent on both sides may and must accordingly determine it. Fourth, ordinarily the life, health, or preservation of so proud, luxurious, and passionate a woman is not worth the saving at so dear a rate as the wasting of a considerable estate that might be used to relieve a multitude of the poor and perhaps to save the lives of many who are worthier to live.

A man's duty to relieve the poor and provide for his family is so great, and the account that all men must give of the use of their talents is so strict, that it must be a great reason indeed that must allow him to give way to very great wastefulness. Unless there is something extraordinary in the case, it is better to deal with such a woman as a lunatic[63] and, if she will be mad, to use her as the mad are used than for a steward of God to suffer the Devil to be served with his Master's goods.

Lastly, I must charge the reader to remember that both these cases are rare. Few women are so liable to so great mischiefs that may not be prevented at cheaper rates; and, therefore, the indulgence given in these decisions is nothing to the greater part of men, nor is to be extended to ordinary cases. But commonly men everywhere sin by omission of a stricter government of their families and by Eli's sinful indulgence and remissness. Though a wife must be governed as a wife, and a child as a child, yet all must be governed. Though it may be truly said that a man cannot hinder that sin that he cannot hinder but by sin or by contributing to a greater hurt, it is to be concluded that every man is bound to hinder sin whenever he is able lawfully to hinder it.

By the same measure, toleration, or not hindering errors and sins about religion in church and commonwealth, is to be judged. No one must commit them or approve them or forbear duty of their own to cure them; but it is not a duty that is destructive that would be a duty when it is a means of edifying.

---

[63] *Bedlam.*

Chapter Nine

Duties of Parents to Their Children

How great importance the wise and holy education of children is to the saving of their souls, the comfort of their parents, the good of church and state, and the happiness of the world I have partly told you before. But no man is able fully to express this. How great that calamity is that the world is fallen into through the neglect of that duty, no heart can conceive. But they who think what a case the heathen, infidel, and ungodly nations are in, and how rare true piety is grown, and how many millions must lie in hell forever will know so much of this inhuman negligence as to abhor it.

Direction 1: Understand and lament the corrupted and miserable state of your children, which they have derived from you, and thankfully accept the offers of a Savior for yourselves and them, resign and dedicate them to God in Christ in the sacred covenant, and solemnize this dedication and covenant by their baptism (see my *Treatise of Baptism*). To this end understand the command of God for entering your children solemnly into covenant with him and the covenant mercies belonging to them (see Rom. 5:12, 16–18; Eph. 2:1, 3; Gen. 17:4, 13–14; Deut. 29:10–12; Rom. 11:17, 20; John 3:3, 5; Matt. 19:13–14).

You cannot dedicate yourselves to God until you dedicate to him all that is yours and in your power, and therefore your children as far as they are in your power. As nature has taught you your power and your duty to enter them in their infancy into any covenant with man that is certainly for their good (and if they refuse the conditions when they come to age, they forfeit the benefit), so nature teaches you much more to oblige them to God for their far greater good, in case he will admit them into covenant with him. That he will admit them into his covenant (and that you ought to enter them into it) is past doubt, as seen in the evidence that the Scripture gives us that from Abraham's time until Christ's it was so with all the children of his people. Nay, no man can prove that before Abraham's time, or since, God had ever a church on earth of which the infants of his servants, if they had any, were not members dedicated in covenant to God, until of late times when a few began to scruple the lawfulness of this. As it is a comfort to you if the king would bestow upon your infant children (who were tainted by their father's treason) not only a full discharge from the blot of the offense but also the titles and estates of lords, though they understand none of this till they come to age, so is it much more a matter of comfort to you, on their behalf, that God in Christ will pardon their original sin and take them as his children and give them title to everlasting life, which are the mercies of his covenant.

Direction 2: As soon as they are capable, teach them what covenant they are in and what are the benefits and conditions that their souls may gladly consent to when they understand it, and you may bring them to renew their covenant with God in their own persons. But the whole order of teaching children I shall give you later by itself and, therefore, shall here pass by all that except that which is to be done more by your familiar converse than by more solemn teaching.

Direction 3: Train them up in exact obedience to yourselves, and break them of their wills. To that end, do not allow them to act irreverently or contemptuously toward you but to keep their distance, for too much familiarity breeds contempt and leads to disobedience. The common course of parents is to please their children so long by letting them have what they want and what they will, until their wills are so used to being fulfilled that they cannot endure to have them denied and so can endure no government because they endure no crossing of their wills. To be obedient is to renounce their wills and be ruled by their parents' wills; to teach them to have their own wills is to teach them disobedience and to harden them and make it difficult for them to obey. Tell them often, familiarly, and lovingly of the excellency of obedience and how it pleases God and what need they have to be governed and how unfit they are to govern themselves and how dangerous it is to children to have their own wills. Speak often with great disgrace of self-will and stubbornness, and tell others in their hearing what has come of self-willed children.

Direction 4: Make them neither too bold with you, nor too strange or fearful; govern them not as servants but as children, making them perceive that you dearly love them and that all your commands, restraints, and corrections are for their good and not merely because you will have it so. They must be ruled as rational creatures who love themselves and those who love them. If they perceive that you dearly love them, they will obey you the more willingly and will be brought to repent of their disobedience. They will obey you in heart and in outward actions, behind your back and before your face. Their love for you, which must be caused by your love to them, must be one of the chief means to bring them to the love of all that good that you commend to them, and so to form their wills sincerely to the will of God and make them holy. For if you are too distant[1] and too harsh,[2] they will fear you only and not much love you; and then they will not love the books or practices that you commend to them. Like hypocrites, they will seek to please you to your face and care not what they are in secret and behind your backs. Nay, it will tempt them to loathe your government and all that good that you persuade them to and make them like birds in a cage that watch for an opportunity to get away and get their liberty. They will be the more in the company of idle children because your anger and distance make them to take no delight in your presence.

Fear will make them liars as often as a lie seems necessary to their escape. Parents who show much love to their children may safely show severity when their children commit a fault. For then they will see that it is their fault only that displeases you and not their persons; and your love reconciles them to you when they are corrected, while less correction from parents who are always distant or angry and show no tender love to their children will alienate them and do no good. Too much boldness in children leads them, before you

---

[1]*Strange.*
[2]*Terrible.*

are aware, to contempt of parents and all disobedience; too much fear and distance deprives them of most of the benefits of your care and government. Tender love, with severity only when they do amiss, and this at a reverent, convenient distance, is the only way to do them good.

Direction 5: Labor much to possess their hearts with the fear of God and a reverence of the Holy Scriptures; then whatsoever duty you command them or whatsoever sin you forbid them, show them some texts of Scripture for it, and cause them to learn them and often repeat them, that so they may find reason and divine authority in your commands. Until their obedience begins to be rational and divine, it will be but formal and hypocritical. It is conscience that must watch them in private, when you see them not; and conscience is God's officer, not yours. Conscience will say nothing to them until it speaks in the name of God. This is the way to bring the heart into subjection and also to reconcile them to all your commands, when they see that they are first the commands of God.

Direction 6: When you talk of God, Jesus Christ, and the Holy Scripture, or of the life to come or any holy duty, speak always with gravity, seriousness, and reverence of the most great and dreadful and most sacred things. For before children come to have any distinct understanding of particulars, it is a hopeful beginning to have their hearts possessed with a general reverence and high esteem of holy matters; for that will continually awe their consciences, help their judgments, settle them against prejudice and profane contempt, and be as a seed of holiness in them. "The fear of the LORD is the beginning of wisdom" (Ps. 111:10; Prov. 1:7; 9:10). The very manner of the parents' speech and carriage, expressing great reverence for the things of God, has great power to leave a similar impression on a child. Most children of godly parents who came to good, I am persuaded, can tell you by experience (if their parents did their duty in this point) that the first good they felt upon their hearts was a reverence for holy things, which the speech and carriage of their parents taught them.

Direction 7: Speak always before them with great honor and praise of holy ministers and people, and with disapproval[3] and

---

[3]*Dispraise.*

loathing of every sin and of ungodly men (see Isa. 3:7–9, 11; Ps. 10:2–4; 15:4; 101), for this is a thing children will quickly and easily receive from their parents. Before they can understand particular doctrines, they can learn, in general, what kind of persons are most happy or most miserable, and they are very apt to receive a liking or disliking from their parents' judgment, which has a great hand in all the following good or evil of their lives. If you instill[4] them with good and honorable thoughts that fear God, they will be inclined to think well of them and to dislike those who speak evil of them and to hear such preachers and to wish themselves such Christians; so it is in this and the foregoing point that the first stirrings of grace in children are ordinarily felt. Therefore, on the other side, it is a most pernicious thing to children when they hear their parents speak contemptuously or lightly of holy things and persons and irreverently talk of God, Scripture, and the life to come or speak disapprovingly[5] or scornfully of godly ministers or people or make a jest of the particular duties of a religious life. These children are likely to receive that prejudice or profane contempt into their hearts that may bolt the doors against the love of God and holiness and make their salvation a work of much greater difficulty and much smaller hope.

Therefore, I still say that wicked parents are the most notable servants of the Devil in all the world, and the bloodiest enemies to their children's souls. More souls are damned by ungodly parents, and next to them by ungodly ministers and magistrates, than by any instruments in the world. And so whole nations are generally carried away with enmity against the ways of God, the heathen nations against the true God and the infidel nations against Christ and the papist nations against the Reformation and spiritual worshippers, because parents speak evil to the children of those they dislike and so instill[6] them with the same dislike from generation to generation. "Woe to those who call evil good and good evil, who put darkness for light and light for darkness, who put bitter for sweet and sweet for bitter!" (Isa. 5:20).

Direction 8: Let it be the principal part of your care and labor in all their education to make holiness appear to them the most neces-

---

[4]*Possess.*
[5]*Dispraisingly.*
[6]*Possess.*

sary, honorable, gainful, pleasant, delightful, amiable state of life and to keep them from apprehending it as needless, dishonorable, hurtful, or uncomfortable. Especially draw them to the love of it by representing it as lovely. Therefore, begin with that which is easiest and most grateful to them, such as the history of the Scripture and the lives of the martyrs and other good men, and some short, familiar lessons. In restraining them from sin, you must go to the highest step at first and not think to draw them from it by allowing them the least degree, for every degree disposes to more, and none is to be allowed, and a general reformation is the easiest as well as absolutely necessary. Yet in putting them upon the practice of religious duties, you must carry them on by degrees and put them at first upon no more than they can bear, either upon the learning of doctrines too high and spiritual for them or upon such duty for quality or quantity as is over-burdensome to them. For if you once turn their hearts against religion and make it seem like slavery and a tedious life to them, you take the course to harden them against it.

Therefore, all children must not be used alike, just as all stomachs must not be forced to eat alike. If you force some to take so much as to overindulge,[7] they will loathe that sort of food as long as they live. I know that nature itself, as corrupt, has already an enmity to holiness, and I know that this enmity is not to be indulged in children. I know that misrepresentations of religion, imprudent education, is the way to increase it and that the enmity being in the heart, it is change of mind and love that is the overcoming of it, and not any such constraint as tends not to reconcile the mind by love. The whole skill of parents for the holy education of their children consists in this, to make them conceive holiness as the most amiable and desirable life by representing it to them in words and practice not only as necessary but also as profitable, honorable, and delightful. "Her ways are ways of pleasantness, and all her paths are peace" (Prov. 3:17).

Direction 9: Speak often to them of the vileness[8] and sinfulness of sensuality and of the greater worth of the pleasure of the mind, which consists in wisdom and doing good. Your chief care must be to save them from pleasing the flesh, which is not only the sum of

---

[7]*Become a surfeit.*
[8]*Brutish baseness.*

all iniquity but that to which children are most prone. For their flesh and sense is as quick as others. They want not only faith but clear reason to resist it, and so, besides their natural depravity,[9] the custom of obeying sense without reason, which is in infancy and almost useless, increases this wicked sin. Therefore, labor to imprint in their minds an odious conceit of a flesh-pleasing life; speak bitterly to them against gluttony, drunkenness, and excess of sport. Let them often hear or read the parable of the glutton and Lazarus in Luke 16; and let them memorize Romans 8:1, 5–9, 13; 13:13–14 and often repeat them.

Direction 10: To this end, and also for the health of their bodies, keep a strict guard upon their appetites, which they are not able to guard themselves. Keep them as exactly as you can to the rules of reason, both in the quantity and quality of their food. Yet tell them the reason of your restraint, or else they will secretly strive to break their bounds. Most parents are guilty of the great hurt and danger of their children's health and souls by overindulging them with food and drink. If I should call them "devils" and "murderers" to their own children, they would think I spoke too harshly; but I would not have them give so great occasion for it as by destroying, as far as in them lies, the souls and bodies of their children. They destroy their souls by accustoming them to gluttony and to be ruled by their appetites, which all the teaching in the world will hardly overcome without the special grace of God. What is all the vice and villainy in the world but the pleasing of the desires of the flesh? And when they are habituated to this, they are rooted in their sin and misery. They destroy their bodies by suffering them to please their appetites with raw fruits and other hurtful things, but especially by drowning and overwhelming nature by excess; and all this is through ignorance, joined with self-conceitedness, which makes them to overthrow themselves.

They think that their appetite is the measure of their eating and drinking and that if they drink but when they are thirsty (as some drunkards are continually) and eat but when they are hungry, it is no excess; and because they are not presently sick or vomit it not up, they think it does no harm but good. You shall hear them like the insane[10] say, "I warrant them, it will do them no harm to eat and

---

[9]*Pravity.*
[10]*Mad people.*

drink when they will; it will make them strong and healthful. I do not see that anyone who keeps a strict diet is any healthier than others." While they do this, they destroy themselves and are brought to an untimely end. Therefore, if you love either the souls or the bodies of your children, teach them temperance from their infancy, and do not let their appetites or cravings, but your own reason, be the measure of their diet. Teach them to eat sparingly, and let it be of the coarser rather than the finer sort of diet. See it measured to them yourselves, and do not let them eat or drink between meals and out of season; and so you will help to overcome their sensual inclinations and give reason the mastery of their lives, and you will, under God, do as much as any one thing can do to help them to a healthful temper of body, which will be a great mercy to them and fit them for their duty all their lives.

Direction 11: For sports and recreations, let them be such and so much as may be needful to their health and cheerfulness, but not so much as may carry away their minds from better things and draw them from their books or other duties, nor such as may tempt them to gaming or covetousness. Children must have convenient sport for the health of the body and alacrity of the mind; such as exercises their bodies is best, and not such as stirs them. Cards and dice and such idle sports are most unfit, tending to hurt both body and mind. Their time must be limited them, that their play may not be their work. As soon as they have the use of reason and speech, they should be taught better things and not left until they are five or six years of age to do nothing but get a custom of wasting all their time in play. Children are capable of learning something early that may prepare them for more.

Direction 12: Use all your wisdom and diligence to root out the sin of pride. To that end, do not, as is usual with foolish parents, please them with making them fine and then by telling them how fine they are, but rather commend humility and plainness to them and speak disgracefully of pride and fineness and teach an averseness to it in their minds. Cause them to learn such texts of Scripture as speak of God's abhorring and resisting the proud and of his loving and honoring the humble. When they see other children who are finely clothed, speak of it as their shame, that they may not desire to be like them. Speak against boasting and every other way of pride to which they are liable. Give them the praise of all that is well, for that is their due encouragement.

Direction 13: Speak to them disgracefully of the gallantry and pomp and riches of the world and of the sin of selfishness and covetousness, and diligently watch against it and all that may tempt them to it. When they see great houses, attendance, and gallantry, tell them that these are the Devil's baits to entice poor sinners to love this world, that they may lose their souls and the world to come. Tell them how much heaven excels all this, and that the lovers of the world will never come thither but only the humble, meek, and poor in spirit. Tell them of the rich glutton in Luke 16 who was clothed in purple and silk and fared deliciously every day; but when he came to hell, he could not get a drop of water to cool his tongue, while Lazarus was in the joys of paradise. Do not behave as the wicked, who entice their children to worldliness and covetousness by giving them money and letting them play for money and promising them to make them fine or rich and speaking highly of all who are rich and great in the world. Rather, tell them how much happier a poor believer is, and withdraw all that may tempt their minds to covetousness. Teach them how good it is to love their brethren as themselves and to give them part of what they have, and praise them for it. Dispraise them when they are greedy to keep or heap up all to themselves, and all will be little enough to cure this wicked[11] sin. Teach them such texts as Psalm 10:3, "For the wicked boasts of the desires of his soul, and the one greedy for gain curses and renounces the LORD."

Direction 14: Watch their tongues, especially against lying, railing, unclean[12] talk, and taking the name of God in vain. Pardon them many lighter faults about common matters sooner than one such sin against God. Tell them of the odiousness of all these sins, and teach them the texts that most condemn them; and never pass it by or make light of it when you find them guilty.

Direction 15: Keep them, as much as possible, from ill company, especially of ungodly playmates. This is one of the greatest dangers for the undoing of children in the world, especially when they are sent to common schools, for there is scarce any of those schools so

---

[11]*Pernicious.*
[12]*Ribald.*

good but they have many rude and ungodly children who speak profanely and filthily and make their unclean[13] and railing speeches a
matter of boasting. Besides fighting, gaming, scorning, and neglecting their lessons, they will make scorn of him who does not follow
them, if not beat and abuse him. There is such tinder in nature for
these sparks to catch upon that there are very few children but when
they hear others take God's name in vain or sing wanton songs or
talk filthy words or call one another by reproachful names quickly
imitate them.

When you have watched over them at home as closely[14] as you
can, they are infected abroad with such vices as they are hardly
after cured of. Therefore, let those who are able either educate their
children at home or in private and well-ordered schools; those who
cannot do so must be the more watchful over them and charge them
to associate with the best. Speak to them of the odiousness of these
practices and the wickedness of those who use them, and speak very
disgracefully of such ungodly children, and when all is done, it is
a great mercy of God if they are not undone. Those, therefore, who
venture their children into the worst[15] schools and company, and
after that to Rome and other profane or popish countries to learn
the fashions and customs of the world, upon pretense that else they
will be ignorant of the course of the world and ill-bred and not like
others of their rank, may think of themselves and their own reasons
as well as they please. For my part, I would rather make a chimney-
sweeper of my son, if I had any, than be guilty of doing so much to
sell or betray him to the Devil.

Question: Is it not lawful for a man to send his son to travel?

Answer: Yes, in these cases: 1. In case he is a ripe, confirmed
Christian who is not in danger of being perverted but is able to resist
the enemies of the truth and to preach the gospel or to do good to others and withal have sufficient business to invite him. 2. Or if he go
in the company of wise and godly persons and the probability of his
gain be greater than of his loss and danger. 3. Or if he goes only into
religious countries, among more wise and learned men than he con-
verses with at home, and has sufficient motives for his course. But to

---

[13]*Ribald.*
[14]*Narrowly.*
[15]*Rudest.*

send young, raw, unsettled persons among papists and profane, licentious people, though perhaps some sober person be in company with them, and this only to see the countries and fashions of the world, is an action unbecoming[16] any Christian who knows the depravity[17] of human nature and the mutability of young, unfurnished heads and the subtlety of deceivers and the contagiousness of sin and error and the worth of a soul and will not do as some conjurers or witches, even selling a soul to the Devil, on condition he may see and know the fashions of the world; which alas, I can quickly know enough of to grieve my heart without traveling so far to see them. If another country has more of Christ and is nearer heaven, the invitation is great; but if it has more of sin and hell, I would rather know hell and its suburbs too by the map of the Word of God than by going there. If such children return not the confirmed children of the Devil and prove not the calamity of their country and the church, let them thank special grace, and not their parents or themselves.

Direction 16: Teach your children to know the preciousness of time, and do not allow them to misspend an hour. Often speak to them how precious a thing time is, how short man's life is, how great his work, and how our endless life of joy or misery depends on this little time. Warn them of the sin of those who play and idle away their time; keep account of all their hours, and suffer them not to lose any by excess of sleep or excess of play or any other way; but engage them in some employment that is worth their time.

Train up your children in a life of diligence and labor, and teach them not to ease and idleness when they are young. Our wandering beggars, and too many of the gentry, undo their children by this means, especially young women. They are taught no calling, nor exercised in any employment, but only such as suits for nothing but ornament and recreation, and therefore should have but recreation hours, which is but a small proportion of their time. By the sin of their parents, they are engaged in a life of idleness, which afterward is difficult for them to overcome. Those who live only to live are taught to live like swine or vermin and accomplish few things in the world; and so they rise, dress, adorn themselves, take a walk, and go to dinner, then to cards and dice or chat and idle talk or to some

---

[16]*Unbeseeming.*
[17]*Pravity.*

play or recreation and so on, the lamentable life of too many who have great obligations to God and greater things to do, if they were acquainted with them.

If they interpose a few hypocritical, heartless words of prayer, they think they have piously spent the day; yea, the health of many is utterly ruined by such idle, fleshly education. So that disuse disables them from any considerable motion or exercise that is necessary to preserve their health. It would move one's heart with pity to see how the houses of some of the higher sort are like hospitals; and education has made many, especially women, like the lame, sick, or bedridden, so that one part of the day that should be spent in some profitable employment is spent in bed and the rest in doing nothing or worse than nothing. Most of their life is made miserable by diseases, so that if their legs are used to carry them about, they are out of breath, and they are a burden to themselves, and few live out little more than half their days. Whereas, poor creatures, if their own parents had not betrayed them into the sins of Sodom, pride, fullness of bread, and abundance of idleness, they might have been in health and lived like honest Christian people, and their legs and arms might have served them good use.

Direction 17: Let necessary correction be used with discretion, according to the following rules: First, do not let it be so seldom as to leave them fearless and so make it ineffectual; and let it not be so frequent as to discourage them or breed in them a hatred of their parents. Second, let it be different according to the different tempers of your children. Some are so tender and timorous and apt to be discouraged that little or no correction may be best; and some are so hardened and obstinate that it must be much and sharp correction that will keep them from dissoluteness and contempt. Third, let it be more for sin against God (as lying, railing, filthy speaking, and profaneness) than for faults about your worldly business. Fourth, correct them not in passion, but wait till they perceive that you are calmed; for they will think else that your anger rather than your reason is the cause. Fifth, always show them the tenderness of your love and how unwilling you are to correct them if they could be reformed any easier way; and convince them that you do it for their good.

Sixth, make them read those texts of Scripture that condemn

their sin and then those that command you to correct them. For example, if lying is their sin, turn them first to Proverbs 12:22, "Lying lips are an abomination to the LORD, but those who act faithfully are his delight" and Proverbs 13:5, "The righteous hates falsehood." These texts as well: "You are of your father the devil. . . . When he lies, he speaks out of his own character, for he is a liar and the father of lies" (John 8:44). "Outside are the dogs and sorcerers and the sexually immoral and murderers and idolaters, and everyone who loves and practices falsehood" (Rev. 22:15). Next turn him to Proverbs 13:24, "Whoever spares the rod hates his son, but he who loves him is diligent to discipline him" and Proverbs 29:15, "The rod and reproof give wisdom, but a child left to himself brings shame to his mother" and Proverbs 22:15, "Folly is bound up in the heart of a child, but the rod of discipline drives it far from him" and Proverbs 23:13–14, "Do not withhold discipline from a child; if you strike him with a rod, he will not die. If you strike him with the rod, you will save his soul from Sheol" and, lastly, Proverbs 19:18, "Discipline your son, for there is hope; do not set your heart on putting him to death." Ask your child whether he would have you, by sparing him, to disobey God, hate him, and so destroy his soul. When his reason is convinced of the reasonableness of correcting him, it will be more successful.

Direction 18: Let your own example teach your children the holiness and heavenliness and blamelessness of tongue and life that you desire them to learn and practice. The example of parents is most powerful with children, both for good and evil. If they see you live in the fear of God, it will do much to persuade them that is the most necessary and excellent course of life, and that they must do so too. If they see you live a carnal, sensual,[18] and ungodly life and hear you curse or swear or talk filthily or complainingly,[19] it will greatly embolden them to imitate you. If you do not speak well to them, they will sooner believe your bad lives than your good words.

Direction 19: Choose such a calling and course of life for your children as tends most to the saving of their souls and to their public usefulness for church or state. Do not choose a calling that is most liable to temptations and hindrances to their salvation, though it

---

[18]*Voluptuous.*
[19]*Railingly.*

may make them rich; rather choose a calling that allows them some leisure for remembering things of everlasting consequence and fit opportunities to get and to do good.

Direction 20: When they are ready for marriage, and you find it needful, look for suitable partners for them. When parents wait too long and do not their duties in this, their children often choose for themselves to their own undoing; for they choose not by judgment, but by blind affection.

Remember these two directions: first, that the mother, who is still present with children when they are young, be diligent in teaching them and reminding them of good things. When the fathers are abroad, the mothers have more frequent opportunities to instruct them and to speak to them that which is most necessary and to watch over them. This is the greatest service that most women can do for God in the world. Many a church that has been blessed with a good minister may thank the pious education of mothers; and many a thousand souls in heaven may thank the holy care and diligence of mothers as the first effectual means. Good women this way, by the good education of their children, are great blessings to church and state. (Some understand "childbearing," 1 Tim. 2:15, to mean "bringing up children for God," but I rather think it is Mary's bearing Christ, the promised seed.)

Second, let children be taught to read; otherwise you deprive them of a singular help to their instruction and salvation. It is a thousand pities that a Bible should signify no more than a chip to a rational creature as to their reading it themselves and that so many excellent books as are in the world should be as sealed or insignificant to them.

If God denies you children and saves you all this care and labor, do not be discontent[20] but be thankful, believing it is best for you. Remember what a deal of duty, pains, and heart's grief he has freed you from, and how few fare[21] well when parents have done their best. What a life of misery children must here pass through, and how sad the fear of their sin and damnation would have been to you.

---

[20]*Repine not.*
[21]*Speed.*

Chapter Ten

Duties of Children to Their Parents

T hough precepts to children are not of so much force as to those of riper age because of their natural incapacity and childish passions and pleasures, which bear down their weak degree of reason, yet something is to be said to them because the measure of reason that they do have is to be exercised and by exercise to be improved. Those of riper years, while they have parents, must know and do their duty to them. God blesses even children as they perform their duties.

Direction 1: Be sure that you dearly love your parents. Delight to be in their company. Do not be like those unnatural children who love the company of their idle playfellows better than their parents' and would rather be about their sports than in their parents' sight. Remember that you have your being from them and come from their loins; remember what sorrow you have cost them, and what care they take for your education and provision; remember how tenderly they have loved you, and what grief it will be to their hearts if you go astray,[1] and how much your happiness will make them glad; remember what love you owe them both by nature and in justice for all their love to you and all that they have done for you. They take your happiness or misery to be one of the greatest parts of the happiness or misery of their lives. Do not deprive them then of their happiness by depriving yourselves of your own; do not make their

---

[1] *Miscarry.*

lives miserable by undoing yourselves. Though they chide, restrain, and correct you, do not abate your love to them, for this is their duty, which God requires, and they do it for your good. It is a sign of a wicked child if he loves his parents less because they correct him and will not let him have his will. Though your parents have many faults themselves, you must love them as your parents still.

Direction 2: Honor your parents in your thoughts, speeches, and behavior. Do not think dishonorably or contemptuously of them in your hearts. Do not speak dishonorably, rudely, irreverently, or saucily either to or of them. Yea, though your parents are never so poor in the world or weak of understanding, yea, though they were ungodly, you must honor them notwithstanding all this. Though you cannot honor them as rich, wise, or godly, you must honor them as your parents. Remember that the fifth commandment has a special promise of temporal blessing: "Honor your father and your mother, that your days may be long in the land that the LORD your God is giving you" (Ex. 20:12; Eph. 6:2). Consequently, those who dishonor their parents have a special curse even in this life, and the justice of God is seen in the execution of it. Those who despise and dishonor their parents seldom prosper in the world. There are five sorts of sinners that God uses to overtake with vengeance, even in this life. First, perjured persons and false witnesses; second, murderers; third, persecutors; fourth, sacrilegious persons; and fifth, those who dishonor their parents. Remember the curse on Ham (Gen. 9:22, 25). It is a fearful thing to see and hear how ungodly children talk contemptuously and rudely to their parents, argue and contend with them, contradict them, and speak to them as if they were equals; and at last they will grow even to abuse and defame them. "The eye that mocks a father and scorns to obey a mother will be picked out by the ravens of the valley and eaten by the vultures" (Prov. 30:17).

Direction 3: Obey your parents in all things that God does not forbid. Remember that as nature has made you unfit to govern yourselves, so God, in nature, has mercifully provided governors for you. Here I shall first tell you what obedience is and then tell you why you must be thus obedient. First, to obey your parents is to do that which they command you and forbear that which they forbid you, because it is their will you should do so. You must 1. Have in your minds a desire to please them and be glad when you can please them and sorry when you offend them. And then, 2. You must not set your wit or your will against theirs but readily obey their commands, without unwillingness, murmuring, or disputing. Though you think your own way is best and your own desires are reasonable, your own wit and will must be subjected unto theirs, or else how do you obey them? Second, for the reasons of your obedience: 1. Consider it is the will of God that it should be so, and he has made them as his officers to govern you; and in disobeying them, you disobey him. "Children, obey your parents in the Lord, for this is right. 'Honor your father and mother' (this is the first commandment with a promise), 'that it may go well with you and that you may live long in the land'" (Eph. 6:1–3). "Children, obey your parents in everything, for this pleases the Lord" (Col. 3:20). "Listen to your father who gave you life, and do not despise your mother when she is old" (Prov. 23:22). "A wise son hears his father's instruction, but a scoffer does not listen to rebuke" (Prov. 13:1). "Hear, my son, your father's instruction, and forsake not your mother's teaching, for they are a graceful garland for your head and pendants for your neck" (Prov. 1:8–9).

2. Consider also that your parents' government is necessary for your own good and it is a government of love. As your bodies would have perished if your parents or some others had not taken care for you when you could not help yourselves, so your minds would be untaught and ignorant, even like animals,[2] if you had not others to teach and govern you. Nature teaches the chickens to follow the hen, and all things, when they are young, to be led and guided by their mothers;[3] else what would become of them? 3. Consider also that they must be accountable to God for you. If they leave you to yourselves, it may be their destruction as well as yours, as the sad example of Eli tells you. Do not rebel, therefore, against those whom God, by nature and Scripture, has set over you. Though the fifth commandment requires obedience to princes, masters, pastors, and other superiors, it names your father and mother only because they are the first of all your governors, to whom by nature you are most obliged.

But perhaps you will say that though little children must be ruled by their parents, yet you are grown up to riper age and are

---

[2]*Brutes.*
[3]*Dams.*

wise enough to rule yourselves. I answer, God does not think so; otherwise, he would not have set governors over you. And are you wiser than he? There are few in the world wise enough to rule themselves; otherwise God would not have set princes, magistrates, pastors, and teachers over them, as he has done. God loves you better than to leave you without guidance,[4] knowing that youth is rash and inexperienced.

Question: How long are children to remain under the command and government of their parents?

Answer: There are several acts and degrees of parents' government, according to the several ends and uses of it. Some acts of their government are to teach you to go and speak, and some to teach you your labor and calling, and some to teach you good manners and the fear of God or the knowledge of the Scriptures, and some to settle you in a course of living in which you shall need their close oversight no more. When any of these ends are attained, and you have all to which your parents' government can help you, then you are past that part of their government. But still you owe them not only love, honor, and reverence but obedience in all things in which they are still appointed for your help and guidance. Even when you are married and separate from them, though you have a propriety in your own estates, and they have not so strict a charge of you as before, yet if they command you your duty to God or them, you are still obliged to obey them.

Direction 4: Be content with your parents' provision for you and disposal of you. Do not rebelliously murmur against them and complain of their use of you, much less take anything against their wills. It is the part of fleshly rebels, and not of obedient children, to be discontent and murmur because they do not fare better or because they are kept from sports and play or because they do not have better clothes or because they do not have money allowed them to spend or use at their own discretion. Are you not under your parents' government, and not of enemies? Are your lusts and pleasures fitter to govern you than your parents' discretion? Be thankful for what you have, and remember that you do not deserve it but have it freely; it is your pride or your fleshly sensuality that makes you murmur, and not any wisdom or virtue in you. Humble your pride and fleshly mind, and

---

[4]*Masterless.*

then you will not be so eager to have your will. What if your parents deal too hardly with you in your food, clothing,[5] or expenses? What harm does it do you? Nothing but a selfish, sensual mind would make so great a matter of it. It is a hundred times more dangerous to your souls and bodies to be bred too high and fed too full and daintily than to be bred too low and fed too hardly. One tends to pride, gluttony, wantonness, and the overthrow of health and life; the other tends to a humble, mortified, self-denying life and to the health and soundness of the body. Remember how the earth opened and swallowed all those rebellious murmerers who grudged against Moses and Aaron (Numbers 16; read it, and apply it to your case). Remember the story of Absalom and the folly of the prodigal (Luke 15). Do not desire to be at your own disposal or be eager to have the vain desire of your heart. While you are content and submit to your parents, you are on God's way and may expect his blessing; but when you insist on your own way, you may expect the punishment of rebels.

Direction 5: Humble and submit yourselves to any labor to which your parents shall appoint you. Take heed, as you love your souls, lest a proud heart makes you murmur and say, "This work is too low for me" or lest a lazy mind and body make you say, "This work is too hard for me" or lest a foolish, playful mind makes you weary of your book or labor, that you may be at your sports, and say, "This is too tedious for me." It is little or no hurt that is likely to befall you by your labor and diligence; but it is a dangerous thing to get a habit or custom of idleness and voluptuousness in your youth.

Direction 6: Be willing and thankful to be instructed by your parents or any of your teachers, especially about the fear of God and the matters of your salvation. These are the matters that you are born and live for; these are the things that your parents have first the charge to teach you. Without knowledge and holiness all the riches and honors of the world are worth nothing; all your pleasures will undo you (read Mr. Thomas White's *A Little Book for Little Children* and Mark 9:36; 10:14, 16).[6] Oh, what a comfort it is to understand-

---

[5]*Raiment.*

[6]Thomas White's *A Little Book for Little Children* was published in 1660. It was a pioneer work in that it attempted to address the very young, whom White addressed as "my dear pretty children." For further information on this genre of children's literature, see Gillian Avery, "Intimations of Mortality: The Puritan and Evangelical Message to Children," in *Representation of Childhood Death*, ed. Gillian Avery and Kimberley Reynolds (New York: Macmillan, 2000), 87–110.

ing parents to see their children willing to learn and love the Word
of God and lay it up in their hearts and talk of it and obey it and
prepare for everlasting life! If such children die before their parents,
how joyfully may they part with them as into the arms of Christ,
who said, "for to such belongs the kingdom of heaven" (Matt. 19:14).
If the parents die first, how joyfully may they leave behind them a
holy seed that is likely to serve God in their generation and to follow
them to heaven and live with them forever! But whether they live
or die, how heartbreaking to parents are ungodly children who love
not the Word and way of God and love not to be taught or restrained
from their own licentious courses.

Direction 7: Patiently submit to the correction that your parents
lay upon you. Consider that God has commanded them to do it to
save your souls from hell and that they hate you if they do not correct
you when there is cause. They must not spare for your crying (Prov.
13:24; 22:15; 29:15; 23:13–14; 19:18). It is not for their delight but for
your own necessity. Avoid the fault, and you may escape the correction. Your parents would rather see you obedient than to hear you
cry! It is not because of them but of yourselves that you are corrected.
Be angry with yourselves and not with them. It is a wicked child who
instead of being made better by correction will hate his parents for
it and so grow worse. Correction is a means of God's appointment;
therefore, go to God on your knees in prayer, and entreat him to bless
and sanctify it to you, that it may do you good.

Direction 8: Do not choose your own company, but use such company as by your parents is appointed you. Bad company is the first
undoing of a child. When, for the love of sport, you choose such playfellows as are idle, licentious, and disobedient and will teach you to
curse, swear, lie, talk filthily, and draw you from your book or duty,
this is the Devil's highway to hell. Your parents are fittest to choose
your company.

Direction 9: Do not choose your own calling or trade of life without the choice or consent of your parents. You may tell them what
you are most inclined to, but it belongs more to them than to you to
make the choice; and it is your part to bring your will to theirs. If
your parents choose a calling for you that is unlawful, you may, with
humble submissiveness, refuse it. If it is only inconvenient, you have

liberty afterward to change it for a better if you can, when you are no longer under their disposal and government.

Direction 10: Do not marry without your parents' consent. Nay, if it may be, let their choice first determine the person, and not your own. Inexperienced youth chooses by fancy and passion, when your experienced parents will choose by judgment. But if they would force you to join yourselves to those who are ungodly and would make your lives either sinful or miserable, you may humbly refuse them. But you must remain unmarried while, by the use of right means, you live in chastity until your parents are in a better mind. If indeed you have a real necessity of marrying, and your parents will consent to none but one of a false religion or one who is utterly unfit for you, in such a case they forfeit their authority at this point that is given them for their edification and not for your destruction; then you should consult other friends who are more wise and faithful. If you suffer your affections to contradict your parents' wills and pretend a necessity that you cannot change your affections, as if your folly were incurable, this is to enter sinfully into that state of life that should have been sanctified to God, that he might have blessed it to you.

Direction 11: If your parents are in want, it is your duty to relieve them according to your ability, yea, and wholly to maintain them if there is need. For it is not possible by all that you can do that you can ever be on even terms with them or ever repay[7] them for what you have received from them. It is base inhumanity, when parents come to poverty, for children to put them off with some short allowance and to make them live like their servants when you have riches and plenty for yourselves. Your parents should be maintained by you as your superiors, and not as inferiors. See that they fare as well as yourselves; yea, though you did not get your riches by their means, yet even for your being you are their debtors for more than that.

Direction 12: Imitate your parents in all that is good, both when they are living and when they are dead. If they were lovers of God and of his Word and service and of those who fear him, let their example provoke you, and let the love that you have to them engage you in this imitation. A wicked child of godly parents is one of the most miserable wretches in the world. With what horror do I look on

---

[7] *Requite.*

such a person! How near is such a wretch to hell! When father and mother were eminent for godliness and daily instructed them in the matters of their salvation and prayed with them and warned them and prayed for them, and after all this the children prove covetous or drunkards or whoremongers or profane and enemies to the servants of God and deride or neglect the way of their religious parents, it makes one tremble to look such wretches in the face. For though there is some hope for them, alas, it is so little that they are next to desperate. When they are hardened under the most excellent means, and the light has blinded them, and their acquaintance with the ways of God has turned their hearts more against them, what means is left to do good to such resisters of the grace of God? The likeliest is some heavy dreadful judgment. Oh, what a woeful day will it be to them when all the prayers, tears, teachings, and good examples of their religious parents shall witness against them! How will they be confounded before the Lord! And how sad a thought is it to the heart of holy, diligent parents to think that all their prayers and pains must witness against their graceless children and sink them deeper into hell!

And yet, alas, how many such woeful spectacles there are before our eyes! How deeply does the church of God suffer by the malice and wickedness of the children of those parents who taught them better and walked before them in a holy, exemplary life! But if parents are ignorant, superstitious, idolatrous, popish, or profane, their children are forward enough to imitate them. Then they can say, "Our forefathers were of this mind, and we hope they are saved; and we would rather imitate them than such innovating reformers as you." They said to Jeremiah, "As for the word that you have spoken to us in the name of the LORD, we will not listen to you. But we will do everything that we have vowed, make offerings to the queen of heaven and pour out drink offerings to her, as we did, both we and our fathers, our kings and our officials, in the cities of Judah and in the streets of Jerusalem. For then we had plenty of food, and prospered, and saw no disaster. But since we left off making offerings to the queen of heaven and pouring out drink offerings to her, we have lacked everything and have been consumed by the sword and by famine" (Jer. 44:16–18). Thus they "have stubbornly followed their own hearts and have gone after the Baals, as their fathers taught them" (Jer. 9:14); and so they "forget my name by their dreams that they tell one another, even as their fathers forgot my name for Baal" (Jer. 23:27). "They and their fathers have transgressed against me to this very day" (Ezek. 2:3); yea, "They did worse than their fathers" (Jer. 7:26).

Thus, in error and sin they can imitate their forefathers, when they should rather remember that it cost Christ his blood to ransom them "from the futile ways inherited from your forefathers" (1 Pet. 1:18). They should penitently confess, as did Daniel, "To us, O LORD, belongs open shame, to our kings, to our princes, and to our fathers, because we have sinned against you" (Dan. 9:8). And as Psalm 106:6 says, "Both we and our fathers have sinned; we have committed iniquity; we have done wickedness." God says, "Because your fathers have forsaken me . . . and because you have done worse than your fathers . . . I will hurl you out of this land" (Jer. 16:11–13). "Have you forgotten the evil of your fathers, the evil of the kings of Judah . . . ? They have not humbled themselves even to this day" (Jer. 44:9–10). "Do not be like your fathers, to whom the former prophets cried out, 'Thus says the LORD of hosts, Return from your evil ways and from your evil deeds.' But they did not hear or pay attention to me" (Zech. 1:4). "From the days of your fathers you have turned aside from my statutes and have not kept them. Return to me, and I will return to you" (Mal. 3:7). "Do not walk in the statutes of your fathers" (Ezek. 20:18). Do not follow your fathers in their sin and error, but follow them as they follow Christ. "Be imitators of me, as I am of Christ" (1 Cor. 11:1).

Chapter Eleven

Duties of Children and Youth to God

Though I put your duty to your parents first, because it is first learned, your duty to God is your greatest and most necessary duty. Learn the following precepts well.

Direction 1: Learn to understand the covenant and vow that, in your baptism, you made with God the Father, Son, and Holy Spirit, your Creator, Redeemer, and Regenerator. When you understand it well, renew that covenant with God and deliver yourselves to him as your Creator, Redeemer, Sanctifier, Owner, Ruler, Father, and happiness.[1] Baptism is not an idle ceremony but solemnly entering into a covenant with God, in which you receive the greatest mercies and bind yourselves to the greatest duties. It is the entering into that way in which you must walk all your lives and an avowing that to God that you must be still performing. Though your parents had authority to promise for you, it is you who must perform it, for it was you that they obliged. If you ask by what authority they obliged you in covenant to God, I answer, by the authority that God has given them in nature and in Scripture as they oblige you to be subjects of the King or as they enter your names into any covenant, by lease or other contract, that is for your benefit. They do it for good, that you may have part in the blessings of the covenant. If you grudge at it and refuse your own consent when you come to age, you lose the benefits. If you think they did you wrong, you may be out of the covenant,

---

[1] *Felicity.*

if you renounce the kingdom of heaven. It is much wiser to be thankful to God that your parents were the means of so great a blessing to you and to do again that which they did for you and openly, with thankfulness, to own the covenant in which you are engaged and live in the performance and in the comforts of it all your days.

Direction 2: Remember that you are entering into the way to everlasting life, and not into a place of happiness or continuance. Therefore, set your hearts on heaven, and make it the design of all your lives to live in heaven with Christ forever. O happy you if God will soon[2] teach you to know what it is that must make you happy and if at your first setting out, your end is right and your faces are heavenward! Remember that as soon as you begin to live, you are hurrying[3] toward the end of your lives. Even as a candle wastes as soon as it begins to burn, and the hourglass as soon as it is turned, hurrying[4] to its end, so as soon as you begin to live, your lives are dying and moving[5] toward your final hour. As a runner, as soon as he begins his race, hurries[6] to the end of it, so are your lives, even in your youngest time. It is another kind of life that you must live forever rather than this trifling, pitiful, fleshly life. Prepare, therefore, for that for which God sent you to prepare. Oh, happy you if you begin and go on with cheerful resolution to the end! It is blessed wisdom to be wise and to know the worth of your time in childhood, before any of it is wasted and lost upon the foolishness[7] of the world. Then you may grow wise indeed and will be treasuring up understanding and growing in sweet acquaintance with the Lord, when others are going backward and daily making work for sad repentance or final desperation. "Remember also your Creator in the days of your youth, before the evil days come and the years draw near of which you will say, 'I have no pleasure in them'" (Eccles. 12:1).

Direction 3: Remember that you have corrupted natures to be cured and that Christ is the Physician who must cure them. The Spirit of Christ must dwell within you and make you holy and give you a new heart and nature, which shall love God and heaven above

---

[2]*Betimes.*
[3]*Hasting.*
[4]*Hasting.*
[5]*In a consumption, and posting.*
[6]*Is hasting.*
[7]*Fooleries.*

all the honors and pleasures of the world. Do not rest, therefore, until you find that you are born anew and that the Holy Spirit has made you holy and quickened your hearts with the love of God and of your dear Redeemer (2 Cor. 5:17; Rom. 8:9, 13; John 3:3, 5–6). The old nature loves the things of this world and the pleasures of the flesh; but the new nature loves the Lord who made, redeemed, and renewed you and the endless joys of the world to come and the holy life that is the way to it.

Direction 4: Take heed of loving the pleasures of the flesh, eating too much or drinking or play. Do not set your hearts upon your belly or your sport; let your meat and sleep and play be moderate. Do not meddle with cards or dice or any bewitching or riotous sports; do not play for money, as it stirs up covetous desires and tempts you to be overzealous, to lie, wrangle, and fall out with others. Do not use food or sports that are not for your health—a greedy appetite entices children to devour raw fruits and to rob their neighbors' orchards and at once to undo both soul and body. An excessive love of play causes them to run among bad companions, loses their time, and destroys their love of books and duty and their parents themselves and everything that is good. You must eat, sleep, and play for health and not for useless, hurtful pleasure (1 Cor. 10:31).

Direction 5: Subdue your wills and desires to the will of God and your superiors, and do not be set upon by anything that God or your parents deny you. Do not be like those self-willed, fleshly children who are importunate for anything that their fancy or appetite would have and cry or are discontent if they do not have it. Do not say, "I must have this or that," but be content with anything that is the will of God and your superiors. It is the greatest misery and danger in the world to have everything you want and to be given to your heart's desire (Ps. 81:10–12).

Direction 6: Take heed of a custom of foolish, filthy railing, lying, or any other sinful words. You think it is a small matter, but God does not think so. It is not a jesting matter to sin against the God who made you; fools make sport with sin (Prov. 14:9; 10:23; 26:19). One lie, one curse, one oath, one debauched,[8] railing, or deriding word is worse than all the pain that your flesh ever endured.

---

[8]*Ribald.*

Direction 7: Take heed of such company and playfellows as would entice and tempt you to any of these sins, and choose such company as will help you in the fear of God. If others mock you, do not care for it more than the shaking of a leaf or the barking of a dog. Take heed of lewd and wicked company, as you care for the saving of your souls. If you hear them rail or lie or swear or talk filthily, do not be ashamed to tell them that God forbids you to keep company with them (Ps. 119:63; Prov. 13:20; 18:7; 1 Cor. 5:12; Eph. 5:11).

Direction 8: Take heed of pride and covetousness. Do not desire to be glamorous[9] or to get all for yourselves, but to be humble and meek and love one another and as glad that others are pleased as yourselves.

Direction 9: Love the Word of God and all good books that would make you wiser and better; do not read plays, tale-books, love-books, or any idle stories. When idle children are at play and engage in foolish behavior,[10] let it be your pleasure to read and learn the mysteries of your salvation.

Direction 10: Remember to keep the Lord's Day holy. Do not spend it in play or idleness. Reverence the ministers of Christ, and mark what they teach you, and remember it is a message from God about the saving of your souls. Ask your parents when you come home to help your understandings and memories in anything that you do not understand or forgot. Love all the holy exercises of the Lord's Day, and let them be more pleasant to you than your meat or play.

Direction 11: Be as careful to practice all as to hear and read it. Remember that all is to make you holy, to love God and obey him; take heed of sinning against your knowledge and against the warnings that are given you.

Direction 12: When you grow up, by the direction of your parents choose such a trade or calling as allows you the greatest helps for heaven and has the fewest hindrances and in which you may be most serviceable to God before you die. If you will practice these few directions (which even your own hearts must say have no harm in them), what happy persons will you be forever!

---

[9]*Fine.*
[10]*Fooleries.*

Chapter Twelve

Directions for the Right Teaching of Children

I here suppose them untaught that you have to do with, and therefore shall direct you what to do, from the beginning of your teaching and their learning. I urge[1] you to study this chapter more than the rest; for it is an unspeakable loss that befalls the church, and the souls of men, for want of parents' skill, will, and diligence in this matter.

Direction 1: Cause your younger children to learn the words, though they are not yet capable of understanding the matter. Do not think as some do that this is to make them hypocrites and to teach them to take God's name in vain; for it is neither vanity nor hypocrisy to help them first to understand the words and signs, in order to [develop] their early understanding of the matter and signification. Otherwise, no man might teach them any language, nor teach them to read any words that are good, because they must first understand the words before the meaning. If a child learns to read in a Bible, it is not taking God's name or Word in vain, though he does not understand it; for it is in order to his learning to understand it; and it is not vain that is to so good a use. If you leave them untaught until they come to be twenty years of age, they must learn the words before they can understand the matter. Do not, therefore, leave them the children of darkness, for fear of making them hypocrites. It will be an excellent way to redeem their time, to teach them first

---

[1]*Beseech.*

that which they are capable of learning; children of five or six can learn the words of a catechism or Scripture before they are capable of understanding them. When they come to years of understanding, that part of their work is done, and they have nothing to do but to study the meaning and use of those words that they have learned already. Whereas, if you leave them untaught until then, they must then be wasting a long time to learn the same words that they might have learned before. The loss of so much time is no small loss or sin.

Direction 2: The most natural way of teaching children the meaning of God's Word, and the matters of their salvation, is by talking with them suited to their capacities. Begin this with them while they are on their mother's laps, and use it frequently. For they are quickly capable of some understanding about greater matters as well as about less. Knowledge must come by slow degrees. Do not wait until their minds are prepossessed with vanity and toys (Prov. 22:6).

Direction 3: By all means, let your children learn to read, though you are never so poor, whatever shift you make. It is a great mercy to be able to read the Holy Scripture, and any good books themselves, and a great misery to know nothing but what they hear from others. They may read almost at any time, when they cannot hear.

Direction 4: Let your children, when they are little ones, read the history of the Scriptures. For though this, of itself, is not sufficient to instill in them[2] any saving knowledge, yet it entices them to delight in reading the Bible, and then they will be often at it when they love it, so that all these benefits will follow: First, it will make them love the Bible, though it is only with a common love. Second, it will make them spend their time in it, when they would otherwise rather be at play. Third, it will acquaint them with Scripture history, which will afterward be very useful to them. Fourth, it will lead them up by degrees to the knowledge of the doctrine, which is all along interwoven with the history.

Direction 5: Take heed that you do not turn all your family instructions into a customary, formal course by bare readings and repeating sermons from day to day without personal application. For it is commonly seen that they will grow sleepy, senseless, and customary under such a dull and distant course of duty, though the mat-

---

[2] *Breed in them.*

ter is good, almost as if you had said nothing to them. Your business, therefore, must be to get with them, and awaken their consciences to know that the matter concerns them, and to force them to make application of it for themselves.

Direction 6: Let none practice a formal preaching to their families unless they are preachers or men who are fit for the ministry; rather, spend time in reading to them the best books and speaking often to them of their souls. Not that I think it unlawful for a man to preach to his family, in the same method that a minister does to his people, for no doubt he may teach them in the most profitable manner he can; and that which is the best method for a set speech in the pulpit is usually the best method in a family. But my reasons against this kind of preaching are these: First, very few masters of families are equipped to do it (even among those who think they are); and then they ignorantly abuse the Scripture, much to God's dishonor. Second, there is scarce any but may read at the same time such lively, profitable books to their families as handle those things that they have most need to hear of, in a far more edifying manner than they themselves are able, unless they are so poor that they cannot purchase such books.[3] Third, the familiar way is most edifying; and to talk seriously with children and servants about the great concernments of their souls commonly more moves them than sermons or set speeches. Yet because there is a season for both, you may sometimes read some powerful book to them and sometimes talk familiarly to them. Fourth, it often comes from pride when men put their speech into a preaching method to show their parts, and as often nourishes pride.

Direction 7: Let the manner of your teaching be often interlocutory, or by way of questions. When you have so many or such persons present as that such familiarity is not seasonable, then reading, repeating, or set speeches may do best; but at other times, when the number or quality of the company does not hinder, you will find that questions and familiar discourse are best. For, first, it

---

[3]Books were much more expensive in the seventeenth century as printing costs were relatively high. With progress in the printing press, the prices of books dropped dramatically. In fact, in the eighteenth century, in his *A Treatise of the Millennium*, Samuel Hopkins (1721–1803) listed cheap books, and their availability to all, as a sign of the Millennium. For a thorough survey of the development of the printing press, see Elizabeth L. Eisenstein, *The Printing Press as an Agent of Change* (Cambridge: Cambridge University Press, 1980).

keeps them awake and attentive when they know they must make some answer to your questions, which set speeches, with the dull and sluggish, will hardly do. Second, it helps them in the application, so that they much more easily take it to heart and see how it applies to them.

Direction 8: Yet prudently take heed that you speak nothing to any in the presence of others that tends to open their ignorance or sin or the secrets of their hearts or that any way tends to shame them, except in the necessary reproof of the stubborn. If it is their ignorance that will be opened by questioning them, you may do it before your children who are familiar with each other, but not when any strangers are present. If it be about the secret state of their souls that you examine them, you must do it alone, lest shaming and troubling them make them hate instruction and deprive them of its benefits.

Direction 9: When you come to teach them the doctrine of religion, begin with the baptismal covenant, as the sum of all that is essential to Christianity. Here teach them, briefly, all the substance of this at once. For though such general knowledge will be obscure, and not distinct and satisfactory, yet it is necessary at first, because they must see truths set together. They will understand nothing truly if they understand it but independently by broken parts. Therefore, open to them the sum of the covenant or Christian religion all at once, though you say but little at first of the several parts. Help them to understand what it is to be baptized into the name of the Father, Son, and Holy Spirit. You must open it to them in this order: you must help them to know who the covenanters are, God and man; and first the nature of man is to be opened because he is first known and God, in him, who is his image. Tell them often that man is not like a beast that has no reason nor free will nor any knowledge of another world nor any other life to live but this, but that he has an understanding to know God and a will to choose good and refuse evil and an immortal soul that must live forever, and that all inferior creatures were made for his service, as he was made for the service of his Creator. Further, tell them that neither man nor anything that we see could make itself, but God is the Maker, Preserver, and Disposer of the entire world. Tell them that this God is infinite in power, wisdom, and goodness and is the Owner, Ruler, Benefactor, Happiness,[4] and End of man.

Tell them that man was made to be wholly devoted and resigned to God as his Owner and to be wholly ruled by him as his Governor and to be wholly given up to his love and praise as his Father, his Happiness,[5] and End; that the tempter having drawn man from this blessed state of life, in Adam's fall, the world fell under the wrath of God and had been lost forever, but that God in his mercy provided us a Redeemer, even the eternal Son of God, who, being one with the Father, was pleased to take the nature of man and so is both God and man in one Person, who, being born of a virgin, lived among men, fulfilled the law of God, overcame the tempter and the world, and died as a sacrifice for our sins to reconcile us unto God. Tell them that all men are born with corrupt natures and that they live in sin until Christ restores them (there is no hope of salvation but in him). Tell them that he has paid for our debt and has made satisfaction for our sins and has risen from the dead, conquered death and Satan, and is ascended and glorified in heaven; tell them that he is the King, Teacher, and High Priest of the church. Tell them that he has made a new covenant of grace and pardon and offered it in the Scriptures and by his ministers to the world; that those who are sincere and faithful in this covenant shall be saved, and those who are not shall be damned because they reject this Christ and grace, the last and only remedy. Here open to them the nature of this covenant: that God offers to be our reconciled God, Father, and Happiness,[6] and Christ to be our Savior, to forgive our sins, reconcile us to God, and renew us by his Spirit, and the Holy Spirit to be our Sanctifier, to illuminate, regenerate, and confirm us; that all that is required on our part is such an unfeigned consent as will appear in the performance in our serious endeavors.

Tell them who are wholly to be given up to be renewed by the Holy Spirit, to be justified, taught, and governed by Christ and to be brought by him to the Father, to love him as our God and End, and to live to him and with him forever. Whereas the temptations of the Devil and the allurements of this deceitful world and the desires of

---

[4] *Felicity.*
[5] *Felicity.*
[6] *Felicity.*

the flesh are the great enemies and hindrances in our way, we must consent to renounce all these, let them go, deny ourselves, and take up with God alone what he sees sufficient[7] to give us and take him in heaven for all our portion. He who consents wholly to this covenant is a member of Christ, a justified, reconciled child of God, and an heir of heaven, and so continuing, shall be saved; he who does not shall be damned. This is the covenant that in baptism we solemnly entered into with God the Father, Son, and Holy Spirit as our Father and Happiness,[8] our Savior and Sanctifier. Teach them these things again and again.

Direction 10: When you have opened the baptismal covenant to them and the essentials of Christianity, have them learn the Apostles' Creed, the Lord's Prayer, and the Ten Commandments. Tell them the uses of them; that man having three powers of soul, his understanding, will, and obedience, these must be sanctified, and therefore there must be a rule for each; and that accordingly the Creed is the summary rule to tell us what we in our understanding must believe, the Lord's Prayer is the summary rule to direct us as to what our wills must desire and our tongues must ask, and the Ten Commandments are the summary rules of our practice; and that the Holy Scripture, in general, is the more large and perfect rule of all; and that all that will be taken for true Christians must have a general, implicit belief of all the Holy Scriptures and a particular, explicit belief, desire, and sincere practice, according to the Creed, the Lord's Prayer, and the Ten Commandments.

Direction 11: Next, teach them a short catechism, by memory, that opens these teachings more fully and then teach them a larger catechism. The shorter and larger catechisms of the Westminster Assembly are very well fitted to this use. I have published a very brief one myself, which in eight articles or answers contains all the essential points of belief and in one answer the covenant consent and in four articles or answers all the substantial parts of Christian duty. Some of the answers are too long for children, but if I knew of any other that had so much in so few words, I would not offer this to you because I am conscious of its imperfections. There are very few

---

[7]*Meet.*
[8]*Felicity.*

catechisms that differ in the substance; whichever ones they learn, help them to understand and to memorize them.

Direction 12: Next, open to them more distinctly the particular part of the covenant and catechism. I think this method most profitable for a family: first, read them the best expositions on the Creed, the Lord's Prayer, and the Ten Commandments, which are not too large to confuse them or too brief so as to be hardly understood. For a summary, Mr. Brinsley's *True Watch* is good;[9] but to read to them, Mr. Perkins on the Creed[10] and Dr. King on the Lord's Prayer[11] and Dod on the Commandments[12] are suitable, so that you may read one article, one petition, and one commandment at a time, and read these to them at different times. Second, in your familiar discourse with them open to them one head or article of religion at a time, and another the next time, and so on, until you come to the end. And here: 1. Open in one discourse the nature of man and the creation. 2. In another, or before it, the nature and attributes of God. 3. In another, the fall of man, and especially the corruption of our nature, as it consists in an inordinate inclination to earthly and fleshly things and a backwardness or averseness or enmity to God and holiness and the life to come; and the nature of sin; and the impossibility of being saved until this sin is pardoned and these natures renewed and restored to the love of God and holiness from this love of the world and fleshly pleasures.

4. In the next discourse, open to them the doctrine of redemption in general and the incarnation and natures and person of Christ.

---

[9]John Brinsley's *The True Watch and Rule of Life; or, A Direction for the Examination of Our Spiritual Estate* (1606) went through several editions throughout the seventeenth century. Brinsley (most active in his writing in 1633), a minister and teacher in Leicestershire, was most famous for this often reprinted work.

[10]William Perkins (1558–1602) was arguably the most popular Puritan minister of the late sixteenth century and has only recently come to receive from historians the attention that was given to him by contemporaries. The work Baxter refers to is Perkins's *An Exposition of the Symbol or Creed of the Apostles according to the tenor of the Scriptures, and the consent of orthodox Fathers of the Church* (1595), which went through several editions in the seventeenth century.

[11]Henry King's (the Bishop of Chichester, 1592–1669) *Exposition on the Lord's Prayer* (1628) was a popular treatise on the subject, though not so well known as others. See Mary Hobbs, *The Sermons of Henry King (1592–1699), Bishop of Chichester* (Aldershot, UK: Scolar Press, 1992). For a survey of texts on the Lord's Supper as genre, see Kenneth W. Stevenson, *The Lord's Prayer: A Text in Tradition* (Minneapolis: Fortress Press, 2004) and Ian Green, *Print and Protestantism in Early Modern England* (New York: Oxford University Press, 2001), 246–247.

[12]John Dod's (c. 1549–1645) *A Plain and Familiar Exposition of the Ten Commandments* (1604) was probably the most popular treatise on the subject in the seventeenth century; it went through several reprints and represents classic Puritan divinity. It was said of Dod, "A grave divine; precise, not turbulent; and never guilty of the churches rent: Meek even to sinners; most devout to God. This is but part of the due praise of Dod." *Memorials of the Rev. John Dod, M.A.* (Northampton, UK: Taylor and Son, 1875), v.

5. In the next, open the life of Christ, his fulfilling the law, and his overcoming the tempter, his humble life and contempt of the world, and the end of all, and how he is exemplary and imitable unto us. 6. In the next, open the whole humiliation and suffering of Christ, and the pretenses of his persecutors and the ends and uses of his suffering, death, and burial. 7. In the next, open his resurrection, the proofs and the uses of it. 8. In the next, open his ascension, glory, and intercession for us and the uses of all. 9. In the next, open his kingly and prophetical offices in general, and his making the covenant of grace with man, and the nature of that covenant and its effects. 10. In the next, open the works or office of the Holy Spirit in general, as given by Christ to be his agent in men on earth, and his great witness to the world; and particularly open the extraordinary gift of the Spirit to the prophets and apostles, to plant the churches and compose[13] and seal the Holy Scriptures; and show them the authority and use of the Holy Scriptures. 11. In the next, open to them the ordinary works of the Holy Spirit, as the illuminator, renewer, and sanctifier of souls and in what order he does all this, by the ministry of the Word.

12. In the next, open to them the office and use and duty of the ordinary ministry and their duty toward them, especially as hearers, and the nature and use of public worship, and the nature and communion of saints and churches. 13. In the next, open to them the nature and use of baptism and the Lord's Supper. 14. In the next, open to them the shortness of life and the state of souls at death and after death, and the Day of Judgment, and the justification of the righteous, and the condemnation of the wicked at that day. 15. In the next, open to them the joys of heaven and the miseries of the damned. 16. In the next, open to them the vanity of all the pleasure and profits and honor of this world and the method of temptations and how to overcome them. 17. In the next, open to them the reason and use of suffering for Christ and of self-denial and how to prepare for sickness and death. After this, go over also the Lord's Prayer and the Ten Commandments.

Direction 13: After all your instructions, make them give you an account, in their own words, of what they understand and remember;

---

[13]*Indite.*

otherwise, the next time to give account of the former. Encourage them for all that is well done in their endeavors.

Direction 14: Labor to keep a wakened, serious attention and to print upon their hearts the greatest things. To that end, for the matter of your teaching and discourse, let nothing be so much in your mouths as, first, the nature and relations of God; second, a crucified and a glorified Christ, with all his grace and privileges; third, the operations of the Spirit on the soul; fourth, the madness of sinners and the vanity of the world; fifth, the endless glory and joy of saints, and the misery of the ungodly after death. Let these five points be frequently urged and be the life of all the rest of your discourse. Then, for the manner of your speaking to them, let it be always with such a mixture of familiarity and seriousness that may carry along their serious attentions, whether they will or no. Speak to them as if they or you were dying and as if you saw God, heaven, and hell.

Direction 15: Take all individually sometimes by themselves, and there describe to them the work of renovation, and ask them whether such a work was wrought upon them. Show them the true marks of grace, and help them to try themselves; urge them to tell you truly whether their love to God or the creature, to heaven or earth, to holiness or flesh-pleasing be more, and what it is that has their hearts, care, and chief endeavor. If you find them regenerate, help to strengthen them; if you find them too much dejected, help to comfort them; and if you find them unregenerate, help to convince them, and then to humble them, and then to show them the remedy in Christ, and then show them their duty that they may have part in Christ, and drive all home to the end that you desire to see; but do all this with love, gentleness, and privacy.

Direction 16: Some pertinent questions that will engage to teach or judge themselves will be of great use. Such questions as these: Do you not know that you must shortly die? Do you not believe that immediately your souls must enter upon an endless life of joy or misery? Will worldly wealth and honors or fleshly pleasures be pleasant to you then? Had you then rather be a saint or an ungodly sinner? Would not you rather be one of the holiest persons whom the world despised and abused than the greatest and richest of the wicked? When time is past and you must give account, would you not rather it had been spent in holiness, obedience, and preparations for the life to come than in pride, pleasure, and pampering the flesh? How could you forget your endless life for so long? Or sleep so quietly in an unregenerate state? If you were to die before conversion, what will become of you? Do you think anyone in hell is glad that they were ungodly? Or does anyone have pleasure in their former merriments and sin? What do you think they would do if they were to do it over again? Do you think, if an angel or saint from heaven should come to decide the controversy between the godly and the wicked, that he would speak against a holy and heavenly life or plead for a loose and fleshly life? Which side do you think he would take? Did not God know what he did when he made the Scriptures? Is he or an ungodly scorner to be more regarded? Do you think every man in the world will not wish, in the end, that he had been a saint, whatever it cost him? Such questions as these urge the conscience and do much to convince.

Direction 17: Cause them to learn one most plain and pertinent text for every great and necessary duty, and against every great and dangerous sin; and have them often repeat them to you. Such texts as, "Unless you repent, you will all likewise perish. . . . I tell you . . . unless you repent, you will all likewise perish" (Luke 13:3, 5); "Truly, truly, I say to you, unless one is born of water and the Spirit, he cannot enter the kingdom of God" (John 3:5); so Matthew 18:3; Romans 8:9; Hebrews 12:14; John 3:16; Luke 18:1, etc.; so texts against lying, swearing, taking God's name in vain, flesh-leasing, gluttony, pride, and the rest.

Direction 18: Drive all your convictions to a resolution of endeavor and amendment, and make them promise you to do that which you convinced them of, and sometimes before witnesses. But let it be done with these necessary cautions: first, that you do not urge a promise in any doubtful point or such as you have not first convinced them of. Second, that you do not urge a promise in things beyond their present strength; as you must not bid them promise you to believe, or to love God, or to be tender-hearted, or heavenly minded, but to do those duties that tend to these, as to hear the Word, read, pray, meditate, keep good company, or avoid temptations. Third, that you are not too often upon this (or upon one and the same strain in the other methods), lest they take them for words of course, and custom teaches them to condemn them. If seasonably and prudently done, their promises will lay a great engagement on them.

Direction 19: Teach them how to pray, by forms or without, as is most suitable to their case and parts; and either yourself or some who may inform you should hear them pray sometimes, that you may know their spirit and how they profit.

Direction 20: Put such books into their hands as are suitable[14] for them and engage them to read when they are alone. Ask them what they understand and remember. Do not hold them, without necessity, to such hard work as to allow them no time for reading by themselves, but drive them to work harder, that they may have some time when their work is done.

Direction 21: Cause them to teach one another when they are together. Let their talk be profitable. Let those who read best read to the rest and instruct them and further their edification. Their familiarity might make them very useful to one another.

Direction 22: Do not tire them with too much at once; give it to them as they can receive it. Narrow-mouthed bottles must not be filled as wider vessels.

Direction 23: Labor to make all sweet and pleasant to them; and to that end sometimes mix the reading of some profitable history, such as *Foxe's Book of Martyrs*[15] and Clarke's *Martyrologie* and *Lives of Eminent Persons*.[16]

Direction 24: Lastly, entice them with kindnesses and rewards. Be kind to your children when they do well, for this makes your persons acceptable first, and then your instructions will be much more acceptable. Nature teaches them to love those who love them and

---

[14]*Meetest.*

[15]John Foxe (1516–1587), an English preacher, published his *Book of Martyrs* in March 1563. Originally titled *Acts and Monuments of These Latter and Perilous Days*, it immediately acquired the popular name *Book of Martyrs*. A second edition was produced in 1570, and a third and fourth in 1576 and 1583. *Book of Martyrs* remains a detailed and historic account of the English Reformation, though some have criticized it for its overtly Protestant motif. There are several popular editions of the work currently available.

[16]Samuel Clarke (1599–1683) was the son of a clergyman and was educated at Emmanuel College, Cambridge. He was often in trouble for nonconformity, and in 1660 he joined Richard Baxter in welcoming the return of the king from exile, but was nevertheless ejected from his London pulpit in 1662. After being ejected, he spent his remaining years attending the parish church of the Church of England and devoting himself to writing. His *Lives of Eminent Persons* (1662) and *A Martyrologie* (1652), here referred to, were popular pieces of seventeenth-century biography; there were some modern editions of these works, but most are now scarce and hard to find. Clarke should not be confused with another Samuel Clarke (1675–1729), a theologian and an exponent of Newtonian physics, best remembered for his influence on eighteenth-century English theology.

do them good, and to listen to those they love. A small gift, now and then, might signify much to the benefit of their souls.

Direction 25: If anyone shall say that there is so much to do in these directions that they cannot follow them, I ask them to ask[17] Christ, who died for them, whether souls are not precious and worth all this labor. Further, consider how small a labor this is in comparison to their everlasting end; and remember that all is gain, pleasure, and delight to those who have holy hearts; and remember that the effects to the church and kingdom of such holy government of families would more than compensate for all the pains.

---

[17]*Consult.*